LANGUAGE BEHAVIOR AND COMMUNICATION

LANGUAGE BEHAVIOR AND COMMUNICATION
An Introduction

Harold J. Vetter UNIVERSITY OF MARYLAND

F. E. PEACOCK PUBLISHERS, INC. · ITASCA, ILLINOIS

Preface

THIS BOOK was originally conceived as an introduction to the systematic study of language behavior and communication processes. It was expressly intended for use by the student and instructor whose mutual interests in language and communication have thus far been handicapped by the lack of an introductory level textbook; for the specialist in the social sciences who is seeking acquaintance with broad developments in fields of research that are related to communication and language; and for the general reader with curiosity and a desire to learn more about the endlessly fascinating topic of language behavior and communication.

I should like to state at once that this book is not intended to supplant the technical references available in various fields; rather, one of its purposes is to provide suggestions for profitable further reading. In a volume of this type, a detailed discussion of technical issues is obviously out of place. Nor has any attempt been made to present a closely reasoned defense of a particular theoretical viewpoint or persuasion. For one thing, such an approach would be highly inappropriate to a book which purports to be introductory in character. For another, given the speed with which developments occur in this field, it would be difficult to hold doctrinaire views on almost any subject pertaining to language and communication.

Any book which deals with language is bound to touch, however lightly, upon a subject area of intense current interest: psycholinguistics, or the psychology of language. This new interdisciplinary field has developed within the past twelve to fifteen years as a result of interaction between sectors of linguistics and psychology. Linguistics is the discipline which is concerned with the scientific study of language. It has identified units of language such as phonemes, morphemes and immediate constituents at the corresponding levels of phonology, morphology and syntax. Recently, the field of linguistics has been undergoing a revolution in its basic conceptions. This revolution involves concepts originating in the approach of *generative grammar,* which postulates the existence of a base structure underlying language and views linguistic utterances as representing transformations of elements in the base.

Linguistics prior to the inception of generative grammar was essentially descriptive and made few suggestions with respect to the processes or mechanisms which the user of language must possess in order to speak and comprehend the language. The generative linguists, however, maintain that their conceptions of the nature of language place definite restrictions and impose certain requirements on the kind of processes which the language user must possess. These conceptions clearly involve psychological assumptions about the user of language.

A number of psychologists, since about 1950, have been interested in the study of language, chiefly with the objective of applying principles of learning to linguistic phenomena. They have been interested, for example, in problems of speech perception, the psychological reality of linguistic units, and the role of associative processes in the generation and interpretation of sentences. A major issue at the present time is the question of whether contemporary psychological theory is capable of providing an account of the language user which is adequate to deal with his functioning as conceived by the generative linguistic theorist.

The professional literature of psycholinguistics is, and will undoubtedly continue to be, a literature of the specialist. One of the distinguishing features of such literature is its preoccupation with issues, controversies and sources of dispute. Debates may range in character from good-natured to acrimonious, but the emphasis is strictly upon differences—of method, of interpretation, of conception. The mere ability to read and comprehend such material presupposes a level of expertise and sophistication that excludes the student, not to mention many specialists themselves. Therefore, I should like to express the hope that the discussion of language presented in the present volume may prove helpful to the student and general reader as an orientation to the more advanced topic of psycholinguistics.

It seems necessary to add a word or two on the relationship between language behavior and communication. Those who are accustomed to think of language in terms primarily of its communicative properties and functions may tend to regard communication and language as nearly synonymous. Our personal experience, however, tells us that a great deal of meaningful human interaction takes place through conduits of communication that are nonverbal. Conversely, there are kinds of linguistic utterance which are largely devoid of communicative significance.

The focus of interest in the present book is the area of convergence between language behavior and communication. According to some current authorities, such a description clearly establishes the limits of the subject matter as defined by *human communication*—an accurate characterization as far as the content of this volume is concerned. While the description and analysis of animal communication processes constitute an engrossing and significant subject in their own right, they are of relevance and interest in the present context only to the extent that they cast some light on human communication. At the same time, I have had to exercise considerable discrimination in selecting suitable topics to fit the rather narrow scope of this book from the vast number of potentially relevant subjects designated by the label *communication*.

I should like to acknowledge my indebtedness to my editor and publisher, Tom LaMarre and Ted Peacock, respectively, for their sustained encouragement throughout the preparation of this manuscript. They are entitled to the credit for most of whatever quality the book displays, just as I am to blame for whatever it exhibits by way of deficiencies.

For their contributions of ideas and material to this project, a sincere note of thanks is due to Carol Fink, Gail Bloch, Don Crook, Mark Taube, Sandy London, Jenny Steinmetz and Hinda Sack. To my wife, Virginia, for her patience, typing skill and willingness to interpret my hieroglyphics without aid of Rosetta Stone, I am indebted threefold.

Finally, I wish to thank the authors, editors and publishers for extending me permission to quote from copyrighted material.

Contents

CHAPTER 1

Language in Historical Perspective

Surely language is the crown of humanity. Man knows of no other tenant of this universe with this gift. It is at once the most unlikely and yet most utilitarian quality of the human mind. It delivers us from isolation, it is the foundation of humanity, it is the web-work in which all social organization is embedded. Language makes us men. (p. 361)

Eugene Galanter*

CIVILIZED PEOPLE have shown an interest in language since antiquity. In places widely separated by space and time, language has figured prominently in creation myths, according to which its unique qualities were accepted as evidence of its divine origin. And in more than one historical epoch, literacy was regarded as a gift too precious to be shared by any but a small priestly elite.

Concern with language has generally been bounded by current social needs and problems. But occasionally such limitations have been transcended by men of authentic genius. As an illustration, we might mention a scholar of language named Panini, a Hindu grammarian of the fourth century B.C., whose treatise on Sanskrit was described by the twentieth century linguist Leonard Bloomfield as "one of the greatest monuments of human intelligence" (p. 11). In this work, Panini achieved a level of sophistication in the description and analysis of

---

* *Textbook of Elementary Psychology,* San Francisco: Holden-Day, 1966.

1

language that remained unequalled until more than two millenia had passed and linguistics had emerged as a rigorous science.

Three centuries earlier than Panini, the Egyptian king Psammetichos is reputed to have conducted the first known experiment on language. He is said to have ordered that two children be raised by shepherds who would never speak to their wards. Apparently, Psammetichos believed that the children would naturally develop a language, and further, that the language they developed could then be considered the prototype of all languages. Tradition informs us that the first word the children spoke was *bekos,* the Phrygian term for bread. Therefore, Phrygian was declared the world's oldest language.

In language, as in so many other areas of intellectual activity, the Greeks—beginning with the pre-Socratic philosophers in the latter part of the sixth century B.C.—were the initiators of systematic inquiry. According to Ivić (1965), they were the first language theorists; they were the first Europeans to concern themselves with the study of written texts; they founded the principles of classical European grammar; and we owe them credit for establishing a tradition of grammatical research which endured the tests of time.

Hellenic interest in language was an outgrowth of philosophical pursuits. It was essentially in response to philosophical questions that Greek scholars speculated on the origin of language, the relationship between words and their meanings, and the application of principles of logic to grammar. Philosophical discussions were often directed toward linguistic problems. One of these discussions, as Ivić (1965) points out, is quite famous—the argument over whether the connection between the meanings of words and their sounds is logical and direct or arbitrary and capricious. The 'analogists' maintained that language is not dependent upon manmade conventions, but is a gift of nature. There is perfect correspondence between the sound of a word and its meaning, in their view, any imperfections in this relationship that have arisen in the course of time can be discovered by etymological research—systematic studies of words, their origins and derivations. The 'anomalists,' on the other hand, rejected the notion of perfect harmony between sound and meaning of words. They buttressed their argument with examples and illustrations of linguistic irregularities which exist at all levels of language relations. The 'anomalists' invoked the authority of Democritus (c. 460–360 B.C.), who had repudiated the conception of the divine origin of speech. Democritus argued that the imperfect nature of language was proven by such evidence as the existence of synonyms and homonyms, the demonstration of linguistic change over time, and the irregularity of grammar.

Plato (427–347 B.C.) in his dialogue *Cratylus*, suggests that the name of an object does not represent the object itself, but rather only represents our idea of the object. On the question of the origin of language, Socrates maintains that "speaking of a divine origin of words is but a contrivance to avoid a scientific examination of the source of names."

Aristotle (384–382 B.C.) displayed the same twofold philosophical and scientific interest in language that he exhibited in other phenomena. He believed that language was found exclusively in humans, with the songs of birds the closest approximation among animals. Children, he considered, are not able to speak as adults only because they have not yet achieved control over their tongues; control is perfected through training. Man's language differs biologically from the vocalizations of animals, in the Aristotelian view, on the basis of a difference in the locus of sound production and the apparatus of articulation: human language is produced by action of the tongue and animal sounds by the impact of air on the walls of the trachea. Human language articulation is unlike the expressive sounds produced by children or animals. These can neither be reduced to syllables nor combined to form syllables, as is possible with human speech. He considered language itself as part of natural order (*physis*) and the meanings of words as man-made (*thesis*).

Aristotle also attempted to establish a means of classifying parts of speech. The basic units of language, he felt, were nouns (*onoma*) and verbs (*rhema*), because only these words have a distinct meaning of their own; all other words merely serve to relate the logical aspects of the thinking process (*syndesmoi*).

Epicurus (341–271 B.C.) was one of the first to concern himself with the origin of language. He believed that language came, not from God or from man's reason, but from Nature.

Greek grammarians who were charged with the task of reinterpreting old manuscripts in the second century B.C. may be credited with the beginning and development of formal grammar. In what became identified as the Alexandrian school, generation after generation of skilled grammarians received training, and there were established fine traditions with regard to both fields of grammatical interest and work methods. It even developed specialized branches with their respective skilled practitioners: lexicographers, scholiasts, glossators, rhetoricians, etc. (Ivić, 1965).

As in so many other spheres of activity, the Romans borrowed liberally from the Greeks in matters pertaining to language. Thus, when a formal grammar was required by the Romans (100 B.C. to 200 A.D.) during the period of their hegemony, in order to unify the empire and compose a Latin literature, the model they chose was Greek.

The early Christian leaders considered language as God-given; and the differences between languages were solely of pragmatic concern whenever a newly discovered country needed Christianizing. Although language theory was dominated by the theme of divine revelation and concern for biblical exegesis, the natural basis of language was not completely abandoned. Some of the most significant theologians who discussed this conception of language were St. Augustine (354–430), Anselm of Canterbury (1033–1109), Peter Abelard (1079–1142), Thomas Aquinas (1225–1274) and Ricobald of Ferrara, who believed in the separation of language capacities and languages and was supported in this belief by witnessing a miracle in 1293. When a deaf mute acquired hearing and speech after praying at the grave of St. Anthony of Padua, he could repeat what was said to him but was unable to understand it. This was said to prove that language capacity was God-given, but that the knowledge of a particular language had to be learned.

Others throughout the Middle Ages and the Renaissance believed that there must be a natural language. Emperor Frederic II (1192–1250) tried to replicate the experiment of Psammetichos, but the children are supposed to have died. King James IV of Scotland (1473–1513) is also claimed to have attempted this experiment. He sought to prove a biblical origin for his country and believed that, if the first utterances of the children were made in a biblical language, the genealogy of Scotland would extend to the days of the Old Testament.

However, there were some men, even within the church, such as Pietro Bembo (1470–1547), secretary to Pope Leo X, and Juan Luis Vives (1492–1540), who proposed that each language has a natural order with which no individual can tamper. Furthermore, these languages undergo changes with time, and the simplest languages are the oldest. Even the skeptic, Montaigne (1533–1592), believed in the natural basis of language.

Marx (1967) noted that the separation between philosophy and science with respect to language began with Descartes (1596–1650). As long as philosophy and natural science were indistinguishable, the philosophic emphasis upon language as the expression of human reason tended to confine to philosophy the consideration of all language elements. However, Descartes drew a further distinction between language and the expression of emotions, which man shares with most animals, and articulation, which he shares with parrots and magpies.

Descartes did not write extensively about language, but his conception of how the mind is related to the body influenced much of the later speculation concerning language. His resolution of the mind-body problem in terms of two substances—"extended," (all objects of the physical world, hence body) and "unextended," (not localized in space, hence mind)—and their interaction at the pineal body, generated the dualistic theory. Thus, mind can be considered as a distinct entity apart from the body (Alkon, 1952).

Certainly another tenet of Cartesian philosophy which affected conceptualizations of language was the postulation of "innate ideas." Examples given by Boring (1950) are God, self, conceptions of time, space and motion.

The twentieth century linguist, Noam Chomsky, paraphrased and quoted Descartes to demonstrate Descartes' belief that language was a species-specific capacity, a specific human ability and independent of intelligence. And, of course, with innate thoughts common to all men, everyone has something to talk about.

> . . . it is a very remarkable fact that there are none so depraved and stupid, without even excepting idiots, that they cannot arrange different words together, forming of them a statement by which they make known their thoughts; while, on the other hand, there is no other animal, however perfect and fortunately circumstanced it may be, which can do the same (1966, p. 4).

It was the use of language in its creative aspect that supposedly convinced Descartes and, after him, Cordemoy, of the limitations of mechanistic explanations for the behavior of humans (Chomsky, 1966).

Leibnitz (1646–1716), considered by Boring to be one of the founding fathers of German psychology, believed that language was natural, not man-made, and that there was a pure, language, "language adamique" which expressed the true nature of things. Of course, in true Teutonic style he stressed the superiority of the German language because of its closeness to "language adamique." He further expounded that language ability was a gift of God and that the form of language was determined by natural instinct. The exceptions to this are Chinese, which could have been invented by a wise man, and some other languages which could have been the result of selecting words from languages already in existence (Marx, 1967).

Locke (1632–1704) rejected the Cartesian notion of "innate ideas," reasserting the Aristotelian conception of the mind as a *tabula rasa*. However, he did accept the dualism in the mind-body postulation and went on to problems of how the mind comes to perceive the world (Boring, 1950; Alkon, 1952). Marx (1967) quoted Locke to illustrate his keen interest in language:

> There is so close a connection between ideas and words . . .
> that it is impossible to speak clearly and distinctly of our
> knowledge, which all consists of propositions, without consid-
> ering first, the nature, use, and signification of language
> (p. 453).

At various points in his writings, Locke considered language to be
God-given, socially conceived and divined by Adam. Thus, he has been
quoted selectively by proponents of each of these views.

Condillac (1715–1780) who spread Locke's conceptions of ideas and
associations to France (Boring, 1950) had a number of things to say
about language. He thought that man's first language consisted of gestures and inarticulated noises that were "based on the construction of our
body instruments." There were some articulated sounds which came to
emphasize gesture language. The next articulated sounds were used in
imitation of natural sounds. Gradually, the articulated sounds replaced
the gesture language. The articulated language was said to differ from
the gesture language solely because ideas were presented in succession
rather than simultaneously.

> Although Nature gave man nearly complete freedom to do
> as he wills in articulated language, she guides us by putting
> the first words in our mouths and we discover other sounds by
> analogy. . . . I have said enough to show that languages are
> the work of nature, that they were formed, so to say, without
> us and that we, as we worked at language, blindly followed
> our way of seeing and feeling (Marx, 1967, p. 454).

His countryman, La Mettrie (1709–1751), saw nothing very unique
about man. He was only the most complex of machines. Chomsky
(1966), in order to refute them later, quoted several of La Mettrie's
choice comments from L'Homme Machine.

> I believe that thought is so little incompatible with organ-
> ized matter, that it seems to be one of its properties on a par
> with electricity, the faculty of motion, impenetrability, exten-
> sion, etc. . . . There should, furthermore, be no obstacle in
> principle to teaching an ape to speak. It is only 'some defect in
> the organs of speech' that stands in the way, and this can be
> overcome with proper training. I have very little doubt that if
> this animal were properly taught he might at last be taught to
> pronounce, and consequently to know a language. Then he

would no longer be a wild man, nor a defective man, but he would be a perfect man, a little gentleman. . . (p. 10).

Chomsky was of course careful to include that La Mettrie had simply not come to grips with the problem raised by Descartes, *viz* the creative aspects of language usage.

The most typical expression in the field of language study during the period of the Enlightenment was, according to Marx (1967), that of DeBrosses (1709–1777) who attributed language to a biological and natural basis, but considered that the contemporary languages were primarily the product of man's reason. It was this assumption which evidently led Jean Jacques Rousseau (1712–1788) to state that man had fashioned language for himself, after he had become an intelligent being, had formed societies and developed his arts. This, of course, implied that man had not been originally a social being.

Ferguson (1722–1816), professor of moral philosophy at Edinburgh, believed, however, that man did begin as a social animal and he ended interest in Psammetichos' experiment.

> Man's use of language and articulate sound, like the shape and erect position of his body, are to be considered as so many attributes of his nature: they are to be retained in his description, as the wing and the paw are in that of the eagle and the lion . . . The exploration of man's mind is not aided by the study of a wild man caught in the woods which would teach us nothing important or new, for the normal development of mental functions is dependent on society (Marx, 1967, p. 456).

Most of the above speculations were by philosophers and based upon reason, not experimentation nor even work with language. Then a physician entered the scene in the person of Franz Joseph Gall (1758–1828), the father of phrenology. Marx quoted Gall as wanting to put an end to the "highhanded generalizations of the philosophers" who had regarded the functions of the soul without consideration for their biological basis. He proposed that language of words in terms of its cause, is not a product of the faculties, but rather, a creation of our *internal* faculties. Language, according to the topography of the mind given in Boring (1950) is in area 33. Language was also considered by Gall to be common to both man and animals, each having sufficient words for his own needs. Workers in aphasia after Gall mapped brain areas intensively, but were twitted by Freud (1856–1939) who told them "there is no justification for the assumption that the physiological correlate of a simple psychological element is also simple and localizable" (Marx, p. 463). Freud certainly thought there was more to aphasia than localized brain damage.

A philosopher whom Gall did not succeed in discrediting (although he is listed in Boring, 1950, only in a post-chapter note) was Wilhelm von Humboldt (1767–1835). His method of bringing language from the sphere of philosophy into the realm of nature was simply to include reason as one of man's endowments. His was the culmination of Cartesian philosophy, for he believed that language was innate in man. As had Descartes, Humboldt felt that the creative aspect of language use was the essential characteristic of human language. There was a constant and unitary "form" of language. Further, the underlying laws of generation were fixed in language. The scope and the manner in which these generative processes might operate in the actual production (or perception) of speech were unknown.

> In developing the notion of 'form of language' as a generative principle, fixed and unchanging, determining the scope and providing the means for the unbounded set of individual creative acts that constitute normal language use, Humboldt makes an original and significant contribution to linguistic theory—a contribution that unfortunately remained unrecognized and unexploited until fairly recently (Chomsky, 1966, p. 22).

According to this early precursor of modern language theorists, language science would, in the future, have to study both man's language capacity and the history of languages. The first of these was considered the primary aim of study. He argued for the biological basis of language capacity on the grounds that all children acquire language at about the same age under myriad circumstances. He also cautioned against the study of language by examination of a corpus of words. However, Marx (1967) quoted him as saying that "it is still too early to attempt an overall theory of human speech . . . or even a general grammar" (p. 459).

From Locke to the Mills, the British empiricists were becoming the British associationists in their search for how man comes to know the world. James Mill (1773–1836) propounded the notion of association into a theory of "mental compounding" which said that every complex idea is composed of the additive association of simple ideas which retain their own properties at the same time that they contribute to the larger structure (Alkon, 1952).

John Stuart Mill (1806–1873) refined his father's theory and generated a theory of "mental chemistry" in which simple ideas generated a complex idea rather than formed the structure of it (Boring, 1950). Carroll (1953) noted that the mental chemistry concept evolved by the father and son reflected their observations of language phenomena, as complex thoughts might be represented by combinations of words and syntactical constructions showing the relations between the lower-order notions expressed by those works. He hastened to add, however, that these interpretations could hardly have rested on any type of sophistication beyond the concepts of subject, object, attribute, etc., popularized by grammarians.

According to Marx (1967) Darwin's theory of evolution was not considered by philosophers to be contradictory to the view that language was unique to man. For Darwin, articulation, association of ideas and the ability to connect definite ideas with definite sounds were properties common to man and beast; man differed from animals in the power of associating together the most diversified sounds and ideas. Originally, man had imitated animal noises, but now, "man has an instinctive tendency to speak, as we see in the babble of our young children, whilst no child has an instinctive tendency to brew, bake or write" (Marx, p. 460).

"William Wundt is the first man who without reservation is properly called a psychologist" (Boring, 1950, p. 316). His school accepted Cartesian dualism, without the interaction at the pineal body. The Wundtian mind-body relationship was a psychophysical parallelism. However, the mind could still be studied without reference to the body, as with Descartes' system. Structural psychology accepted the mental chemistry propounded by John Stuart Mill. Also, of course, structural psychology was associationistic (Alkon, 1952). In his *Grundzeuge der physiologischen Psychologie,* Wundt (1832–1900) proposed a scientific approach to determine the internal and external conditions under which language comes about. He thought that comparative linguistics and Voelkerpsychology would describe the laws of the development of language and its influence on the thinking of the individual and society (Marx, 1967).

Actually Wundt had quite a bit to say about language in his *Elements of Folk Psychology* (1916). First, he held that language was bound up with thought, and from the phenomena of language, one might draw inferences concerning the most general characteristics of thought. He also thought that the development of language did not keep pace with that of other forms of culture. Primitive forms of thought and the verbal expression which they received were thought to persist long after the external culture was relatively advanced.

Wundt wrote also of gesture language which he considered quite different from verbal language but intelligible to all. He considered "child-language" to be much more similar to gesture language than other types of language, in that the sounds are fitted to the meaning. Because of this, he felt that child language had little to teach concerning the development of thinking and speaking.

As noted by Alkon (1952), both the schools of Gestalt psychology and behaviorism came into being as protests against the structural tradition. Gestalt psychology accepted the experimental method and introspection, but it rejected the analysis of the total perceptual experience into sensory elements. Rather, these psychologists advocated a phenomenological description of immediate experience and appeared to be favorable to the Cartesian notion of innate ideas, but in an updated form. The social-behavioral view of the nature of language as described by McCarthy (1946) has come from this Gestaltian tradition, and is reflected in culture and language studies. Piaget (Flavell, 1963) wrote that representational thought does not begin with and result from verbal signs from the social environment. The first signifiers are the private, nonverbal symbols. However, language is a vehicle *par excellence* of symbolization, without which thought could never become really socialized and thereby logical. He treated language behavior as the dependent variable with cognition as the independent variable. Thus, he utilized the study of language as a means of understanding the thoughts of the child. It was Piaget who noted a difference, developmentally, between egocentric speech and socialized speech in the child. Related in many ways to this group are the functionalists such as Dewey who expressed interest in language primarily as communication in a particular social setting. Sapir (1921) could have been nurtured in this tradition. He wrote:

> Language is a purely human and noninstinctive method of communicating ideas, emotions, and desires by means of a system of voluntarily produced symbols. These symbols are, in the first instance, auditory and they are produced by the so-called 'organs of speech.' There is no instinctive basis in human speech as such, however much instinctive expressions and the natural environment may serve as a stimulus for the development of certain elements of speech. . . . (p. 8).

Most people, asked if they can think without speech would

probably answer, 'Yes, but it is not easy for me to do so. Still I know it can be done.' It is, indeed, in the highest degree likely that language is an instrument originally put to uses lower than the conceptual plane and that thought arises as a refined interpretation of its content (p. 15).

This last, of course, (a) sounds like Watson's (1925) analysis of thought as being "subvocal speech," (b) is diametrically opposed to Piaget's interpretation and, more importantly, (c) served as a forerunner of the Whorfian hypothesis (1956) which stated that one analyzes and perceives the world through and, in a way peculiar to, one's native language.

In the camp of behaviorism, Leonard Bloomfield has been the leading figure in the development of modern linguistics. According to Alkon (1952), Bloomfield was so impressed by William James' criticism of structural psychology that he reexamined his position, and thereupon adopted the study of language utilizing only observable behavior. Wells (1954) noted that in actuality Bloomfield was applying John Stuart Mill's method of experimental inquiry which was really nothing more than a stimulus-response concept. Wells considered this too reductionistic. Alkon wrote (1952) that the most far reaching result in this change in method and interest is the:

. . . now-familiar assumption that linguistic study must begin with the phonology of the language under consideration, and then proceed to describe the morphological and syntactic features in terms of structure within the system, rather than in terms of any causal interrelationships between such formal features of the language and the 'mental life' of the speech community in question (p. 38).

Apart from this type of study, there has been an enormous volume of research on language development in children. McCarthy's section headings take one from developmental stages to language and intelligence, sentence structure and grammatical form, functions of language, effects of environment, and so forth.

This, of course, was all in the period we might designate B.C.—before Chomsky. Chomsky (1966) chides Bloomfield and others who attribute the creative aspects of language use to "analogy" or "grammatical patterns" and insists they employed these terms in a completely metaphorical way, with no clear sense and no relation to the technical usage of linguistic theory. He believes that now, finally, there is a renaissance of interest in some of the classic concerns of the seventeenth, eighteenth and nineteenth centuries—concerns that were too long ignored by modern linguistics which, according to him, "self-consciously dissociated itself from traditional linguistic theory and has attempted to construct a theory of language in an entirely new and independent way" (p. 1).

REFERENCES

ALKON, P. K. Behaviourism and linguistics: an historical note. *Language and Speech*, 1952, 2, 37–51.

BLOOMFIELD, L. A set of postulates for the science of language. *Language*, 1926, 2, 153–164.

BORING, E. G. *A history of experimental psychology*. New York: Appleton-Century-Crofts, 1950.

CARROLL, J. B. *The study of langugage*. New York: John Wiley and Sons, 1953.

CHOMSKY, N. *Syntactic structures*. The Hague: Mouton, 1957.

CHOMSKY, N. Review of B. F. Skinner's *Verbal behavior. Language*, 1959, 35, 26–58.

CHOMSKY, N. *Cartesian linguistics*. New York: Harper and Row Publishers, 1966.

FERSTER, C. B. and PERROTT, M. C. *Behavioral principles*. New York: Appleton-Century-Crofts, 1968.

FLAVELL, J. H. *The developmental psychology of Jean Piaget*. Princeton: D. Van Nostrand, 1963.

HOCKETT, C. F. The foundations of language in man, the small-mouthed animal. *Scientific American*, 1967, 217, 141–144.

IVIĆ, M. *Trends in linguistics*. The Hague: Mouton, 1965.

LENNEBERG, E. H. *Biological foundations of language*. New York: John Wiley and Sons, 1967.

McCARTHY, D. Language development in children. In L. Carmichael (Ed.), *Manual of child psychology*. New York: John Wiley and Sons, 1946.

MARX, O. The history of the biological basis of language. In E. H. Lenneberg (Ed.), *Biological foundations of language*. New York: John Wiley and Sons, 1967.

SAPIR, E. *Language*. New York: Harcourt, Brace, & World, 1921.

SKINNER, B. F. *Verbal behavior*. New York: Appleton-Century-Crofts, 1957.

SKINNER, B. F. Operant behavior. In W. Honig (Ed.), *Operant behavior: areas of research and application*. New York: Appleton-Century-Crofts, 1966.

WATSON, J. B. *Behaviorism*. New York: Norton, 1925.

WELLS, R. Meaning and use. *Word*, 1954, 10, 235–250.

WHORF, B. L. Science and linguistics. In J. B. Carroll (Ed.), *Language, thought and reality*. Cambridge, Massachusetts: John Wiley and Sons, 1956.

WUNDT, W. *Elements of folk psychology*. (Translated by E. L. Schaub). London: George Allen and Unwin, 1916.

CHAPTER 2

Design Features of Language

> But nature it was
> Urged men to utter various sounds of tongue,
> And need and use did mould the names of things . . .
>
> Lucretius: *De Rerum Naturae*

THE USER OF A LANGUAGE must be able to do two things: speak and listen. Putting it more formally, he must possess *productive* and *receptive control* of his language.

To state matters in this fashion is to emphasize the primacy of language in its vocal and auditory aspects. No anthropologist has ever discovered a culture which lacks a spoken language, although any number of cultures have been described which failed to develop a written language.[1] Nor does any culture rely on nonverbal signs for more than auxiliary communication. Says Galanter (1966), "Language seems to be as natural and genetic an endowment of men as flight is of birds" (p. 362).

Obviously there is much more to language than the capacity to produce and respond to sounds. Primates, for example, can both produce

---

[1] The usual basis for stigmatizing a culture as "primitive" is an invidious comparison with those cultures, Eastern as well as Western, that have managed to achieve a high level of efficiency in the technological exploitation of natural resources. There is no valid linguistic criterion, including the presence or absence of a written language, for characterizing a culture or a language as primitive.

13

and react to a range of vocalizations that signify fear, anger, pleasure, etc. Such vocalizations, moreover, may play a significant role in the social activities of these animals, e.g., in maintaining the integrity of their social organization.

But communication alone is not a sufficient criterion for defining language, for organisms much lower on the phylogenetic scale than man are capable of some rather intricate and elaborate patterns of communicative behavior. A striking example of the potentiality for complex communication behavior in infrahuman species is the "body language" of the honeybee. The studies of the German naturalist von Frisch (1955) have shown that bees are able to convey the location and direction of food discoveries to others in the swarm by means of a series of maneuvers as stylized, in some respects, as the figures in classical ballet.

Von Frisch constructed a hive with glass walls that permitted him to observe the behavior of the bee tenants when they returned from a food-seeking flight. When the source of the nectar was close, say within 100 feet or less, the finder bee would perform a "dance" consisting of a circular movement. To indicate longer distances, the bee would run in a straight line while moving its abdomen rapidly from side to side, then make a turn and repeat the maneuver. For distances in excess of 200 yards, the number of turns made by the bee decreased. A run followed by only two turns, for example, might indicate that the food source was several miles away.

After observing this behavior, the other bees were able to fly directly to the food. It was apparent that they received cues to the location of the food from the direction of the "run" made by the finder bee. An upward vertical run in the hive indicated that the food source would be found by flying into the sun, whereas a downward vertical run indicated that the food source was away from the sun. Von Frisch found that bees which were restricted to a horizontal surface and deprived of sunlight were unable to communicate the direction of their finds.

Of more direct relevance to language problems are the studies of the great apes because of their structural similarities to humans. Chimpanzees, gibbons, orangutans and gorillas have all been studied intensively by naturalists and psychologists. Two American investigators, Keith and Cathy Hayes (1951), actually raised a chimpanzee in their home from the age of three days through four years.[2] The chimp, named Viki, and the subject of Mrs. Hayes's book *The Ape in Our House,* was treated as nearly as possible like a human child with regard to such activities as

---

[2] Sadly, we must report that Viki died of a virus infection before the experiment had ended.

feeding, toilet training, discipline and play. Viki not only learned to imitate much of the behavior of the adult humans with whom she lived, but also learned to respond to spoken commands.

At the beginning of the experiment, Viki produced only the kind of vocalizations that chimpanzees normally make when they are excited. The initial problem, therefore, was to get her to produce nonemotional sounds. According to Munn (1966):

> This seemed hopeless. Efforts to induce Viki to 'speak' for her milk were also, at first, in vain. Accordingly, milk was withheld in the hope that Viki would 'say' something. But Mrs. Hayes and Viki looked at each other, or at the milk, and Viki made no sound. When the milk was about to be taken away, Viki let out worried little 'oo-oo's,' typical reflex vocalizations. For making such sounds, emotional as they were, she was given a sip of milk. In the excitement over getting milk, Viki made some reflex barking sounds, and was given more milk. Then, as her appetite wore off, she was silent again (p. 433).

When she was about ten months old, however, she succeeded with much effort in producing a sound like "ahhh" just before reaching for milk. Mrs. Hayes calls this her "asking sound." The only words that Viki ever learned to mouth were "papa," "mama," and "cup"—the latter a combination of the sounds [k] and [p] uttered in rapid succession.

Outside the family circle of primates, the most promising infrahuman candidate for communication honors is the bottle-nosed dolphin or porpoise. Equipped with a brain that is larger than the human brain, the dolphin shows some amazing capacities for complex learning. In addition, it possesses an elaborate and variegated set of soundmaking capabilities. From the respiratory blowhole in its head, the dolphin produces both whistles and a sound that has been likened to a "raspberry" or Bronx cheer. It can also produce a series of clacks by gnashing its needle-pointed teeth. But its chief soundmaking apparatus is a voice box that compares in complexity with human vocal equipment. From this voice box it can emit a tremendously complicated range of barks, squawks, whistles, mewings, creakings and other sounds that are more difficult to identify. They range from deep bass to a supersonic pitch far beyond the limits of human auditory receptivity.

Dr. John C. Lilly of the Communications Research Institute of Miami, Florida, is acknowledged to be one of the world's foremost authorities on dolphin behavior. Dr. Lilly is convinced, after more than a decade of research, that dolphins are capable of not only intelligent communication but even of language. One of his more startling findings was that dolphins appear to possess mimetic capabilities. By reducing the playback speed of tape recorded dolphin vocalizations, Lilly (1962) found that he could distinguish sounds that resembled a baby crying, the plucking of a banjo, human laughter and other sounds one normally associates with human beings. So far, however, Dr. Lilly has not succeeded in establishing the type of linguistic communication between himself and his aquatic subjects that would confirm even his more modest expectations of their vocal capacities. Nevertheless, the evidence on the dolphin is as yet incomplete.

Infrahuman communication is an interesting and absorbing subject in its own right, apart from the question of its possible relevance to the understanding of language. Nearly every species that has been studied has revealed a capacity for communication, and this ability to communicate is a vital aspect of the forms of social organization these animals have developed. We may note, however, that none of the examples cited above displays the deliberate and intelligent use of symbols that characterizes human language behavior. In these illustrations we can identify the utilization of "signaling reflexes" or reflex vocalizations rather than words or symbols. As Klineberg (1954) points out:

> The main difference between human language and that of all other animals seems to lie mainly in the fact that the language of animals can express only what is present at the time; it occurs mainly in response to an emotional situation; it may on occasions indicate desires or types of object or action. As far as we can tell, however, it can have no abstract or symbolic meaning, nor can it to any extent describe what has happened in the past or what is to happen in the future (p. 36).

Whatever else he shares with the rest of the animal kingdom, man is unique in his possession of the means whereby he can escape imprisonment in the events of the present. As we consider at a later point some attempts at the formal definition of language, we shall have occasion to note that the twofold capacity for time-binding and abstraction is generally regarded as an indispensable property of human language.

THE ORIGINS OF LANGUAGE

The intriguing mystery of how language originated has proven a source of perennial fascination for linguistic scholars and scientists throughout the centuries. But unless or until the science fiction writer's dream of a practicable device for time travel is realized, we are obviously barred from any first-hand knowledge of this epochal development in human history. Did language make a sudden and dramatic appearance in human life or did it mark the culmination of process that extended over eons and eons of time? The sheer impossibility of finding empirical answers to such questions has never been a deterrent to speculation about the origins of language. More recently, as Roger Brown (1958) has noted, the fact that speculative theories of language origin have been "trivialized" by epithets such as the "bow-wow" theory (the onomatopoetic notion that words may have originated as attempts to represent the sounds made by animals), the "ding-dong" theory (that language originated in reflex associations between particular objects and a corresponding vocal response), or the "yo-heave-ho" theory (that language began as the rhythmical vocalizations accompanying some cooperative activity like pulling or rowing) has tended to make the whole subject a matter of distaste to language scholars and scientists. Nevertheless, such speculative theories of language origin have contributed indirectly to progress toward understanding language phenomena by stimulating research on a variety of topics. Investigations of *phonetic symbolism,* for example, have added much valuable information about the affective properties of language, although they originated in speculation about the origins of language. We shall pursue this topic in Chapter 7: SOUND SYMBOLISM IN LANGUAGE.

THE DEFINITION OF LANGUAGE

Before proceeding further, it seems appropriate to consider some of the various attempts that have been made to provide a formal definition of language. One of the earliest and best known of these attempts is that of Sapir (1921). Language, according to his definition, is a "purely human and non-instinctive method of communicating ideas, emotions and desires by means of a system of voluntarily produced symbols" (p. 7). Sapir indicates that these symbols are vocal in nature and are produced by the articulatory apparatus of speech. The term "voluntarily produced" emphasizes the fact that symbols represent learned, rather than instinctual, bases for communication, as contrasted with modes of communication among infrahuman species.

For Brown (1958):

> . . . language, in the full, is nothing less than an inventory of all the ideas, interests, and occupations that take up the attention of the society (p. 156).

Katz (1966) provides a somewhat more formally worded characterization:

> Natural languages are vehicles for communication in which syntactically structured and acoustically realized objects transmit meaningful messages from one speaker to another (p. 98).

Hill (1958) presents an inclusive definition which incorporates a number of significant features:

> Language is the primary and most highly elaborated form of human symbolic activity. Its symbols are made up of sounds produced by the vocal apparatus, and they are arranged in classes and patterns which make up a complex and symmetrical structure. The entities of language are symbols, that is, they have meaning, but the connection between symbol and thing is arbitrary and socially controlled. The symbols of language are simultaneously substitute stimuli and substitute responses and can call forth further stimuli and responses, so that discourse becomes independent of an immediate physical stimulus. The entities and structure of language are always so elaborated as to give the speaker the possibility of making a linguistic response to any experience (p. 9).

Implicit in this definition are these ideas: (1) that language is *vocal*, composed of sounds produced by the mechanism of human speech; (2) that language is *human*; (3) that language is *arbitrary*, with no pre-ordained reasons for any symbol to possess a particular meaning; (4) that language is a *system*, i.e., a set of rules or a code; and (5) language is *complete*, meaning that it possesses inexhaustible resources for generating appropriate responses to any novel experience.

The fact that language is vocal frees the organs and other parts of the body not directly engaged in the production or reception of speech for other activities. Thus, speaking and listening may take place concurrently with other actions.

The fact that language is arbitrary implies that it is unpredictable in terms of the relations between word symbols and meanings in a given speech community.[3] In addition, as Hill (1958) comments:

---

[3] While it is true that the relation between sound and meaning is "arbitrary," many other important aspects of language are most likely not arbitrary (e.g., the universals of syntax). To say that "language is arbitrary" is to disregard the fact that there is more to language than reference. This kind of position is clearly wrong.

> . . . the sounds of speech and their connection with entities of experience are passed on to all members of any community by older members of that community. Therefore, a human being cut off from contact with a speech community can never learn to talk as that community does, and cut off from all speech communities never learns to talk at all. In essence, to say that language is arbitrary is merely to say that it is social (p. 3).

The fact that language is a system is not easily demonstrated. Most of the remainder of this chapter is given over to an inspection of the characteristics which stamp language as a system.

To the above properties of language, Hockett (1960) has added several other design features, including *specialization, productivity, discreteness, interchangeability,* and *duality of patterning.* The significance and meaning of the latter are explained by Saporta (1967):

> The term is used to refer to the fact that natural languages not only consist of signs, that is, meaningful units, referred to as morphemes, but also of distinctive units, without meaning, which serve to distinguish signs. These two units form the basis of the division of a grammar into a syntactic component or syntax, which provides the rules for the sequencing of signs, and the phonological component or phonology which provides the rules for the formation of signs, and the pronunciation of the sequences generated by the syntax. One of the requirements of the phonology is that it make explicit, in a way parallel to the syntax, that there are restrictions on the combinatorial possibility of phonological segments. Thus, any speaker of English knows that although neither occur as signs, *fet* is a possible sequence but *fte* is not: the former conforms to the phonological rules; the latter violates them (p. 6).

We shall now proceed to examine the language system on the two levels of phonology and syntax.

THE PHONOLOGICAL COMPONENT

If a linguistically untrained person were asked to identify the most basic sound constituents of his language, he might respond by naming letters. This would be incorrect, of course, for letters are not sounds themselves but merely a means for the graphic representation of sounds. With a bit of prompting, he might amend his answer to consonants and vowels. And this would be a step closer to the truth; consonants and vowels are the raw material out of which words are built.

But our subject would have overlooked a set of sound features that are equally as important as vowels and consonants in the language system. These are the phonetic elements of *stress, pitch* and *juncture* that define patterns of pronunciation and intonation in language. In a dictionary, they may be partially indicated by conventional markers, but they are not supplied in the conventional written context because it is assumed that they are known implicitly to a native speaker.

This is one of the many weaknesses of an alphabet such as ours, which is a very imperfect approximation to the sound patterns of our language. If it proves vexatious for a youngster learning his own language in school, consider how great a source of frustration it can be to a foreigner struggling with the irregularities of English pronunciation. The story is told that Voltaire, who was living in exile in London and trying unsuccessfully to cope with English, upon discovering that *plague* had one syllable and *ague* two, wished that plague would take one half of the English language and ague the other half.

Everyone is familiar with the fact that custom rather than logic often dictates both pronunciation and syntax. For example, ask someone to pronounce *ghoti,* and observe his reaction when he is informed that it may be pronounced *fish:* the *gh* sound in cou*gh,* the *o* in w*o*men, and the *ti* in na*ti*onal.

Consonants, vowels, semi-vowels, and the elements of stress, pitch and juncture together constitute what the linguists have designated *phonemes.* A phoneme is not a sound but an abstraction—the element or feature common to a group of sounds. It may be thought of as a *class* of sounds with a predictable range of variations "which are automatic and which are reacted to as the 'same sound' by the native speaker of the language" (Pittenger and Smith, 1957, p. 63). Thus, in the words *pen, spend* and *cup,* the sound of /p/[4] is recognizably "different" in each case; but all of the variations, technically called *allophones,* can also be recognized by a native speaker as being the "same" sound, namely /p/.[5]

Phonemes are divided into two groups: *segmental phonemes,* which

---

[4] It is conventional practice in linguistic transcription to represent phonemes by inclusion within slants, e.g., /p/, which should be read as "phoneme *p,*" and ordinary sounds (*phones*) by inclusion within brackets, e.g., [p].

[5] It is necessary to note that even single allophones (e.g., /p/ in *pen*) are not acoustically invariant, as shown by sound spectrographic analysis. Of course, this type of invariability is of a different sort from allophonic variability.

include the vowels, semi-vowels and consonants; and *suprasegmental phonemes,* which include stress, pitch and juncture. These are shown in the chart on the next page.

It will be noted that stress, pitch and juncture are all described as having four degrees or levels. To see how these levels apply in everyday speech, let us consider a few examples of actual utterances.

STRESS. The relative degree of intensity with which a syllable is pronounced defines its stress level. Using the markers given above, we can indicate the four degrees of stress in English by the following variations on the word *content* (Carroll, 1964), p. 16):

> I am còntént.
> It is devoid of cóntênt.
> The table of cóntènts. (In some dialects.)
> Satisfaction and cònténtmĕnt.

Carroll points out that stress has an interesting function in adding an honorific designation to famous people and places:

> An ordinary person on the street might be named Clárk Gáble, just like Jóhn Dóe. But make him a movie star and your have Clàrk Gáble. Similarly, compare Ábraham Líncoln, Âbraham Líncoln; whîte hóuse, Whíte Hòuse; Thírd Âvenue, Fifth Ávenue (p. 16).

PITCH. Pitch is defined as the relative tonal height with which a sound is spoken. In the sentence *Are you feeling hungry?,* we can note a sequence of pitches that fall to a low pitch on *hun-* and then rise on *-gry.* Or consider the following interchange among three hypothetical speakers concerning an intended trip by a mutual friend:

> 2 He's going to 3 Pittsburgh 1
> 2 He's going to 3 Pittsburgh 3
> 2 Why's he going to 4 Pittsburgh 1

The first sentence is a statement of fact; the second indicates that the speaker has heard the statement and repeats it by way of confirmation; the third speaker has also heard perfectly, but registers something akin to surprise, as though to say, "Why Pittsburgh, instead of New York or Chicago?"

As compared with what are called *tonal languages,* English exhibits a minimal emphasis upon pitch variation. But in a tone language, as

TABLE 2.1
ENGLISH PHONEMES AND SOME WORDS AND SENTENCES EXEMPLIFYING THEM (AS IN THE AUTHOR'S DIALECT) (CARROLL, 1964, PP. 14–15)

33 SEGMENTAL PHONEMES

20 Consonants		4 Semivowels	

Occurring as initial, medial, or final:

		As Consonant	In Diphthong
/b/ as in *buy*	/s/ as in *so*		
/d/ as in *do*	/t/ as in *toe*	/h/ as in *hoe*	*bah* /bah/
/f/ as in *foe*	/v/ as in *vow*		
/g/ as in *go*	/z/ as in *zoo*	/r/ as in *roe*	*err* /ər/
/k/ as in *key*	/θ/ as in *thigh*		
/l/ as in *lie*	/ð/ as in *thy*	/w/ as in *woe*	*now* /naw/
/m/ as in *my*	/š/ as in *show*		
/n/ as in *no*	/č/ as in *chow*	/y/ as in *you*	*boy* /boy/
/p/ as in *pay*	/ǰ/ as in *Joe*		

Occurring only as medial or final:

/ž/ as in *pleasure, rouge*
/ŋ/ as in *singer, thing*

9 Vowels

Simple Vowel + Consonant	Followed by Semivowels				
	/-y/	/-w/	/-h/	/-r/	/-yr/
/i/ as in *pit*	pea	*	*	*	pier
/e/ as in *pet*	pay	*	*	*	pare
/æ/ as in *pat*	*	*	/æh/ †	*	*
/ɨ/ as in *roses*	*	*	*	*	*
/ə/ as in *putt, but*	*	*	/əh/ **	purr ††	*
/a/ as in *pot*	pie	now	pa	par	pyre
/u/ as in *put, look*	buoy	coo	boo!	poor	*
/o/ as in *	boy	low	oh!	pore	*
/ɔ/ as in *	*	*	law	war	*

12 SUPRASEGMENTAL PHONEMES

4 Pitches: /¹/ (lowest), /²/, /³/, /⁴/ (highest).
4 Stresses: / ´ / (primary), / ˆ / (secondary), / ` / (tertiary), / ˇ / (weak).
4 Junctures: /⁺/ (internal), /|/ (level), /‖/ (rising), /#/ (falling, terminal).

A SAMPLE TRANSCRIPTION

He: /²dìǰə + sɨyðə + ³hwáythàws³‖/
She: /²nów³‖²kə̀zay + wɔ̂hntɨd + tə + vîzɨtðə + smlə̀sôwnɨyən + myùw³zíyəm²|
²ðə + làybrəriyəv + ³káhŋgrɨs³|²ænðə + ǰéfərsən + mə³móhrɨyəl²‖
⁴ɔ̂hl²|²in + tûw + ⁴áwrz²#/
He: /²im⁴páhsɨbəl¹#/

> *He:* Didja see the White House?
> *She:* No, 'cause I wanted to visit the Smithsonian Museum, the Library of Congress, and the Jefferson Memorial—(*excitedly*) all in two hours!
> *He:* (*incredulously*) Impossible!

---

* Does not occur as a monosyllable in the author's Lower Connecticut Valley dialect, but may occur in other dialects of English.
† An interjection of frustration or disgust.
** The hesitation form.
†† In the author's dialect, this is a single *r*-like vowel, but it fits best into the pattern if considered a diphthong with /ə/.

Robins (1964) observes, "in which the pitch levels or the rising and falling pitches are properties of the words as lexical items, the substitution of a different word in a sentence may change the pitch sequence, if the two words concerned are different in tonal composition" (p. 112). As an example, the sequence /ta/ in Mandarin Chinese may represent four different words, according to tone: level tone, "to raise"; rising tone, "to penetrate"; rising-falling tone, "to hit"; falling tone, "great."

JUNCTURE. A juncture signals various types of transition—of getting from one utterance to another, from one syllable or clause to another. A slight break called an open transition (symbolized / + /) occurs between the phonemes /t/ and /r/ in *night–rate*, thus distinguishing it from *nitrate*. Three other types of juncture, called *single bar juncture* / | /, *double bar juncture* / ‖ /, and *double cross juncture* / # / can be described with reference to their role in the termination of an utterance in accordance with whether the last pitch phoneme maintains its level, / | /, rises slightly, / ‖ /, or falls slightly, / # /. Pitch and juncture, therefore, operate together to provide the *intonation* patterns of English.

SEGMENTAL PHONEMES: VOWELS AND SEMI-VOWELS. Vowels can be classified with respect to the relationship between tongue and lips, on the one hand, and the mouth cavity, on the other. Thus, a vowel produced by the front part of the tongue raised and almost touching the alveolar ridge behind the upper teeth would be called a *high front vowel*. A vowel pronounced with the back part of the tongue is a *back vowel*, and would also be described in terms of whether the tongue is in high, mid, or low position. In addition, if the vowel is pronounced with the lips pursed, we would characterize it as *rounded;* if the lips are spread, we would call it *unrounded*. These three variables (height of the tongue, position of the tongue, position of the lips) permit us to diagram the *short* or *simple* vowels of English as follows:

	FRONT	CENTRAL	BACK
HIGH	/i/	/i/	/u/
	pit	"jist"	put
MID	/e/	/ə/	/o/
	pet	putt	"gonna" (N.E.)[6]
LOW	/æ/	/a/	/ɔ/
	pat	pot	pot (N.E.)

The sounds characterized as *semi-vowels* (/h/, /r/, /w/, /y/) are variously produced within the oral cavity by a gliding motion of the tongue. These semi-vowels, when added to the simple vowels, produce a

---

[6] As pronounced by a native speaker of the northeastern part of the United States.

complex repertoire of vocalic syllable nuclei to describe the possible varieties of vowel phonemes that can be found within the English language. This is certainly a far cry from the "a,e,i,o,u" of the elementary school memories.

SEGMENTAL PHONEMES: CONSONANTS. As in the case of the vowels and semi-vowels, we describe the consonants in terms of the articulatory apparatus and movements of that apparatus required to produce the sounds. The following chart from Carroll (1964) presents the systematic

TABLE 2.2

CHART OF SOME ENGLISH CONSONANT PHONEMES*

(Carroll, 1964, p. 17)

Place of Articulation †	Type of Articulation †			
	Stop $V - V+$	Nasal $(V+)$	Fricative $V - V+$	Affricate $V - V+$
Bilabial	p b	m		
Labiodental			f v	
Dental			θ ð	
Alveolar	t d	n	s z	
Alveopalatal			š ž	č ǰ
Velar	k g	ŋ		

$V-$: Voiceless
$V+$: Voiced

* To avoid complications, the semivowels r, y, w, and h and the lateral l have been omitted.

† The meanings of terms such as *alveolar, fricative*, etc., can be found in most standard dictionaries, or you can attempt to infer these meanings from the characteristics of the sounds themselves. For the meaning of the phonemic symbols, see Table 2.1.

differences in sound as a function of the place of articulation (labial, dental, alveolar, palatal and velar) and type of articulation (stop, nasal, fricative and affricate). Although many of the consonantal phonemes correspond to the letters of the alphabet, it is necessary to represent others by means of phonetic symbols.

THE SYNTACTICAL COMPONENT

FORMS. Once the linguist has identified the phonemes of the language he is studying, his next task is to determine the forms that operate in the language as functional grammatical units. A neutral term like *form* is preferable to one with a more specific meaning, like *word*, because words obviously cannot be regarded as minimal grammatical units. The word *greeted*, for instance, differs in meaning from *greet* by virtue of the addition of the suffix *-ed*. While *greet* can stand alone, the suffix *-ed* would not be encountered apart from a linguistic context in which it operated to change the tense of a verb from present to past. Both forms, however, possess distinct grammatical functions.

Prefixes as well as suffixes, and extended as well as single units, can function as forms. Consider the following examples:

dis-	light	merry-go-round
connect	house	forget-me-not
-ed	lighthouse	
disconnected		

One of the problems that the linguist faces is trying to determine whether a particular sequence of forms ought to be considered a form itself, i.e., a self-contained unit. In the list above, the expression *merry-go-round* seems to function as a unit, and it is doubtful whether a similar form (e.g., happy-go-round) would be freely constructed.

We can define a form that is not further divisible into two or more other forms as a *morpheme*. Morphemes, like forms, which operate independently are classified as *free;* those which occur only in combination with other forms or morphemes are called *bound*.

As we have seen already in the case of phonemes, morphemes show both free and conditioned variation. Carroll (1964) observes:

> The morpheme -*ing* in *working, being* and so forth shows more or less free variation with -*in'*. (At least, a speaker could say *working* in some situations and *workin'* in others; any variables that control this would be extralinguistic.) But the pluralizing suffixes spelled -*s, -es, -en, -i,* in *rocks, dogs, roses, oxen* and *alumni* and pronounced /-s, -z, -in, -ay *or* -iy/ can be thought of as conditioned variants of a single morpheme which may be symbolized {Z} (p. 19).

The branch of linguistics which deals with the systematic study of forms is *morphology*.

An investigator named Jean Berko (1958) made an effort to discover what is learned by children in the acquisition of English morphology. If a young child can supply the correct plural ending for an ordinary noun, it may be merely a demonstration that he has memorized the correct form. If, on the other hand, he is able to give the correct plural ending /-z/ for a nonsense word (e.g., *gutches* as the plural for *gutch*), it suggests that the child has internalized a working system of plural *allomorphs,* conditional variants, and is able to generalize to new cases and select the right form.

Berko was also interested in the manner in which these morphological rules evolve. Is there a progression from simple, regular rules to more irregular and qualified rules that are adequate to fully describe English?

The experiment began with an examination of actual vocabulary. The 1,000 most frequent words in a first grader's vocabulary were selected from a standardized list. These were examined to see what features of English morphology were commonly represented in the vocabulary of a child of this age. Based on actual vocabulary samples, estimates were then made of the kind of morphological rules children might be expected to have acquired, and from these items a list was constructed. In order to gather some idea of the notions children form about compound words in their language, it was decided to ask them directly about a selection of such words.

Thus, from within the framework of a child's vocabulary, a test was devised to explore the child's ability to apply morphological rules to new words. Subjects were called upon to inflect, derive, compound and analyze words.

Nonsense words were made up according to the rules for possible sound combinations in English. Pictures were then drawn on cards to represent these nonsense words. There were 27 of these pictures— brightly colored, and depicting objects, cartoon-like animals, and men performing various actions. Several actual words were also included. The text, omitting the desired form, was typed on each card. The following is an example of the card to test for the regular plural allomorph in /-z/.

THIS IS A WUG.

NOW THERE IS ANOTHER ONE.

THERE ARE TWO OF THEM.

THERE ARE TWO _____.

FIGURE 2.3–The plural allomorph in /-z/.
(From Berko, 1958, p. 154.)

Each child was brought to the experimenter, introduced and told that he was going to look at some pictures. The experimenter would point to the picture and read the text. The child was asked to supply the missing item, and his responses were phonemically transcribed. After all the pictures had been shown, the child was asked why he thought the things denoted by the compound words in the list (e.g., newspaper, Thanksgiving, fireplace, airplane, etc.) were so named. The general form of these questions was, "Why do you think a blackboard is called a blackboard?" If the child answered, "Because it's a blackboard," he was asked, "But why do you think it's called that?"

The answers given by the children were not always correct as far as the English language is concerned, but they were consistent and orderly answers. The evidence strongly supports the conclusion that children in this age group operate with clearly delimited morphological rules. The children did not treat new words according to idiosyncratic patterns. They did not model new words on patterns that appear infrequently. Where they provided inflexional endings, they did best with those forms that are the most regular and have the fewest variants. With morphemes that have several allomorphs, they could handle forms calling for the most common of those allomorphs long before they could deal with allomorphs that appear in a limited distribution range.

GRAMMATICAL STRUCTURES AND SYNTACTIC RELATIONS. With the exception of a relatively small number of fixed formulas (such as salutations, clichés about the weather, polite phrases, etc.), most of the sentences one hears or utters occur for the first time. Yet the native speaker of English would show little hesitation in accepting a word string like *All mimsy were the borogoves, and the mome raths outgrabe* as being an utterance in his mother tongue, albeit a strange one, and rejecting as a candidate for admission to membership a string like *Label break to calmed about and.* Somehow, on an intuitive basis, the speaker is able to understand and produce an indefinite number of previously unobserved utterances. The fact that one is able to do this at all is one of the remarkable features of language behavior. When one considers that an individual of normal capabilities exhibits practically all of the complexities of adult language behavior in his speech by the time he has reached the age of six years or less, the implications for linguistic theory are readily apparent.

The objective of linguistic theory is to provide a formal statement of the coherence and consistency of a given language. The term in linguistics for such a statement is *grammar.* Those to whom grammar connotes a dull, laborious series of drills on how to speak and write "proper English" may be somewhat surprised by this meaning of the term, but for some time now grammar has been used in a descriptive rather than prescriptive sense among language specialists.

An older generation of structural linguists assumed that it was possible, given an adequate corpus of utterances by a native speaker, to *infer* the essential features of consistency and coherence that characterize the grammar of a particular language. Such a statement might require a volume approaching the size of an unabridged dictionary. How, then, could we reconcile anything so voluminous and elaborate with the effective linguistic performance of the six year old child? Says Carroll (1964), "Either the feat of the child is actually greater than we think it is, or there is something wrong with the assertion that a grammar of a language needs to be voluminous" (p. 23).

Each new reported study tends to deepen our appreciation for the impressiveness of the child's feat in learning his native language. But without detracting from the magnitude of such an accomplishment, there is the still unanswered question of the relationship between linguistic behavior and linguistic theory. Is it really possible to start with the slips, false starts, fragmentary sentences and incomplete utterances of ordinary language behavior and arrive at the coherence and consistency of the language system?

At least one group of language specialists, those who are identified by one variety or another of *generative* approach, maintain that it is inherently impossible to get from linguistic performance to linguistic *competence*, meaning by competence the organized totality of an individual's intuitive "knowledge" of his language. The precise meaning of "knowledge" in this context is beyond specification at the present time. It is assumed that a native speaker's intuitions about his own language represent some kind of implicit rules or "hypotheses" derived from the complex interactions between innate predispositions toward language acquisition and the stimulus inputs of his early social and linguistic environment. Thus, linguistic competence is construed as an abstract model of the language, whereas actual language behavior or performance is subject to a number of constraints such as motivation, memory, intelligence, etc.

Chomsky (1956, 1957) demonstrated that two of the three models proposed as devices for generating language utterances are unsuitable for reasons which involve inherent limitations on their operations. The first of these, a *finite-state grammar*, conceptualizes sentences as sequences of items selected from a large inventory and arranged in such an order that antecedent selections determine the conditional probabilities of subsequent choices, i.e., each selection that is made at some point in the sequence reduces the *potential* number of choices available at later stages. The following diagram is intended as a representation of a grammar which, by means of a closed loop, generates an infinite set of sentences like *The little boy comes; The very little boy comes; The very little boys come; etc.* Such a grammar makes use of a finite inventory of

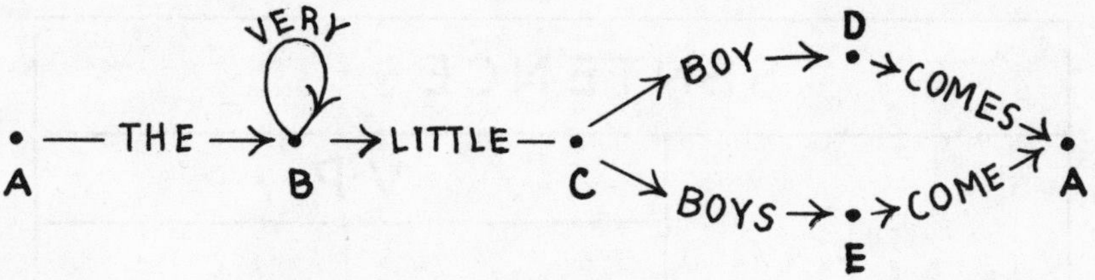

FIGURE 2.4

elements and a finite number of rules. These rules are of the form: A → a, B → b, etc., where the capital letters may be considered as representing states and the lower-case letters transitions between states. If the probability of occurrence of the total sequence from A to A were expressed as a numerical value of 1.0, it can readily be seen that the probability of occurrence of each segment would necessarily be some fraction thereof; and increasing the magnitude (i.e., the probability of occurrence) of one segment, B to C, for example, would automatically diminish the values (probabilities) of the remaining segments.

Chomsky (1956, 1957) has shown that constructions of various kinds occur in natural languages which cannot be accounted for by this kind of model. An example would be English, which has sentences in the form of $a^n b^n$. With respect to such a sentence, Saporta (1966) notes:

> There is no way for a finite-state grammar without a counter to insure that the number of b's is exactly the same as the number of a's. But precisely such restriction occurs in English in sentences of the type. If S_1, then S_2, since S_I may itself be a sentence of the *if-then* type, and so on, yielding arbitrarily many if-clauses followed by exactly the same number of then-clauses (p. 9).

An alternative to the finite-state model is the *phrase-structure grammar*, which makes provision for the fact that language has hierarchical as well as linear organization of the sentence as a series of constructions or *immediate constituents* at successive levels. Words are grouped into smaller constituent noun phrases (NP) and verb phrases (VP), and so on, until the ultimate constituents (usually morphemes) are reached. Figure 2.5 represents this kind of description diagrammatically. A phrase-structure grammar makes use of an analytical device called a

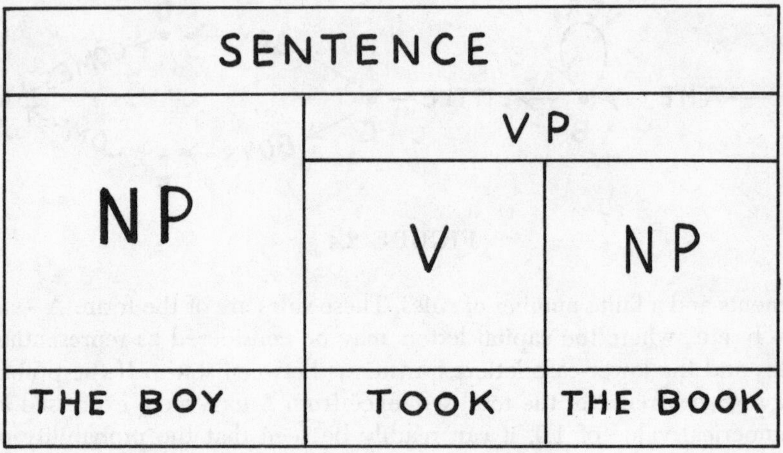

FIGURE 2.5

rewrite rule, which is expressed symbolically as $X \rightarrow Y$, and means "X is to be rewritten as Y." In this formulation, X may be understood as any construction and Y an expansion of X or its replacement by some substitute construction, e.g., a different selection of words that still conforms to the same superficial pattern. We might begin with a basic sentence:

$$\text{Sentence (S)} \rightarrow \text{Subject} + \text{Predicate}$$

and derive a series of more elaborate sentences using the following rewrite rules:

> Subject → Noun, Pronoun or Noun Phrase (NP)
> Predicate → Verb or Verb Phrase (VP)
> Noun Phrase (NP) → Determiner + Noun
> Verb Phrase (VP) → Verb + Noun Phrase (NP)

The relationships among these constructions and levels may be depicted as a tree-like structure:

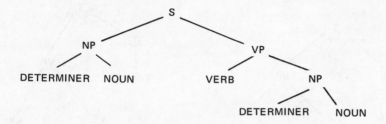

If we now extend our rewrite rules as follows:

> Determiner → a, an, the
> Noun → man, apple, bicycle
> Verb → ate, rode, sold

we can generate sentences such as:

> A man ate an apple.
> The man rode the bicycle.
> The bicycle ate an apple.
> The apple rode a man.

It is obvious that further rules are needed to exclude nonsense sentences such as the third and fourth examples above, but there are no theoretical obstacles which prevent the addition of such rules.

A more serious limitation of phrase-structure grammar, however, is posed by what Chomsky (1956) identifies as *constructional homonymity*. In attempting to construct the simplest possible phrase-structure grammar for English, we would have to include such rules as:

> Verb → are + barbecuing
> Verb → are
> NP → they
> NP → chickens
> NP → barbecuing + chickens

to account for such sentences as *They are barbecuing chickens* (NP + verb + NP) and *Barbecuing chickens are delicious* (NP + verb + adjective), etc. But these rules would supply two derivations of the sentence *They are barbecuing chickens* that are non-equivalent:

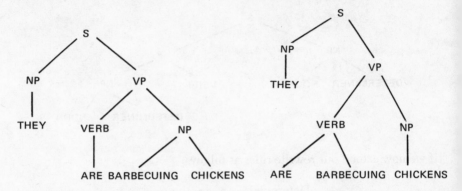

Chomsky's proposal for dealing with such phenomena involves the assumptions that: (1) an adequate grammar makes most parsimonious use of a relatively small number of basic elements or *kernel sentences* from which an indefinitely large number of derived sentences may be generated; (2) the rules applied to the base elements for generating further sentences are necessarily of a less restricted and therefore more powerful kind than those we have already described as rewrite rules. Let us examine the inadequacies of phrase-structure grammar in the light of these assumptions, with a view toward resolving the problem of constructional homonymity in the preceding ambiguous sentence.

The second assumption recognizes the necessity of incorporating into grammars such devices as *morphophonemic rules,* which convert strings of morphemes into strings of phonemes. In English, for example, we have:

$$will \frown past \rightarrow would$$
$$take \frown ing \rightarrow taking$$
$$be \frown en \rightarrow been$$
$$walk \frown ed \rightarrow walked$$

and so forth. Even this simple formulation exceeds the capacities of phrase-structure grammar, as Chomsky (1956) shows by an analysis of the verb phrase.

If we choose an intransitive verb (e.g., 'come,' 'occur,' etc.), we cannot select be⁀en as an auxiliary. We cannot have such phrases as 'John has been come,' 'John is occurred,' and the like. Furthermore, the element be⁀en cannot be chosen independently of the context of the phrase 'Verb.' If we have the element 'Verb' in the context 'the man—the food,' we can have 'the man is eating the food,' 'the man would have been eating the food,' etc., but not 'the man is eaten the food,' 'the man would have been eaten the food,' etc. On the other hand, if the context of the phrase 'Verb' is e.g., 'the food—by the man,' we are *required* to select be⌢en. We can have 'the food is eaten by the man,' but not 'the food is eating by the man,' etc. (p. 148).

The fact that every active sentence ("the man ate the food") has a corresponding passive ("the food was eaten by the man") provides a way to incorporate sentences with be⌢en into the grammar, by addition of the following rule (Chomsky, 1956):

> If S is a sentence of the form NP_1—Auxiliary—V—NP_2, then the corresponding string of the form NP_2—Auxiliary⌢be⌢en—V—by⌢NP_1 is also a sentence (p. 148).

When we apply this rule to the active sentence "the man—past—eat the food" (NP_1—Auxiliary—V—NP_2), we derive the passive sentence "the food—past—be⌢en—eat—by the man" (NP_2—Auxiliary⌢be⌢en—V —by⌢NP_1). A rule of this kind, which rearranges the components of the string to which it applies, provides the means for a considerable simplification of the grammar. Such rules, called *transformations,* involve operations like additions, deletions, permutations, combinations, etc., which convert a sentence with a given constituent structure into a new sentence with a derived constituent structure. It adds immeasurably to our analytic capabilities if our grammar makes further provision for distinguishing *optional transformational rules* from *obligatory transformational rules*.

The stated rule above specified a transformation which converts the sequence affix-verb into verb-affix. Whether or not the transformation is applied, we still have a sentence. Therefore, we must regard the passive as an optional transformation. Says Chomsky (1956):

> This distinction between optional and obligatory transformations leads us to distinguish between two classes of sentences of the language. We have, on the one hand, a *kernel* of basic sentences that are derived from the terminal strings of the phrase-structure grammar by application of only obligatory transformations. We then have a set of derived sentences

that are generated by applying optional transformations to the strings underlying kernel sentences (p. 150).

If we apply the concepts of optional and obligatory transformations to the ambiguous sentence *They are barbecuing chickens,* we can immediately see that the phrase *barbecuing chickens* could have two possible sources: one from an expression X *barbecues chickens,* in which the word *barbecuing* functions as an inflected verb form, and the other from *barbecuing chickens,* in which *barbecuing* operates as an adjective modifying the noun *chickens.* Since there are comparable expressions X *prepares salads* and *Movies are interesting* but not *salads prepares* and X *interests movies,* the expressions *preparing salads* (barbecuing chickens$_1$) and *interesting movies* (barbecuing chickens$_2$) are each generated once and from different underlying constructions.

More detailed consideration of these and related issues in linguistic theory is somewhat beyond the scope of the present discussion. The interested reader is referred to Lenneberg's (1967) provocative discussion of the concept of transformation and Chomsky's (1957, 1966) formal statements of the theory of generative grammar. We may note, by way of conclusion, that a theory—any theory—seeks to account for the largest number of facts with the smallest number of assumptions and principles. As measured by this criterion, generative grammar is superior to all previous approaches in terms of the explanatory power it derives from a parsimonious set of postulates and operations. To this extent, generative grammar fulfills a fundamental requirement of language theory by providing the kind of apparatus or device which can potentially account for an indefinite number of grammatically acceptable sentences and none that are ungrammatical.

REFERENCES

BERKO, J. The child's learning of English morphology. *Word,* 1958, 14, 150–177.

BROWN, R. *Words and things.* New York: The Free Press, 1958.

BROWN, R., BLACK, A. H., and HOROWITZ, A. E. Phonetic symbolism in natural languages. *Journal of Abnormal and Social Psychology,* 1955, 50, 388–393.

CARROLL, J. B. *Language and thought.* Englewood Cliffs, New Jersey: Prentice-Hall, 1964.

CHOMSKY, N. Three models for the description of language. *Proceedings of the Symposium on Information Theory, IRE Transactions on Information Theory,* 1956, 2, 113–124. Reprinted in Smith, A. G. (Ed.) *Communication and culture.* New York: Holt, Rinehart and Winston, 1966.

CHOMSKY, N. *Syntactic structures*. The Hague: Mouton, 1957.

GALANTER, E. *Textbook of elementary psychology*. San Francisco: Holden-Day, 1966.

HAYES, C. *The ape in our house*. New York: Harper and Row, Publishers, 1951.

HILL, A. *An introduction to linguistic structures*. New York: Harcourt, Brace and World, 1958.

HOCKETT, C. F. The origin of speech. *Scientific American*, 1960, 203, 89–96.

KATZ, J. *The philosophy of language*. New York: John Wiley & Sons, 1966.

KLINEBERG, O. *Social psychology*. New York: Holt, Rinehart & Winston, 1954.

LENNEBERG, E. H. *Biological foundations of language*. New York: John Wiley and Sons, 1967.

LILLY, J. C. *Man and Dolphin*. Garden City, N.Y.: Doubleday & Co., 1961.

MUNN, N. L. *Psychology*. Boston: Houghton Mifflin, 1966.

NEWMAN, S. Further experiments in phonetic symbolism. *American Journal of Psychology*, 1933, 45, 53–75.

PITTENGER, R. E., and SMITH, H. L. A basis for some contributions of linguistics to psychiatry. *Psychiatry*, 1957, 20, 61–78.

REVESZ, G. *The origins and pre-history of language*. New York: Longmans, Green, 1956.

ROBINS, R. H. *General linguistics: an introductory survey*. London: Longmans, Green, 1964.

SAPIR, E. *Language*. New York: Harcourt, Brace, and World, 1921.

SAPIR, E. A study in phonetic symbolism. *Journal of Experimental Psychology*, 1929, 12, 225–239.

SAPORTA, S. Linguistics and communication. In L. Thayer (Ed.), *Communication, theory and research*. Springfield, Illinois: Charles C. Thomas, 1967.

TSURU, S. Sound and meaning. Unpublished manuscript cited in R. Brown, *Words and things*. New York: The Free Press, 1958.

VON FRISCH, K. *The dancing bees*. New York: Harcourt, Brace and World, 1955.

CHAPTER 3

Biological Bases of Language

. . . a biological investigation of language must not only study the organism that speaks but must also study the behavior itself—language—much the same way the zoologist who studies the badger must study its physique together with its habits in order to give a complete picture of that animal (p. 3).

Eric Lenneberg*

THE DEVELOPMENT of the vocal-auditory communication system of man dates back to around the beginning of the Pleistocene Age, about a million years ago, with the appearance of primates called *hominids*, or man-like apes. The archaeological traces of these proto-men are the object of intensive study at present; however, the origin of genus *homo* remains obscure. For instance, even the number of species that may have existed in these prehistoric times is largely a matter of guesswork.

Primordial men may have varied in many respects, but it seems reasonable to assume that they possessed certain common features: they were slow to mature, with long-dependent offspring and therefore some type of family structure, omnivorous in diet, highly vocal, upright in posture, flat of face, and with frontally situated eyes that could fixate on the hands (Howells, 1959). Their ancestors, the *hominoids*, had long since descended from the trees, and they could use their hands and eyes in various ways. A million years permitted a great deal of mutation and adaptation of these characteristics.

---

* *Biological Foundations of Language,* New York: John Wiley and Sons, 1967.

During this long period, hominid animals were afforded many opportunities to acquire skills—hunting with weapons, the use of fire, the invention of clothing, the utilization of shelter—as "a means for the maintenance of homeostasis in the interaction between his internal energy system and his external energy field" (Arnold, 1961, p. 94). One of the major developments of this period was the emergence of vocal-auditory communication in these hominid animals. Suddenly or gradually, the voice itself came to be used as a tool. Instead of merely indicating the species, identity and emotional state of the animal, the vocal cries of the hominid came to specify also something external to the animal and in its common environment.

Quite possibly other types of motor expression besides the vocal participated in this radical development. Gestures of the hands, such as pointing, could easily come to have an external reference. Movements of the head and eyes or the face might come to indicate something in the world, as well as expressing emotion. Mimicry may have accompanied or even preceded the development of speech; the essential factor was that expression, vocal or gestural, acquired a further meaning. Gradually there was a progression from the representative use of preverbal sounds to the arbitrary symbols of language (Arnold, 1961).

CHARACTERISTICS OF SPEECH

According to a Pavlovian formula, vocal sounds make up another and more powerful "signaling system." In other words, they become *coded*. If words are used specifically and conventionally for external events, they can substitute for the visual, tactual or other kinds of stimuli from these sources. Words, like gestures, can then be used to direct the sense organs of the hearer toward parts of the environment he would not otherwise perceive, and to induce perception of sectors of the larger second-hand perception of parts of the larger environment that the speaker has perceived but the hearer has not.

As man's use of speech developed, the vocalizations which were uttered possessed expressive as well as symbolic qualities. The qualities of vocal sounds called expressive specify types and subtypes of human emotions, moods and feelings. The crying of a baby or the laughter of a young person are sounds that are unmistakable. There are moans of pain and sighs of relief, growls of anger and grunts of effort, shouts of triumph and murmurs of love. We must assume that these types of vocalization existed long before speech. It was probably from this repertory of spontaneous unlearned utterances in our hominid ancestors that conventional speech sounds developed. It remains the function of these expressive qualities to reveal the mood, feeling, intentions and temperament of the speaker.

Vocal speech also contains the symbols which carry the meanings of things in the common environment of all individuals. These symbols, according to Gibson (1966), enable men "to think of the same things, to have concepts in common, and to verify their concepts jointly" (p. 88). Symbolic meaning is on a different level from perceptual meaning. The cry "wolf" has an entirely different function from either the cry of alarm at actually seeing a wolf or the baying of the wolf itself.

The relation of a perceptual stimulus to its causal source in the milieu is of one genre, while the relation of a symbol to its referent is of a different sort. The former depends on the laws of physics and biology; that is, on the "ecology of stimulation." The latter depends on a "linguistic community," which is a unique invention of the human species. The relation of perceptual stimuli to their source is an innate relation such as one of projection. But, the relation of symbols to their referents is an arbitrary one of social agreement. The conventions of symbolic speech must be learned, but the child can learn one language just as easily as another. The connections between stimuli and their sources may well have to be learned in part, but they do not make a language. The language code is cultural, traditional and arbitrary; the connection between stimuli and their sources is not.

PHYSIOLOGICAL ASPECTS OF SPEECH

The source of acoustical speech sounds is the human vocal apparatus backed up by the human nervous system. This apparatus is probably the most complex sound-maker in the world. The sounds arise from a series of exhalations produced by the breathing muscles of the chest and diaphragm. These may or may not be accompanied by movements of the mouth, jaw, lips, tongue and velum (Gray and Wise, 1959). The series of concurrent movements produces what is called the "segmentation of speech"—that is, the fact of segments in the flow of sound. This flow, voiced or unvoiced, is modified in spectral composition so as to make vowels. It is also cut by pauses, stops and transitions so as to make consonants. The vowels and consonants are the units of articulation.

The muscular movements that create phonemes tend to be stereotyped. If these phonemes are thought of as both the responses of a speaker and the stimuli for a listener, it could be predicted that each speaker of a community would be compelled to make the same phonemes as others in order to be intelligible (Gibson, 1966). This phenomenon is generally viewed as part of what children do when they "learn to speak"—that is, they learn to pronounce in accordance with their language or their dialect, under social pressure from playmates, parents and school.

In other words, the process of speech development could be conceptualized as beginning with the possession by the child of a large repertoire of speech sounds (many not included in his native language). Gradually, through processes that seem to involve both maturation and learning, this repertoire is reduced to contain the sounds necessary in his language—sounds which are not reinforced by the speech of his verbal environment are eliminated and the child is left with a repertoire which contains his approximation of the sounds he hears. As the neuromusculature and sound discrimination processes mature, the child refines and polishes his repertoire into the sounds of his native tongue, gaining voluntary control over their production (Osborn, 1961). The sounds, having been stereotyped for the community, can be said to have a valid objective reality, "anchored in the habitual resonances, stops, frictions, and explosives of conventional articulation and specified by certain invariant properties of the wave trains of vibrating fields in the air" (Gibson, 1966, p. 94).

One physiological process involved in how the infant learns how to speak is referred to by Simon (1957) as "kinesthetic and auditory feedback." Buhler (in Brain, 1961), noting that the child hears the sounds that it produces, said:

> . . . the psychologically important fact is the formation of strong associations between the auditory impression and the movements which produce it, for this is the essential basis of the later imitation of the sounds the child hears, in which it has to translate what it has heard into vocal movements of its own (p. 154).

This approach represents an old theory which proposes that the human infant, in the babbling stage of speech development, learns associations between the sounds of speech and the acts of speech, or conditioned reflexes connecting a certain auditory stimulus to a certain vocal response. This is taken to be the basis of vocal imitation, and to explain why deaf children do not learn to speak. It is assumed by association theorists, therefore, that children must learn the correspondence of hearing and speaking.

It is perfectly true that any single elementary muscle contraction does not correspond to any single elementary sensory datum. But the pattern of contractions and the change of nervous output at the muscles do correspond to the pattern of excitation and the change of nervous input at the cochlea (Gibson, 1966). There is no need for these to be associated, since they are identical. What probably happens during the babbling stage is the differentiation of pattern and change in the muscular output along with a parallel differentiation of pattern and change in the cochlear input. As the child learns to articulate the invariants of sound, he learns to discriminate them. The practicing of vocal-auditory activity permits learning, but it is not associative learning (Gibson, 1966).

The function of auditory self-stimulation is, therefore, probably best understood if it is conceived not as a kind of audition but as a kind of proprioception. It monitors the flow of speech in the same way that other modes of proprioception keep track of the flow of other types of behavior. It thus enables articulation to be controlled. The next syllable depends on the previous one; feedback yields a concurrent record of how far the speech has progressed.

NEUROPHYSIOLOGICAL ASPECTS OF SPEECH

From a neurophysiological standpoint, the expressive and symbolic qualities of language are merely manifestations of what Head (1926) considered the basic processes of symbolic formulation and expression. Brock and Krieger (1963) point out that in its most complete form, this symbolic thinking and expression becomes a function of the entire cerebral cortex. However, it is largely through the work of Penfield that the true complexity of the speech mechanism has been revealed.

Penfield and Roberts (1959) have demonstrated that the human cerebral hemispheres are never twice the same in form and in the patternings of convolutions and fissures. At the time of birth, the motor and sensory areas of the brain are beginning to take on their function as transmitting stations. At that time the speech areas are "blank slates on which nothing has been written" (p. 198). Generally three cortical speech areas, as shown below in Figure 3.1, will be developed in the left hemisphere. Although it is quite rare, the right hemisphere may become dominant with respect to localization of the speech centers. In addition, a small lesion in infancy may produce some displacement of the expected location of the areas within the left hemisphere. A large lesion in the posterior speech area may cause the whole speech apparatus to be developed in the right hemisphere where the cortical areas take up homologous positions.

In the cerebral cortex of the human adult there are areas devoted to the control of speech musculature, and there are other areas devoted to

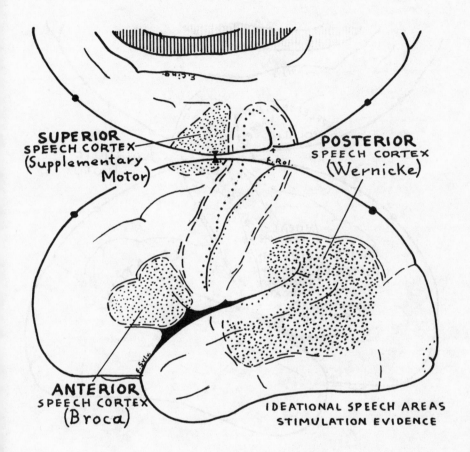

FIGURE 3.1—Summarizing map of the areas of cortex in the dominant hemisphere which are normally devoted to the ideational elaboration of speech. Conclusions derived exclusively from the evidence of electrical speech mapping. Reprinted by permission of Princeton University Press. Source: W. Penfield and L. Roberts, *Speech and Brain Mechanisms* (Princeton University Press, 1959).

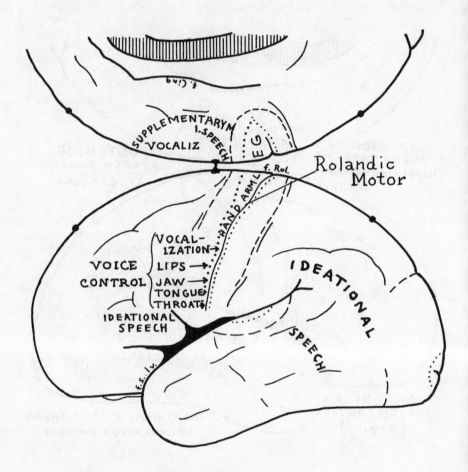

FIGURE 3.2—Speech mechanisms in the dominant hemisphere. Three areas are devoted to the ideational elaboration of speech; two areas, devoted to vocalization. The principal area devoted to motor control of articulation, or voice control, is located in lower precentral gyrus. Evidence for these localizations is summarized from the analysis of cortical stimulation and cortical excision. Reprinted by permission of Princeton University Press. Source: W. Penfield and L. Roberts, *Speech and Brain Mechanisms* (Princeton University Press, 1959).

the ideational processes of speech. Each of these areas will be discussed separately.

Information about the motor mechanism of speech has been obtained by Penfield and others from the electrical stimulation of the cortex of conscious subjects. Vocalization (Penfield and Jaspers, 1954) has been found to be the response of a small area between the upper face movement and the lip movement on the precentral Rolandic gyrus (*see* Figure 3.2). Subsequently it was shown that vocalization could be produced in the supplementary motor area of either cerebral hemisphere (Penfield and Rasmussen, 1950). A gentle electrical current in one of these specific cortical areas causes a patient, who is lying fully conscious on the operating table, to utter a long-drawn vowel sound which he is completely helpless to stop until he runs out of breath. Then, after he has taken a breath, he continues helplessly as before.

One of the major differences between the cortical motor responses of man and animals is manifested in human voice control. Cortical control of the voice, including articulatory movements and vocalization, is located between the two principal areas for ideational speech, one posterior and the other anterior (*see* Figure 3.1). It would appear that the Rolandic area of voice control can serve the purposes of speech on either side alone. This conclusion is drawn from the fact that the excision of one of the vocalization areas alone does not permanently interfere with speaking.

The areas of cortex utilized in the ideational elaboration of speech have been outlined by applying a gentle electrical current to the proper areas of the cortex of the dominant hemisphere in conscious human beings. The interfering current causes the patient to become aphasic until the electrode is withdrawn.

Three areas have been outlined (*see* Figure 3.1):

1. A large area in the posterior temporal and posterior-inferior parietal regions—Wernicke's area;

2. A small area in the posterior part of the third frontal convolution, anterior to the motor voice control area—Broca's area;

3. A part of the supplementary motor area within the midsagittal fissure and just anterior to the Rolandic motor foot area—supplementary speech area.

All three of these cortical areas, organized to function in one hemisphere only, play roles in the ideational speech mechanism under normal condi-

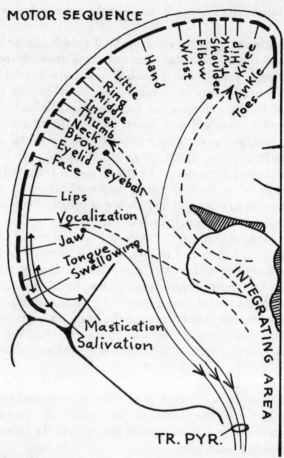

FIGURE 3.3—Voluntary motor tracts. Cross-section through right hemisphere along the plane of the precentral gyrus. The pathway of control of voluntary movement is suggested from gray matter, somewhere in the higher brain stem, by the broken lines to the motor transmitting strip of the precentral gyrus. From there it runs down the cortico-spinal tract, as shown by the unbroken lines toward the muscles. The sequence of responses to electrical stimulation on the surface of the cortex (from above down, along the motor strip from toes through arm and face to swallowing) is unvaried from one individual to another. The drawing is taken from W. Penfield and H. H. Jasper, *Epilepsy and the functional anatomy of the human brain*, Boston: Little, Brown and Company, 1954.

tions. The primary function of these areas of the cortex is the "memory" of words.

In addition, the temporal cortex, chiefly on the superior and lateral surfaces of both lobes and probably extending a little way into the parietal lobe, plus parts of the hippocampal gyrus, assume the function of interpreting experiences—interpretive cortex. Referring to these areas, Penfield and Perot (1963) concluded the following:

> There is within the adult human brain a remarkable record of the stream of each individual's awareness. It is as though the electrode cuts in, at random, on the record of that stream. The patient sees and hears what he saw and heard in some earlier strip of time and he feels the same accompanying emotions. The stream of consciousness flows for him again, exactly as before, stopping instantly on removal of the electrode. He is aware of those things to which he paid attention in this earlier period, even twenty years ago. He is not aware of the things that were ignored. The experience evidently moves forward at the original pace. This was demonstrated by the fact that when, for example, the music of an orchestra, or song or piano, is heard and the patient is asked to hum in accompaniment, the tempo of his humming is what one would expect. He is still aware of being in the operating room but he can describe this other run of consciousness at the same time.
>
> The patient recognizes the experience as having been his own, although usually he could not have recalled it if he had tried. The complete record of his auditory and visual experience is not subject to conscious recall, but it is evidently used in the subconscious brain-transaction that results in perception. By means of it, a man in normal life compares each succeeding experience with his own past experience. He knows at once whether it is familiar or not. If it is familiar, he interprets the present steam of consciousness in the light of the past (pp. 695–96).

There is, apparently, no overlap of the boundaries that separate speech cortex (which endows one with memory of words) and the interpretive cortex which gives one access to the memory of past similar experiences and thus enables one to understand the present (Penfield, 1965).

LENNEBERG ON BIOLOGY AND LANGUAGE

In a recent publication, Eric Lenneberg (1967) has attempted a critical survey of facts and theories pertaining to the biological bases for language; and a careful reading of this book is indispensable for the reader who wishes to pursue the topic at further length. At the risk of doing violence to the coherence and sequential order of his presentation, we shall try to summarize some of the major aspects of Lenneberg's views on the biological foundations of language.

Comparison with other primates of man's peripheral anatomy reveals a large number of specializations of the vocal tract and face which can hardly be explained as an adjustment to diet or as adaptations to any other vital function. But it is possible that some aspect of speech making might have played into the evolutionary history and development of man. However, there is no data to indicate the direction of the relationship, whether the morphological variables caused speech or whether the already existent acoustic abilities caused the morphological changes, or whether both variables were caused by an, as yet, undetermined variable.

Comparative studies also show marked differences between man and infrahuman in the central nervous systems. One that is directly related to language is lateralization of function, i.e., left-hemisphere dominance. Language and speech motor functions are not only represented in the cortex, but involve subcortical and midbrain structures also. Therefore, the capacity for language cannot be assigned to any specific neurological structure. Lenneberg suggests that perhaps the peculiar organization of the brain, rather than its structure, is more important for language, and that insight into the language function could better be accumulated through the study of developmental processes and growth rather than a study of mass. He further suggests that organization within the brain is itself a developmental process with structural correlates on a molecular level. In this sense, language would have a concrete biological structural basis.

In the realm of language disorders, there is substantial argument for the biological basis of language, and no evidence that these disorders are based on a fragmentation of associately-linked simple precepts. Most of the symptomatology is seen by Lenneberg as a disorder of temporal organization. This particular hypothesis can be a very useful tool for further research.

Notwithstanding his biological approach, Lenneberg is no reductionist. Language is a qualitatively different and unique phenomenon despite its biological basis. Lenneberg presents a very interesting and enlightening view, that the uniqueness of language is to be expected from the evolutionary process as well as from genetic mechanisms, and that there is nothing unbiological about recognizing this uniqueness of human language.

The emergence of speech habits as a function of maturational changes within the growing child seems to be the best biological explanation of language, since a great variety of environmental conditions leaves the age of onset unaffected. Furthermore there is much evidence that language development is interlocked with other maturationally-based behavior such as stance, gait and motor coordination, although it is independent of these other processes, i.e., not caused by, or a cause of, these processes. Also there is no evidence that training procedures can advance the rate of language learning. A critical period of language acquisition is linked with an initial lack of maturation; its termination is related to a loss of adaptability and the inability for reorganization in the brain, as a function of the cerebral lateralization of function. As the specific neurophysiological correlates of language are still unknown, the emergence of the critical period of language readiness cannot be attributed directly to any one maturational process. The prerequisite for the eventual discovery of these specific neural phenomena is a knowledge of the exact brain states before, during and after this critical language period. Some factual evidence is available for the supposition of a correlation between full maturation of the brain and the end of the critical period, but a causal relationship cannot be inferred.

Aside from the correlational aspects of the process, just how does language develop? Lenneberg presents a more convincing argument with regard to how it does *not* develop than with respect to how it does. To say that language is a discrimination learning process, or that it is a function of secondary reinforcement, or that it is mediated by stimulus generalization, are oversimplifications which are contrary to observable facts and rest on hypothetical constructs. There is some evidence that linguistic development is a process closely related to other principles of organization of behavior which are biologically based. Sensory data are grouped into undifferentiated global classes and these are subsequently differentiated into more specific patterns. Both perceived patterns and self-produced patterns become organized in this way.

Lennenberg's biological conception of semantics is extremely interesting and well-formulated. The hallmark of the human semantic system is its openness; therefore the idea that names stand for specific objects or even invariant classes of objects is self-contradictory. Concepts are not the products of cognition, but conceptualization is the cognitive process itself and words are the labels for these processes, i.e., words or names are the products of conceptualization. He rejects the view that words are developed into concepts through association with other words or things. The process is basically the ability to make a similar response to different stimuli or stimulus situations, which is based in the individual's ability to abstract the common denominators of experience. This ability has biological limits for all species and, in the species-specific case of man, has resulted in an ability to attach labels to these processes. Within these limits however, natural languages vary to a great degree but not so great as to result in an impossibility of one's learning another language. Naming in all languages has similar formal properties and once one has some idea as to the cultural characteristics of a language group it is fairly obvious as to what is nameable in that group. Where there are great differences between languages (in certain grammatical categories), cognitive processes seem least affected and there is no evidence to support the Whorfian view that different languages affect thought processes differentially. Although the relationship between language and cognition cannot be investigated experimentally, except for a very restricted area, Lenneberg's approach seems to be the most factually-based of any semantic theory (usually metaphysical or social reform in approach). At least his explanation is supported by some experimentation and his inferences are direct (i.e., not too far removed) conclusions from the evidence.

At the present time the only real evidence for the biological basis of language is language universals: commonality of age of onset, universality of the ontogenetic process of language, and the universality of syntactic structure (concatenation of morphemes) in a non-random manner. Lenneberg examines other evidence and discusses the implications with respect to the possibility that in the near future research would provide verification for much of what is presently mere supposition. The contention that language is biologically based seems well-supported, theoretically and experimentally, but it is only preliminary to the more basic question of the identity of the specific biological mechanisms involved. The chief virtue of Lenneberg's thoughtful marshaling of facts and theories is his clarification of the kinds of questions which need to be raised in further research efforts. Finally, what are some of the implications of the position that language is biologically based?

It should be emphasized, as could be ascertained from a careful reading of the book, that language and thought are tied to specific biological units, inasmuch as we are lacking adequate explanations of conceptual thought and language in terms of neurological action. Rather, language and thought are based in an organization, a system, an interdependence of biological material; and there is fundamental interdependence among biology, maturation and environmental conditions. Stated or qualified, in these terms, Lenneberg's theory is not as revolutionary as the title of the book might imply. If one goes further than the title, it becomes apparent that the theory fits in with the research and thought of the past two decades in linguistics, with only a stronger emphasis on biological systems than was heretofore the case.

So, then, the implications of the theory are that the study of language entails not only a description of language, not only a social psychological or experimental analysis of verbal learning, but an analysis of man as an organic system of interdependent variables. It implies that the study of language is the study of an organization of biological, psychological and environmental variables. The science of language is the science of man.

CONCLUDING OBSERVATIONS

An outline of the neurophysiological basis for speech seems to be well established. The three speech areas have been clearly mapped out and their function in word-recall has been described. Although the location may be different from person to person, their presence is definite. The existence of an interpretive cortex acting to complement the function of the speech centers has been demonstrated by Penfield. The interpretive cortex has the function of presenting a background of experience against which the individual can compare and interpret his present situation. To integrate these speech mechanisms, connecting pathways link them together, to other areas of the cortex, and to the thalamus. It is the thalamus (plus the hypothalamus and limbic system) that functions as the integration center for all bodily functions.

The neurophysiological aspects of speech are still far from completely worked out. As van der Berg (1961) has stated:

> The present data show a certain degree of specialization in the tremendous number of neurons and associated interconnecting structures. A large number of 'centers' seems to be imbedded in a vast network of multi-purpose neurons. The topography becomes gradually better known and with it a rough outline of the channels interconnecting the 'centers,' but we are yet far away from the point where it would be possible to build an electrical analog (p. 66).

Until more research is performed and more facts are found, man's understanding of the neurophysiological and psychological aspects of the production of speech will remain incomplete. A greater insight into the controlling mechanism of the subcortical structures as well as how the patterns of neural excitation correlates with words and concepts is sorely needed.

REFERENCES

ARNOLD, G. E. Phylogenetic evolution and ontogenetic development of language. *Logos,* 1961, 4, 86–99.

BROCK, S. and KRIEGER, H. P. *The basis of clinical neurology.* Baltimore: Williams and Wilkins, 1963.

BUHLER, W. R. The neurology of language. *Brain,* 1961, 84, 145–166.

GIBSON, J. J. *The senses considered as perceptual systems.* Boston: Houghton Mifflin, 1966.

GRAY, G. W. and WISE, C. M. *The bases of speech.* New York: Harper and Row, Publishers, 1959.

HEAD, H. *Aphasia and kindred disorders of speech.* London: Cambridge University Press, 1926.

HOWELLS, W. *Mankind in the making.* New York: Doubleday, 1959.

LENNEBERG, E. H. *The biological foundations of language.* New York: John Wiley and Sons, 1967.

MORGAN, C. T. *Physiological psychology.* New York: McGraw-Hill, 1965.

OSBORN, S. S. Concept of speech development. *Journal of Speech and Hearing Disorders,* 1961, 26, 391–392.

PENFIELD, W. Conditioning the uncommitted cortex for language learning. *Brain,* 1965, 88, 787–798.

PENFIELD, W. and JASPER, H. H. *Epilepsy and the functional anatomy of the human brain.* Boston: Little, Brown and Company, 1954.

PENFIELD, W. and PEROT, P. The brain's record of auditory and visual experience: A final summary and discussion. *Brain,* 1963, 86, 695–696.

PENFIELD, W. and RASMUSSEN, T. *The cerebral cortex of man.* New York: MacMillan, 1950.

PENFIELD, W. and ROBERTS, L. *Speech and brain-mechanisms.* Princeton, New Jersey: Princeton University Press, 1959.

SIMON, C. T. The development of speech. In L. E. Travis (Ed.), *Handbook of speech pathology.* New York: Appleton-Century-Crofts, 1957.

VAN DER BERG, J. W. Physiological basis of language. *Logos,* 1961, 4, 56–66.

WALKER, E. The thalamus of the chimpanzee. IV: Thalamic projections to the cerebral cortex. *Journal of Anatomy,* 1938, 73, 37–93.

CHAPTER 4

The Ontogenesis of Language

The child may begin as a parrot imitating what others say, but he will end as a poet able to say things that have not been said before but which will be grammatical and meaningful to his community. (p. 1)

Roger Brown and Jean Berko*

ADVANCES DURING THE PAST SEVERAL YEARS in the systematic study of language have stirred controversy, not only with respect to a number of complex issues in linguistic theory, but also in regard to the presumed bases for the entire process of language development. One group of parties to the controversy includes those who endorse the viewpoint we identified earlier as a *generative* approach toward language. The most articulate spokesman for this group, as well as one of its principal founders, is the brilliant and original linguistic theorist, Noam Chomsky.

The opposition, on the other hand, includes those whose approach to the acquisition of language derives essentially from *learning theory*. Among this group we find a predilection for models which conceptualize language as a hierarchical structure of complex elements built up out of more simple constituents, and a reliance upon reinforcement, stimulus

---

* Word association and the acqustion of grammar. *Child Development,* 1960, 31, 1–14.

control, and mediated generalization as explanatory principles accounting for the salient features of linguistic acquisition.[1]

The above distinction does not neatly divide linguists from psychologists. Although most linguists today in the United States appear to have accepted generative grammar, at least those aspects of the theory which involve *transformational* analysis, the approach is not without its critics. Thus, in a recent review article, Hockett (1967) refers to Chomsky as a "neo-medieval philosopher."

Nor do psychologists exhibit anything approaching unanimity of agreement on the adequacy of contemporary psychological theories, specifically learning theory, in accounting for language acquisition. Miller (1965) possesses impeccable credentials as a psychologist, yet he yields to no one in the vigor of his criticism of reductionist conceptualizations of language. Perhaps it would be more accurate to say that the distinction between the adherents of generative grammar and those who endorse a view based on learning theory involves some pervasive and deep-seated differences in philosophy of science, the dimensions of which are outside the limits of the present discussion. Some of the issues, however, cannot be postponed so easily, especially those that relate to the developmental features of language. To avoid some of the learning lab connotations that seem to attach to a term like language acquisition, we shall emphasize the emergence of language as part of the life cycle of the individual by referring to the process as *linguistic ontogeny*.

The question which divides the groups distinguished above is much more complex than whether or not one "learns" a language. Obviously, everyone who speaks a language—English or Swahili—had to learn it at some time or another. But learning in this sense is a trivial aspect of linguistic ontogeny. Assuming structural integrity on the part of the "learner," it is just as easy to learn one language code as it is to learn another. What is of true significance, therefore, are the fundamentals of a process which seems to operate identically to turn out an accomplished language user, given the most unpromising and sketchy types of "inputs" from the environment. If parents were compelled to give their children special instruction in phonology, morphology and syntax, language skill would be a rare attainment indeed, because relatively few parents possess any acquaintance with such matters. The fact that children can acquire language so easily and with an absolute minimum of specific instruction argues an inborn predisposition toward these types of func-

---

[1] Perhaps it should be emphasized that one can readily accept the validity and explanatory power of such concepts as reinforcement and generalization as they apply to various aspects of language behavior without endorsing them as a basis for language acquistion.

tions and skills. This, in turn, suggests that "evolution has prepared mankind in some very special way for this unique human accomplishment" (Smith and Miller, 1966, p. 3).

In a sharply contrasting version of linguistic acquisition, Jenkins and Palermo (1964) describe the process as beginning with a "form of imitation" followed by the addition of a "number of S-R connections between verbal labels and salient features of the environment" with which they become associated. As Weksel (1965) tartly observes:

> In these few sentences Jenkins and Palermo succeed in glossing over some of the crucial problems facing not only the formulation of a theory of language acquisition, but any attempt to establish a theory of language (p. 696).

If all that a theory of language had to account for was "simple S-R connections between verbal labels and salient features of the environment," such connections might easily be dealt with on the basis of some "form of imitation." The deficiencies of the Jenkins-Palermo type formulation become manifest when it is called upon to deal with the fact that children, in the natural course of language development, are required to produce various types of linguistic structures in the absence of appropriate and explicit examples of such structures in their linguistic habitats. Weksel (1965) categorically excludes from consideration as potential candidates for a theory of language ontogeny any and all extensions and modifications of current learning theory, including sophisticated mediation models. He suggests that the exigencies of the situation demand nothing less than a revolution in psychological theory to match the one that has already taken place in linguistics with the advent of generative grammar.

Before we can even begin to discern the outlines of such revolutionary modifications in psychological theory, it seems quite apparent that we shall need a massive supplementation to our current inventory of empirical facts on linguistic ontogeny. At the present time, we are woefully deficient in hard data, particularly those relating to the earliest period of language development. Nevertheless, there are several observations that one can make about the kinds of problems a psychological theory of linguistic ontogeny will have to attempt to resolve.

As Carroll (1964) reminds us, at least three interrelated sequences in the process of language acquisition can be identified: (1) *cognitive development*, "a child's capacity to recognize, discriminate and manipulate the features and processes of the world around him"; (2) *psychoacoustic discrimination*, "development of the capacity to discriminate and comprehend the speech he hears from others in his environment"; (3) *productive ability*, "development of ability to produce speech sounds and sequences of speech sounds that conform more and more closely to the patterns of adult speech" (p. 31). An adequate psychological theory of language development will be required to make provision for the understanding of these three sequences in both their independent and integrated functioning.

A second fundamental issue in language acquisition concerns the distinction between competence and performance. Something akin to this distinction is implicit in many of the dichotomous classifications that language specialists have used in the past: *la langue* vs. *la parole*, language code vs. speech signal, etc. It is suggested by Miller's (1965) analogy of the relation between population (language) and sample (utterance), and recalls the observation attributed to the 19th Century philosopher Von Humboldt that language uses finite means to achieve infinite ends. According to McNeill (1966, a):

> Our concern in the study of language acquisition is with the development of competence; only after we have understood this to some degree can we hope to understand performance. First, consider the general distinction. Competence is an abstraction away from performance; it represents the knowledge a native speaker of a language must have in order to understand any of the infinitely many grammatical sentences of his language; it represents a native speaker's linguistic intuitions —his realization that *the man hit the ball* is grammatical but *the man virtued the ball* is not. Performance is the expression of competence in talking or listening to speech. One is competent to deal with an infinite number of grammatical sentences; but one's performance may be distracted in various ways. Performance operates under constraints of memory, which is finite, and time, which must be kept up with. Such limitations are irrelevant to competence (pp. 16–17).

With regard to child language, the same distinction between competence and performance must be preserved. If our goal is to account for the emergence of linguistic competence, we defeat our purpose by confusing performance with competence. In addition, McNeill states,

> . . . we are interested in eventually accounting for a child's linguistic performance, and this, too, requires that we rigorously maintain the performance-competence distinction. It is

possible to describe performance, we must show how it derives from competence; that is, how the regularities in a
child's grammatical knowledge produce regularities in his
overt linguistic behavior. Nothing short of this will suffice (p.
17).

A generation of psychologists reared in the rigorous empiricist and
operationist tradition of post-Watsonian behaviorism can be counted on
to respond to the invitation to deal with "a native speaker's linguistic
intuitions" as their principal source of data with a spectrum of emotions
ranging from dismay to out and out disbelief. But if McNeill is correct,
such a reaction is Thermopylaean. A grammatical description of child
language is not the same as an account of linguistic ontogeny; and
someone—the psychologist or the psycholinguist—must forge the necessary links between the two.

Finally, one of the incontrovertible facts of linguistic ontogeny is its
rapidity. Says McNeill (1966, b):

At the age of eighteen months or so, children begin to form
simple two- and three-word sentences. At four they are able to
produce sentences of almost every conceivable syntactic type.
In approximately thirty months, therefore, language is acquired, at least that part of it having to do with syntax (p.
99).

The process of acquisition, McNeill (1966) suggests, is consequently one of
invention: "On the basis of a fundamental capacity for language, each
generation creates language anew, and does so with astonishing speed"
(p. 99). In short, linguistic ontogeny recapitulates linguistic competence. On the basis of evidence gathered thus far, one seems compelled
to conclude that *a system of rules and exceptions to the rules* (a necessity in any language) *is acquired for generating structured linguistic
utterances.* Preceding this process is a sequence of stages of prelinguistic
vocalization, in which practicing and listening to a variety of human
vocalizations seems to facilitate the later development of normal speech.
We turn to this prelinguistic developmental phase, therefore, as the first
stage in our descriptive outline of linguistic ontogeny.

PRELINGUISTIC DEVELOPMENT

Eisenson, Auer and Irwin (1963) have differentiated five stages of prelinguistic vocalization ("speech"). The first stage suggested is that of

undifferentiated crying. This is the first reaction to the environment and is the result of reflexive, total bodily responses. These reflexive oral responses to discomfort lack specificity and direction, according to Eisenson, and are produced by the expiration of breath.

The second stage in this prelinguistic developmental sequence is *differentiated crying.* Differentiation in the sounds of crying may become discernible after the first month of the infant's life. Crying continues to be a total bodily response to a situation, but the stimulating conditions are capable of eliciting characteristic qualities of the sound response. The so-called "hunger cry," for example, seems to be characterized and differentiated from other types of vocalizations by its particular rhythms.

By the third or fourth month of life, the normal infant enters the third state of prelinguistic vocalization, *babbling.* This is the stage of vocal play in which sounds are produced randomly. Differentiated crying also still occurs during this stage. Repetition of various sounds also occurs with increasing frequency in the babbling stage. In this stage, the infant begins to show responsiveness to the sounds of others around him. The child both listens to and produces sounds during the babbling stage. With training, a listener may acquire the ability to distinguish specific sounds and combinations in the infant's vocal productions, such as some back consonants, some frontal consonants, and the vowel combination [œ].

The alleged importance of the babbling stage for later linguistic development has been argued on the basis of scanty evidence from a few cases of isolated or *feral* children (Davis, 1940; Itard, 1932; Singh and Zingg, 1942). Of the thousands of reports written on language acquisition, only these very unusual cases deal with the effects of delay in language learning opportunities beyond the normal period of linguistic acquisition. Obviously, no responsible parent or experimenter would conceive of subjecting a child deliberately to a type of deprivation which could produce an alingual child.

In addition, the available literature has failed to generate much recent interest for several reasons: (1) in the few reported cases of isolated children, expert care was administered in only one case; (2) in none of the cases reported was it possible to accurately assess the native intelligence of the child; thus, it would be impossible to say whether the socially deprived child was congenitally defective in relation to the norm to which we wish to compare him; (3) in the reported cases there is no way to even estimate either the degree of isolation present or the amount of training instituted subsequently. Notwithstanding the limitations of the literature, it is instructive to examine it in search of evidence concerning maturation and language development.

The few well-reported examples of isolated children are limited to Itard's description of the "wild boy of Aveyron," Singh's account of Amala and Kamala, two children found in the company of wolves, and Anna and Isabelle, subjects of Davis' work.

Itard's "Wild Boy," whom he called Victor, was found at the age of twelve living in the forest. Victor was apparently not raised by animals, but rather was abandoned at an age where he could find food enough to keep himself alive. Victor learned to recognize the meanings of several hundred words, but was almost totally unsuccessful at producing speech. As Brown (1958) pointed out, although Victor's intellectual capabilities might have been equal to the task of language mastery, he may have been unable to cope with the intricacies of articulation and phonation. He suggests that the "impulse to babble" which is evident in infants "must receive social support when the readiness is there or the impulse will die" (p. 189).

Amala and Kamala were believed to be feral from birth or near-birth. Amala was one and one-half years old when discovered, and showed great promise at learning to speak. However, she died one year after her discovery and so her case tells us little. Kamala was about eight years old when discovered and lived ten years in human society. During this time she learned to utter a few words and to understand many, though her training apparently was less than expert.

Anna, the first subject of Davis' article (1940), was an isolated child who was discovered and taken to a welfare home at the age of six years. Anna was taught to speak several sentences but never gained a normal fluency in recognition or production of language.

The foregoing examples illustrate isolated children who were unable to acquire normal language usage after experiencing a varying amount of social isolation. Does this mean that social isolation completely prohibits language acquisition?

The case of Isabelle, cited by Davis (1940), contradicts this hypothesis. Isabelle was raised to the age of six and one-half years in nearly complete isolation from everyone but her deaf-mute mother. Isabelle's behavior was animal-like when she was taken from her home, but with expert care and training she was able to achieve a normal I.Q. by the time she was eight and one-half years old. In two years she learned what normally takes six years. Had Isabelle benefited from a normal environment what sort of development would she have displayed? It is possible that she might have been very superior in intelligence. Or perhaps she progressed better than the others because her environment included more necessary social factors and thus she was more predisposed to further socialization.

It is possible, even probable, that the other children were congenitally doomed to inferior performance. Also, the others did not receive the expert training given Isabelle.

We are working here on an unscientific basis. There are no controls on either the inherited or environmentally-induced characteristics of these children. Yet the evidence points to the conclusion that at least six years and probably more (Davis suggests as many as fifteen years) of isolation from society can be overcome with proper training.

The case of Isabelle clearly illustrates that language can be learned at an accelerated rate after the maturation stage has been passed. Language learning thus conforms to the pattern of walking and other forms of behavior which have been demonstrated to take place at an accelerated rate when training begins at an advanced stage of maturation.

There are many gross behavior patterns besides the linguistic which are affected by isolation. As Brown (1958) states, sexual depression is one of the definitive characteristics of feral man; sexuality "appears, like speech, to be a function that a society must develop" (p. 187). Presumably sexual behavior would return with socialization, although no record was found to substantiate this.

If there is a limit to the length of time a child can endure isolation from society and still attain normal fruition of his linguistic talents, what is that period? More important, what are the underlying neurophysiological factors involved in socialization which are affected by isolation? Was Victor physically different from the person he would have been under more normal circumstances? Considering the case of Isabelle again, it is difficult to put aside the possibility that isolation is not causally related to neurophysiological change.

Neurophysiological differences between individuals cause behavioral differences, but do behavioral differences, in this case, cause neurophysiological differences? We do not have enough evidence to say that isolation causes neurophysiological changes effecting language acquisition. If an irreversible change does take place, when does it begin? For how long after the onset of change does the possibility of reversal exist? Once the change has advanced to a critical stage how can it be bypassed?

As important as such questions are to an understanding of rather basic issues in language development, there seems little likelihood that answers will be found in the near future.

There are certain trends in the pattern of sounds produced by the babbling infant (Irwin, 1946), but their importance for the further development of speech has been questioned recently by linguistic investigators. For example, Lenneberg (1964) has reported that sound spectrographic analysis has revealed objective differences between the babbling sounds of children and the speech sounds of adults. This observation casts some doubt on the assumption that the earliest motivation for speech development derives from the infant's discovery of the similarity between his own sounds and those produced by his mother while attending to his needs. In addition, noting that mothers have been shown to be unable to imitate the babbling sounds of their children with any degree of success, Lenneberg concludes that the child is "innately equipped" to hear similarities between his own vocalizations and those of his mother where there are definite differences, or else sound imitation is a "mere fiction" (p. 19). Further, Lenneberg (1962) cites the findings from a case study of an 8-year old child with a congenital neurological defect for speech articulation, who is nevertheless able to understand spoken English. This child has never babbled or attempted word imitation. Therefore, Lenneberg sees little basis for the learning theory assumption that language acquisition "is a gradual process in which verbal responses of some primitive nature (e.g., babbling) are the essential prerequisities for language development (1964, p. 125).

Some children stop babbling about the time they begin to learn their first words. The first sounds apparent to an adult in an infant's babbling are vowels, the first of which is apt to be some variety of "a" repeated at length. The consonantal sounds begin with the labials and are followed in order by gutturals, dentals and finally nasals (Irwin, 1946).

Lallation is the fourth stage identified by Eisenson, et al. (1963), and it occurs during the second six months of life. They define lallation as the "repetition of heard sound complexes and syllables." The infant in this stage of prelinguistic vocalization learns to imitate his own accidental productions. Also during the period of lallation, the infant's response to others becomes more selective in that he will not interrupt his vocal play when some adult speaks to him.

The fifth and final stage of prelinguistic speech is that of echolalia. This stage begins in about the ninth or tenth month and is characterized by the "initiation by the infant of sounds which he hears others make, but which he does not comprehend." According to Eisenson, et al. (1963), "It is unlike lallation in that another individual provides the stimulus for the repetition of a sound." As the authors point out:

> The lallation and echolalic periods are of tremendous importance because during these stages the child acquires a repertoire of sound complexes which ultimately he will be able to produce at will, and which he must have before he can learn to speak or acquire a language in the adult sense (p. 195).

To some extent, echolaic behavior continues throughout life.

The sequential character of these prelinguistic activities is one of the strongest arguments for the large biological component of language behavior. Referring to Lenneberg (1966):

> The hallmarks for maturationally controlled emergency of behavior are four:
> 1. regularity in the sequence of appearance of given milestones, all correlated with age and other concomitant developmental facts;
> 2. evidence that the opportunity for environmental stimulation remains relatively constant throughout development but that the infant makes different use of such opportunities as he grows up;
> 3. emergence of the behavior either in part or entirely, before it has any immediate use of the individual;
> 4. evidence that the clumsy beginnings of the behavior are not signs of goal-directed practice (p. 220).

Studies have demonstrated that the emergence of speech and language meets these criteria.

LINGUISTIC DEVELOPMENT

The period of actual linguistic development does not divide itself readily into stages as visible as those which characterize prelinguistic development. Eisenson and his associates (1963) simply subsume the entire linguistic development sequence under the term *verbal utterance*. This term refers to "the establishment of conventionalized speech patterns as specific responses to socially presented stimuli" (p. 195). Implicit to this definition is the assumption that a period of verbal comprehension without meaningful vocal responses has preceded the emergence of actual utterances. Linguistic development for Eisenson, then, consists of gradual increases in both receptive and productive speech ability.

The period of verbal utterances can, however, be partitioned in terms of the degree to which the child's vocalizations approach an adult level of grammatical structure. According to this criterion, one may discern on an impressionistic basis three levels of linguistic development.

The first stage is that of the word sentence and lasts for several months after the child begins to speak. Single word utterances are considered to be word sentences because they serve to express a complete thought for the child. Any single "word sentence" may have a multiplicity of meanings, depending upon the type of vocal expression, inflection, or situation in which it is used.

The second stage of linguistic development might be called that of the multi-word sentence. Most children reach this stage only after two years of age. The earliest multi-word sentences are most apt to be composed of a noun and a verb which, nevertheless, convey full subject-predicate implications. "Baby go" and "Baby eat" are noun-verb combinations which typically may be produced by children between the ages of fifteen and twenty-seven months. The multi-word sentences at this stage, however, are not correct grammatically. Under two years of age, children tend to omit articles, prepositions, conjunctions, etc.

A third stage might be delineated as the period of grammatically correct verbal utterances. This period begins sometimes around three years of age for most children. Correct grammatical usage, of course, is acquired only gradually and therefore, it would not be applied consistently to all of the child's utterances.

As we mentioned earlier, children appear to master all of the essential grammatical structures of their language in the incredibly short period of 30 months (McNeill, 1966, b). Our support for such statements is derived largely from a body of recent research which incorporates the latest advances in psycholinguistics. Says McNeill:

> The past half-dozen years have seen a great change in the study of child language. Formerly, attention was concentrated on surveys of vocabulary, frequency counts of various grammatical classes, and case histories of the gradual elimination of errors in speaking. The basic assumption appears to have been that child language was adult language filtered through a great deal of cognitive noise and impoverished of vocabulary. The scholar supposed that he knew the child's grammar in advance and that it was reasonable to use categories of adult grammar to describe child language. The change from this point of view has been simple but fundamental and mainly methodological. Recent studies look upon a young child as a fluent speaker of an exotic language. The psycholinguist's problem, therefore, is analogous to the problem faced by a field linguist (p. 16).

Despite the many problems involved in the study of child language, investigators like Brown and Bellugi (1964), Brown and Fraser (1963), Ervin and Miller (1964) and Menyuk (1963) have managed to demonstrate that almost all of the basic structures used by adults to generate sentences are discernible in the language behavior of three-year-olds.

A study by the latter investigator examined the hypothesis that children have incorporated the generative rules of their grammar and are able to understand and produce sentences in accord with these rules, thereby extending their behavior systematically without additional instruction if additional memory aids are given. Menyuk (1963) obtained a language sample from each of her nursery school and kindergarten children in various stimulus situations: conversation with an adult, conversation with peers and responses to the Blacky Pictures projective test. The children were then asked to repeat a set of sentences representative of the various "restricted forms"—Menyuk's term for grammatically incorrect sentences produced originally by children the same age as the subjects—and a set of sentences representative of various transformation types, i.e., sentences which go beyond the simple active declarative type, that were found in their usage of grammar.

Older children were found to be able to perform the task of repeating the sentence sets regardless of the structure of the sentences. The dates appear to confirm the hypothesis that the children in this age group (3 years) have incorporated most of the basic generative rules of the grammar that we have thus far been able to describe and are capable of using these rules to understand and produce sentences.

Fraser, Bellugi and Brown (1963) attempted to determine whether understanding does actually precede productive capability in the process of language development. Twelve children ranging in age from 37 to 43 months served as subjects in this investigation. The task involved 10 grammatical contrasts created by the use of two utterances which are identical for some grammatical feature. Understanding was operationalized as the correct identification of pictures named by contrasting sentences. Production was operationalized as the correct limitation of contrasting features in sentences applied appropriately to pictures. The drawings specified by the investigator followed the general principle that the representations of paired utterances should be identical in every respect except the one coded by the grammatical contrast. The pictures were mounted side by side in a transparent loose-leafed photograph album. The order of the problems was counterbalanced and randomized. Four practice items preceded the test. Two to three sessions were necessary for all but 3 children to take all 3 tasks. The remaining 3 took only one session. Records consisted of one on tape and one written on the scene. Two scorers independently scored all of the data (720 items).

Results indicated that production, meaning the correct production of contrasting features in sentences applied appropriately to pictures, proved to be less advanced than understanding in 3-year-old children. However, production in the sense of imitation proved to be more advanced than understanding. It would appear that the highly systematic speech system is under more complete control at 3 years than is the less systematic and more complex referential system. The outcome suggests that children undergo considerable learning about referential patterning, the stimulus control of grammatical forms, before they produce the forms themselves.

VOCABULARY DEVELOPMENT AND PARTS OF SPEECH

The first word that makes its appearance in the child's vocabulary is usually a noun, followed shortly thereafter by verbs. Pronouns, adjectives and adverbs appear rather late in the developmental sequence; prepositions, articles and conjunctions are the last to appear. Even after they have been learned, these later parts of speech are often omitted in speech. According to Eisenson *et al.*, (1963):

> Nouns, interjections, and verbs precede the other word categories probably because these words, alone or in utterance that approximate conventional sentences, most easily express the child's feelings about his own needs and his reactions to the potencies of words, or really, his potency as a user of words. The word forms get done what needs to get done! (p. 208)

Early vocabulary development is a slow process. Following the utterance of his first meaningful word, months may pass and the child may still know a very small number of words. He reaches a stage, however, in which the acquisition of vocabulary proceeds at an accelerated pace. This occurs, according to Carroll (1964), "when in his cognitive development the child has reached the point of perceiving that things, events, and properties have 'names'" (p. 32). During what might be called this "naming stage," the child may prove a trial for his parents and others with endless questions of "What is that?" The results of this constant quiz process, however, are evident in the following figures on vocabulary development compiled by Smith (1926):

Year Level	Mean Number of Words that Child Can Produce and Respond to
1	3
2	272
3	896
4	1,540
5	2,072
6	2,562

The child's linguistic process is marked by features other than vocabulary growth. McCarthy (1960) reported an increase in sentence length: from an average of 1.2 words at 18 months to an average of 4.6 words at 54 months. Another investigator by the same name (Smith, 1941) noted an increase in "recognition" vocabulary from 23,000 words at the age of 6 (first grade) to approximately 80,000 words at age 17 (12th grade). The absolute validity of such figures is, of course, highly suspect; but from these and similar studies, we gather a general impression that vocabulary development occurs at its swiftest rate between the ages of 2 and 4 years, thereafter proceeding at a more moderate pace.

REFERENCES

BELLUGI, U. and BROWN, R. (Eds.), *The acquisition of language*. Lafayette, Indiana: Child Development Publications, 1964.

BROWN, R. Linguistic determinism and the parts of speech. *Journal of Abnormal and Social Psychology*, 1957, 55, 1–5.

BROWN, R. *Words and things*. New York: The Free Press, 1958.

BROWN, R. and BELLUGI, U. Three processes in the child's acquisition of syntax. *Harvard Educational Review*, 1964, 34, 133–151.

BROWN, R. and BERKO, J. Word association and the acquisition of grammar. *Child Development*, 1960, 31, 1–14.

BROWN, R. and FRASER, C. The acquisition of syntax. In C. N. Cofer and B. S. Musgrave (Eds.), *Verbal behavior and learning*. New York: McGraw-Hill & Co., 1963.

CARROLL, J. B. *Language and thought*. Englewood Cliffs, New Jersey: Prentice-Hall, 1964.

DAVIS, K. Extreme social isolation of a child. *American Journal of Sociology*, 1940, 45, 554–565.

EISENSON, J., AUER, J. J., and IRWIN, J. V. The psychology of communication. New York: Appleton-Century-Crofts, 1963.

FRASER, C., BELLUGI, U., and BROWN, R. Control of grammar in imitation, comprehension, and production. *Journal of Verbal Learning and Verbal Behavior*, 1963, 2, 121–135.

HOCKETT, C. F. The foundations of language in man, the small-mouthed animal. *Scientific American*, 1967, 217, 141–144.

IRWIN, O. C. Infant speech: Vowel and consonant frequency. *Journal of Speech Disorders*, 1946, 2, 123–125.

ITARD, J. M. G. *The wild boy of Aveyron*. New York: Century, 1932.

JENKINS, J. J. and PALERMO, D. Mediation processes and the acquisition of linguistic structure. In U. Bellugi and R. Brown (Eds.), *The acquisition of language*. Lafayette, Indiana: Child Development Publications, 1964.

LENNEBERG, E. H. Understanding language without ability to speak: A case report. *Journal of Abnormal and Social Psychology*, 1962, 65, 419–425.

LENNEBERG, E. H. Speech as a motor skill with special reference to non-aphasic disorders. In U. Bellugi and R. Brown (Eds.), *The acquisition of language*. Lafayette, Indiana: Child Development Publications, 1964.

LENNEBERG, E. H. The natural history of language. In F. Smith and G. A. Miller (Eds.), *The genesis of language*. Cambridge, Mass.: MIT Press, 1966.

LENNEBERG, E. H. *The biological foundations of language*. New York: Wiley, 1967.

McCARTHY, D. *Language development and language disorders*. Yellow Springs, Ohio: Antioch Press, 1960.

McNEILL, D. Developmental psycholinguistics. In F. Smith and G. A. Miller (Eds.), *The genesis of language*. Cambridge, Massachusetts: MIT Press, 1966. (a)

McNEILL, D. The creation of language by children. In L. Lyons and R. J. Wales (Eds.), *Psycholinguistics papers*. Edinburgh: Edinburgh University Press, 1966. (b)

MENYUK, P. A. A preliminary evaluation of grammatical capacity in children. *Journal of Verbal Learning and Verbal Behavior*, 1963, 2, 429–439.

MENYUK, P. A. Alternation of rules in children's grammar. *Journal of Verbal Learning and Verbal Behavior*, 1964, 3, 480–488.

MILLER, G. A. Some preliminaries to psycholinguistics. *American Psychologist*, 1965, 20, 15–20.

MILLER, W. and ERVIN, S. The development of grammar in child language. In U. Bellugi and R. Brown (Eds.), *The acquisition of language*. Lafayette, Indiana: Child Development Publications, 1964.

SINGH, J. A. L. and ZINGG, R. M. *Wolf children and feral man*. New York: Harper, 1942.

SMITH, F. and MILLER, G. A. (Eds.), *The genesis of language*. Cambridge, Mass.: MIT Press, 1966.

SMITH, M. *An investigation of the development of the sentence and the extent of vocabulary in young children*. University of Iowa Studies in Child Welfare, 1926, No. 5.

SMITH, M. K. Measurement of the size of general English vocabulary through the elementary grades and high school. *Genetic Psychology Monographs*, 1941, 24, 344.

WOOD, N. E. *Delayed speech and language development*. Englewood Cliffs, New Jersey: Prentice-Hall, 1964.

WEKSEL, W. Review of U. Bellugi and R. Brown (Eds.), *The acquisition of language. Language*, 1964, 41, 692–709.

CHAPTER 5

Aspects of Meaning

We come then to the conclusion that meaning is practically everything. We always see meanings as we think, act in terms of meaning when we act. Apparently we are never directly conscious of anything but meanings.

W. B. Pillsbury[*]

I T HAS BECOME COMMONPLACE to suggest that there are as many meanings of "meaning" as there are disciplines which deal with language. There must, in fact, be more than this, for the experts within a particular discipline rarely agree with one another on the definition of meaning. Moreover, the concept of meaning has wider reference than to those areas which pertain only to language and the disciplines dealing with linguistic matters.

Part of the difficulty that psychologists seem to experience with meaning may be reflected in the impression one receives from the literature, that somehow meaning has been dealt with inadequately unless or until it has been exhaustively analyzed in all of its shades, varieties and nuances. Psychology, in this respect, may have suffered unduly from a crisis in self-confidence engendered by statements such as this one by Titchener (1915): "If the translation out of common sense into science is to be made at all, psychology is the science in which the equivalent of

[*] Meaning and image. *Psychological Review,* 1908, 15, 156.

66

meaning will be found" (p. 118). The implication of this statement is that there is only one kind of meaning. Fries (1954) notes that, in English usage, the term meaning has signified such diverse matters as:

> . . . 'the denotation of a name,' 'the connotation of a symbol,' 'the implications of a concept,' 'the neuromuscular and glandular reactions produced by anything,' 'the place of anything in a system,' 'the practical consequences of anything,' 'the usefulness of anything,' 'that to which the interpreter of a symbol does refer,' 'that to which the interpreter of a symbol ought to be referring,' 'that to which the user of a symbol wants the interpreter to refer,' 'any object of consciousness whatever' (p. 63).

Attempts to classify and define meaning from the standpoint of the meaning content of utterances in general pose even more formidable problems. Fries (1957) quotes a segment of an analysis of utterances in terms of meaning content:

> Thus in the case of certain sorts of indicative, interrogative, imperative, and optative sentence-utterances . . . it seems possible to distinguish a number of factors, each of which may be and has been referred to as the meaning or part of the meaning of the utterance. These are:
>
> 1. the primary conceptual content symbolized, i.e., presented and evoked;
> 2. the propositional attitude (with regard to this) expressed and evoked;
> 3. the secondary conceptual content presented and evoked;
> 4. the propositional attitudes (regarding this) expressed and evoked;
> 5. the emotions and conative attitudes expressed;
> 6. the emotional tone;
> 7. the emotions and attitudes revealed;
> 8. other kinds of effects;
> 9. the purpose (p. 63).

To complicate matters even further, "meaning" is itself a linguistic term. As Carroll (1964) points out, "we must explicate the use ('meaning') of this word at the very same time that we are explicating the concepts to which it corresponds, or the situations in which it arises"

(p. 34). It is for this reason that Carroll refers to the process as a "bootstrap operation."

One final *caveat* must be stated. According to Laffal (1965):

> We are accustomed to thinking that meaning is a phenomenon, a fact of life, and we believe that it is up to the linguist, the psychologist, and the philosopher to specify where it is located and how it functions. However, anyone who undertakes such an investigation will only discover what he has already assumed. This is so because meaning is essentially *a theory* applied to a set of data—utterances or acts—which defines some point of view about the relation of these phenomena to their users (p. 20).

Earlier we characterized language as a system of arbitrary vocal signs. The area of systematic inquiry which deals with signs, *semiotic*, divides its subject matter into: (1) *syntactics*, the study of relations between signs and other signs; (2) *semantics*, the study of relations between signs and their referents; and (3) *pragmatics*, the study of relations between signs and behavior. Although Laffal seems to suggest an emphasis upon pragmatics in the passage quoted above, it is obvious that all three types of relations are involved in the question of meaning. We must also dismiss any temptations to view this threefold analytic program as representing a division of labor among linguistics, philosophy and psychology.

In the pages which follow we shall try to review selectively some of the approaches which psychologists have employed in their investigations of meaning. Those who wish to pursue an interest in this phase of research are referred to Creelman's (1965) comprehensive review of the professional literature on experimentation in meaning. Miss Creelman's review is noteworthy for its extensive coverage of Russian studies, some of which parallel American efforts and some of which attack problems of meaning from a markedly different perspective.

MEANING AND ASSOCIATION

It will be recalled that Freud developed the therapeutic technique of *free association* as a result of his dissatisfaction and disappointment with hypnotic methods of treatment. Free association encouraged the patient to verbalize the contents of consciousness in the emotional security of the analytic relationship and setting, with two avowed objectives. First of all, the verbal expression of affect-laden associations could be expected to achieve some diminution of the emotional charge through catharsis.

Secondly, the persistence of certain associations interrelated in thematic form might provide the analyst with significant clues pertaining to repressed material.

Although Freud's clinical use of association represented an original contribution, he had been preceded by Galton (1879) in the experimental application of associational techniques. Other early researchers[1] with *word-association* methods included Kraepelin (1892), Munsterberg (1907), Wundt (1911) and Jung (1906). The technique employed by Jung involved the presentation of a stimulus word to a subject who was instructed to respond with the first word that came to mind. His original list included 100 words, among which were included: boat, death, friendly, marry, sad, woman, window. The words obviously cover a broad spectrum of categories.

According to some of Jung's findings, adults tend to respond to the stimulus words with opposites, while children show tendencies to respond with a word that completes a phrase. Jung placed considerable emphasis on reaction time (RT) and conducted studies of typical RTs for various types of stimulus words, e.g., concrete nouns yield the shortest RT, with verbs next, and abstract words last. He found that women tend to have longer RTs than men; that educated or intelligent subjects produce shorter RTs than subjects with less education or lower I.Q.; and that there are intrafamilial similarities in associational patterns as, for instance, between mother and daughter.

Word-association procedures were adapted to the study of insanity by Kent and Rosanoff (1910). As normative data they obtained the associations of 1,000 normal subjects to a list of 100 common English nouns and adjectives. Certain responses proved to be very common: "home" to "house," "thread" to "needle," etc. Not all of the associations to a word are controlled by a semantic relationship, of course. As Osgood (1953) observes, the verbal response is not necessarily mediated by the meaning of the stimulus word. For example, one of the most frequent associations to a word is its opposite; other associations are rhyming or "clang" reactions. Thus, the stimulus word "man" may evoke either the clang reaction "pan" or the opposite reaction, "woman." Mediated associations, on the other hand, would include such responses as "male," "boy" or "masculine." Associations are not meanings; they can provide only one avenue of approach to the complexities of meaning.

A quantitative method for measuring *meaningfulness* (as distinct from meaning) was proposed by Noble (1952), who counted the number of

---

[1] Their contributions are mentioned in Anderson, H. and Anderson, G. (Eds), *An introduction to projective techniques.* Englewood Cliffs: Prentice-Hall, 1951.

associations that individuals produced to a stimulus word during a 60-second period. This research was an extension of work done earlier by Glaze (1928), who determined the association value of nonsense syllables. Noble found that the more commonly used English words (e.g., "table") evoked more associations than did less frequently used words (e.g., "probate"). Words differ in their usefulness; thus, we might expect a relationship between richness of meaning and the frequency with which a word is used. Meaningfulness is increased by higher frequency of usage to the extent that more occasions are provided on which new associations can be acquired to a given word. By the same token, a word that becomes useful will be employed more frequently and, hence, may become more meaningful. "Pop" expressions and slang typify the latter process. Although their meanings are assigned arbitrarily, their rapid circulation in daily speech leads to a marked increase in probability of occurrence and growth of additional associations.

MEANING AND CONDITIONING

In the early experimental work of Pavlov it was found that conditioned responses could be elicited by stimuli which differed to some extent in quantitative respects from the original conditioning stimulus. For example, a conditioned response might be obtained by using a stimulus which varied from the original stimulus along the dimension of amplitude. As Pavlov (1927) noted, "If a tone of 100 d.v. (double vibrations) is established as a conditioned stimulus, many other tones acquire similar properties, such properties diminishing proportionally to the intervals of these tones from the one of 100 d.v." (p. 110).

This phenomenon of *stimulus generalization* has proven nearly as important for psychology in terms of its implications as the original formulation by Pavlov of conditioning itself. For purposes of the present discussion, we may note that one interesting dimension along which stimulus generalization has been shown to operate is related to language. This area has been variously referred to as *verbal generalization* (Bousfield, Whitmarsh, and Danick, 1958), *semantic conditioning* (Razran, 1939), *semantic generalization* (Osgood, 1953), or *mediated generalization* (Bugelski, 1956; Broen, 1966). These terms are largely synonymous and do not differ significantly in operational or empirical respects.

Almost all of the studies in this area of inquiry employ experimental situations in which a response is conditioned to a word following which other related words (synonyms, antonyms, associations, etc.) are presented. If the original conditioned response in varying degrees appears, then generalization has been said to occur. The conditioned responses in these studies have included salivation, changes in skin resistance, numbers, lights, buzzers, etc. The different types of responses are said to serve as mediators; they serve as connections between the original verbal stimulus and the material used to test for generalization.

The basic experimental paradigm used in the study of verbal generalization is as follows:

$$S \quad R$$
$$A \quad B$$
$$C \quad B$$

In the above diagram B is learned to A. After learning is complete, C, which is somehow related to A, is presented and generalization is obtained in the instance in which the subject responds with B to the stimulus C. Mink (1963), Cofer and Foley (1942), Osgood (1953) and Bousfield, *et al.* (1958) have all presented formulations which illustrate ways in which language could mediate generalization. The majority of the studies in verbally mediated or verbal generalization have made use of either a classical conditioning technique (Razran, 1939; Feather, 1965) or a paired associate transfer design (Horton and Kjeldergaard, 1961). We shall confine our detailed discussion to the first of these two procedures.

SEMANTIC CONDITIONING

In 1939, Gregory Razran introduced the expression *Semantic Conditioning* and reported some of his earlier work on this phenomenon. His approach in the original (1939) experiment involved conditioning the salivary response to several different words. Subjects were then tested for transfer to homophones. This study clearly pointed out that the dimension of meaning can be more important—at least to some categories of subject—than the visual or vocal dimension of the word in determining similarity. Razran's results were given support by the work of Riess (1940). Later research has confirmed this relation in sign-sign generalization studies. In particular, the Russian investigators Shvarts (1954, 1961) and Vinogradova and Eysler (1959) have been active in this area of investigation. Shvarts tested subjects using a vasoconstrictive UCR. His results showed more transfer to words that were semantically related to the training word than to those phonetographically related. Vinogradova and Eysler also tested transfer using a vasoconstrictive UCR. They found generalization to all of the semantically related words, to only one of the phonetographically related words and to none of the neutral words.

Another interesting line of study was followed by the Russian experimenters. Volkova (1953) conditioned the salivary response to the word for "good." The subject was also taught to differentiate it from "bad." In testing for transfer the generalized response was obtained to sentences with the word "good" in them, to sentences containing synonyms, and to sentences expressing ideas which were acceptable or "good."

In a study attacking the same area from the opposite direction, Elkin (1955) conditioned subjects to give the finger withdrawal response to certain sentences. Generalization was then carried out by testing separate words of the sentence. The results showed that the greatest transfer occurred to the word or words carrying the meaning load of the sentence. Razran (1952) in a similar line of investigation tested for generalization to different parts of conditioned sentences. His data indicate that the greatest transfer is given to the verb and the direct object of the sentence. The findings of these studies suggest that the role assumed by various word forms is different and may indicate that different learning phenomena are involved in the acquisition of signs whose meanings are of central explanatory value and those whose inclusion in language behavior is primarily of grammatical importance. Further investigation along this line, including developmental studies, could yield valuable information about the processes involved in the acquisition and use of different grammatical forms of the language.

Razran has further pursued the study of some of the complex relationships involved in meaning. He has demonstrated that there is a continuum of meaning along which varying amounts of transfer occur (Razran, 1935). The greater the meaning attributed to the word, the greater is the transfer which will be obtained.

In examining the effect of different semantic relations on transfer, Razran (1949a) has found that word derivatives yield more transfer than any other relations. Supraordinates of the conditioned word were found to yield only about 50 percent as much transfer as subordinates. Contrasts were found to lead to more transfer than any other type of semantic relation with the exception of word derivatives and subordinates. Little generalization was found between parts of compound words. Further research of this kind might lead to valuable data on interactions among words which are semantically related in various ways. Developmental studies in this area might yield information on why such relations exist, how they are learned, and how they influence language behavior.

The results from sign-sign generalization studies thus far seem fairly clear. The adult human subject has built up some sort of response hierarchy which determines that the meaning of verbal stimuli is responded to before the auditory component. Given the nature of language learning, this is a fairly predictable result. Nor is it surprising that generalization will occur to a sentence containing the same approximate meaning as the test word. The sentence may be seen as merely an elaboration on the word-meaning. In a similar manner, generalization from a sentence to words of the sentence is due to the inclusion of the sentence-meaning in the word summary form.

Riess (1946) and Luria and Vinogradova (1959) have studied sign-sign generalization from a developmental viewpoint. Riess examined the effect of chronological age on generalization. The groups tested had mean CA's of 7–9, 10–8, 14–0 and 18–6 years. Riess tested his subjects for transfer to homophones, synonyms and antonyms. The 7–9 year old group showed the most transfer to the homophones and least to the synonyms. By age 10–8, the position of the homophone and the antonym had reversed, although the synonym still elicited the least transfer. At age 14–0 the greatest amount of transfer was obtained to the synonym and the least to the homophone. The 18–6 year old group showed this same relation, although in a more clearly differentiated manner.

Luria and Vinogradova (1959) tested normals and retardates with semantically and phonetographically related words. Unfortunately they did not test antonyms, so no comparison with Riess's 10–8 year old group is possible. The results of this study showed that normals gave transfer only to semantically related words. As retardation increased, the relation gradually reversed itself, until only phonetographic transfer was obtained.

One possible explanation for the shift in the type of transfer obtained in the above two studies is that at the lower levels of functioning the meaning of the stimulus is not known or weakly developed. Razran's (1935) work does indicate that less semantic transfer occurs to less meaningful words. However, it hardly seems possible in the Riess study, for example, that 7–9 year old subjects did not know that the words "father" and "dad" had the same meaning, while "father" and "farther" had different meanings.

A more probable explanation is that for some reason the semantic similarity was placed second to the auditory or visual similarity. In the preverbal child it is naturally likely that the transfer found would be to homophones. Words such as "father" and "farther" will sound almost identical. The preverbal subject will have no other basis for differentiating the words and, therefore, will tend to give the same response to both stimuli. In the process of acquiring language, the individual must shift his attention from purely auditory cues to symbolic cues. By the age of 14 (Riess, 1946) this process seems to be fairly complete. But what is occurring between the start of language acquisition and age 14? Why do 7 year old subjects who use language with a fair amount of proficiency still show homophone transfer?

One possible explanation is that in language acquisition emphasis is placed on the acquisition of meaning, although no extinction of similar response to homophones is taking place. The strength of the response to meaning must grow relative to the homophones and eventually surpass them in the response hierarchy. This still does not fully explain why Riess's group with a mean age of 7–9 years did not show semantic generalization when their use of language is obviously rather well developed. It may be that in the development of language behavior concentration takes place during the first stages not only on the acquisition of meaning, but also on the differentiation between concepts of highly similar meaning. The child learning language may learn the word "cat," for example, and thereafter may refer to all four-legged animals as cats. His task then becomes one of establishing the finer discriminations involved in differentiating cat from dog and attaching the proper verbal sign to each referent. Therefore, in the early stages of language learning the emphasis is more on discrimination and differentiation than on similarity of meaning. This emphasis might help account for the fact that the younger subjects in Riess's study did not give transfer responses to the semantically related words. Although it is likely that they knew the meanings of the words and could point out the similarities, the meanings were not seen on a continuum as were the sounds.

It is possible that language development goes through two stages. The first of these is the acquisition of fine perceptual discriminations which enable differentiation between similar objects and their signs. The concentration is not on the similarity of meaning, but on differentiation. Once this stage is completed, a second stage begins in which the individual comes to see words of similar meaning as being along a continuum of meaning. Along this continuum are words which can be used interchangeably and words which are opposites. This stage of learning leads to greater proficiency and sophistication in the use of language. The results from Riess's 10–8 group (showing the most transfer to antonyms) seems to indicate that the development of the meaning continuum begins with the recognition of the polarity of opposites. The further development of the continuum leading to the recognition of words of greater and greater similarity appears to begin after the recognition of polarity is achieved. As witnessed by Riess's two oldest groups, the emphasis on similarity and the development of the continuum continues at least until age 18. It seems possible, due to the hypothesized method of development of meaning, that the transfer of the 10–8 group to antonyms is as much a semantic transfer as is synonym transfer, but on a different level.

The results obtained from object-sign transfer studies are not as clear as the sign-sign results. Kotliarevsky (1936) and Kapustnik (1930) both found generalization from the referent to its word-sign. In the former experiment a bell was used. In the latter both auditory and visual stimuli were tested. Both of these experiments were conducted on children under 15. Keller (1943) also tested for generalization from object to sign but failed to find evidence for transfer.[2] Since the Keller study used adult subjects, the discrepancy among the above cited studies may further point out certain factors in the development of language behavior. As discussed previously, in the early stages of language development the subject is concentrating on the differentiation of meanings. Necessarily this requires the sign to be more closely tied to its referent. Only through discrimination of various differences among objects is the individual able to differentiate word meanings and apply signs appropriately. However, as this differentiation develops more fully and the subject is able to see words in relation to each other, the sign becomes less tightly bound to its referent. Therefore, object-sign transfer would be expected to occur in the earlier stages of language development, but not in adult subjects. This is just what the above cited studies demonstrate.

The above is a tentative analysis of the implications of the semantic conditioning work for the study of language behavior. Its purpose is to point out the fact that this area may be a rich source of data for the psycholinguist. Analysis of the semantic relations among different words and their referents, in addition to the study of the development and change in these relations, may shed considerable light on the complex process of language acquisition.

MEANING AS REPRESENTATIONAL MEDIATION

In a classic experiment on concept formation, Clark Hull (1920) presented a group of subjects a series of Chinese characters, each of which contained a distinctive identifying component or "radical" sign. Depending on the radical which it contained, a nonsense syllable was pronounced by the experimenter and repeated by the subject upon the presentation of each character. Gradually the subjects built up associa-

---

[2] Although Osgood (1953) has classified Keller's study as a sign-sign study, there is equal logic in characterizing it as an object-sign experiment. Despite the fact that a picture was used rather than the object itself, generalization occurred from the referent to the sign.

tions between the nonsense syllables and the radicals, to the extent that they were then able to anticipate correctly the appropriate nonsense syllable for a new character they had never seen. Thus, the radical became the "meaning" of a nonsense syllable in this experiment; and one could account for this meaning by describing the conditions under which the association was learned and reinforced (Osgood, Suci, and Tannenbaum, 1957).

The learning paradigm which fits the above case is the familiar paradigm of classical conditioning. Saporta (1967) feels that there are severe limitations to the usefulness and validity of attempts to deal with meaning on this level.

> According to this view, just as the presence of a buzzer preceding the electric shock causes the dog to jump, so the presence of the word *milk* is alleged to elicit behavior similar to that formerly associated with the thing "milk." The objections to this view are based both on the facts and on the theory. Such associations cannot be the basis of the meaning of words like *to, hello,* or *unicorn,* since the "things" to which such signs allegedly refer are non-existent. Furthermore, not all the behavior associated to "milk" can be transferred to *milk,* e.g., no matter how much a mother talks to a child about milk, she does not have to burp him. In short, only part of the behavior can be transferred at best, and there seems to be no general way of specifying what part in a way that is not tautological. (p. 5.)

Other psycholinguists have been sharply critical of the kind of oversimplified view of language acquisition that equates "verbal behavior" with non-language (including infrahuman) behavior in terms of analogues derived from conditioning. Said Miller (1965):

> *The meaning of an utterance should not be confused with its reference.* I take this to imply that the acquisition of meaning cannot be identified with the simple acquisition of a conditioned vocalization in the presence of a particular environmental stimulus. It may be possible to talk about reference in terms of conditioning, but meaning is a much more complicated phenomenon that depends on the relations of symbol to other symbols in the language. (pp. 17–18.)

measured. The following is an example of the manner in which the concept GIRLFRIEND might be subjected to semantic differentiation:

GIRLFRIEND

good |___|___|___|___|___|___|___| bad

hard |___|___|___|___|___|___|___| soft

slow |___|___|___|___|___|___|___| fast

The first of the three scales represents the *evaluative* dimension of meaning; the second represents the *potency* dimension; the third represents the *activity* dimension. (These three dimensions of meaning have emerged from analyses of many descriptive terms and may be presumed to represent some quite basic dimensions of psychophysical judgment.) Any term or concept can be rated on as many bipolar adjective scales as the investigator can supply, the number being limited only by the investigator's ingenuity and verbal facility. But in practice only three or four pairs of adjectives for each of the three dimensions are generally sufficient to render an adequate account.

To show the SD in operation, let us consider some actual data: the ratings given to a series of scales by student supporters of Hubert H. Humphrey and Richard Nixon during the 1968 presidential election campaign. Six concepts were examined, one of which was MYSELF. It is evident from Figure 5.2 that the students perceived themselves in quite similar terms, except on the liberal-conservative dimension. If we group the responses according to the three dimensions of meaning represented by the different scales, it appears that all of the students viewed themselves as *good, strong,* and *active.*

How did these same students perceive the office for which the two political candidates were contending, namely the Presidency? Figure 5.3 shows the results that were obtained when the same students who evaluated themselves with the SD also expressed their reactions to "the Presidency."

The students, who perceived themselves in essentially similar ways regardless of their political preferences, displayed some marked differences in the meanings they attributed to the Presidency. Humphrey supporters viewed the office of President as more optimistic, more active, stronger, fairer, and more liberal than did the supporters of Richard Nixon. It seems apparent from these ratings that political convictions may influence the meaning of a related concept (e.g., a political office).

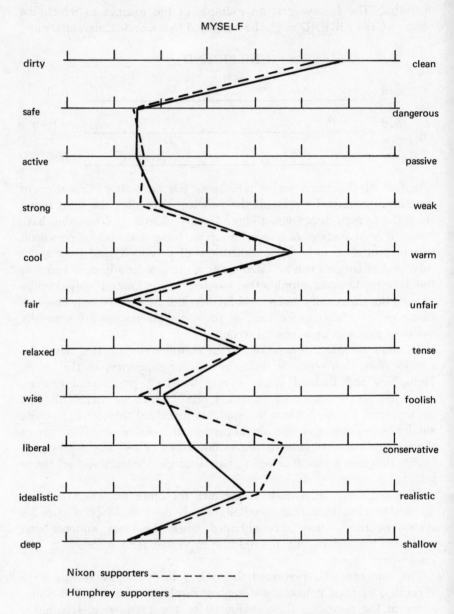

FIGURE 5.2—The semantic differential applied to the concept "myself" by pre-election supporters of Hubert H. Humphrey and Richard M. Nixon. Results are averaged over the 42 students in each group.

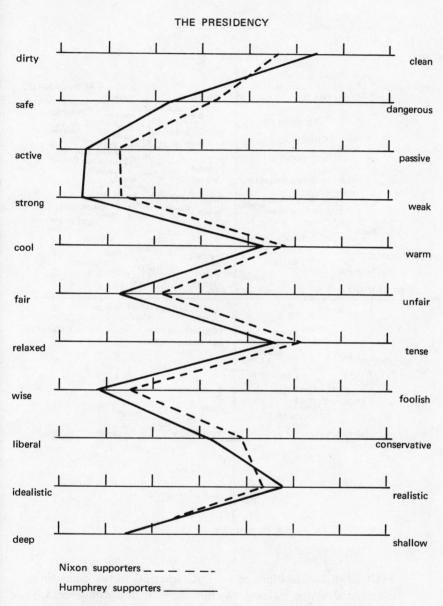

THE PRESIDENCY

FIGURE 5.3—The semantic differential applied to the concept "the Presidency" by pre-election supporters of Hubert H. Humphrey and Richard M. Nixon. Results are averaged over the 42 students in each group.

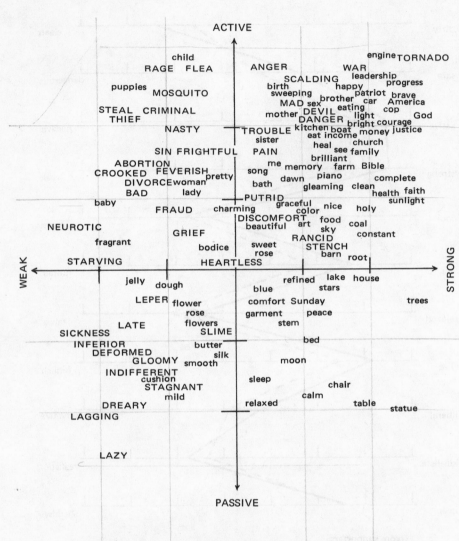

FIGURE 5.4—Locations of selected concepts in the semantic differential space defined by the three scales *strong-weak, active-passive,* and *good-bad.* Concepts rated *good* are in lower-case letters, concepts rated *bad* are in capitals. (Data of J. J. Jenkins *et al.* An atlas of semantic profiles for 360 words. *Amer. J. Psychol,* 1958, **71,** 688–699.)

As far as the SD is concerned, self-concepts do not appear to vary as a function of political preference.

If we assume that the three general factors of evaluation, potency, and activity account for a significant proportion of the meaning of most concepts, then we can locate a particular concept within a "semantic space" whose dimensions are defined by these three factors. It is then possible to map the relationships and clusterings among various concepts and identify those concepts which are similar and those which are dissimilar among a given set of concepts. Carroll (1964) has presented (Figure 5.4) a graphic location of selected concepts in the semantic space defined by the three scales: *strong-weak, active-passive,* and *good-bad.* Concepts rated *good* are given in lower-case letters; concepts rated *bad* are in capitals. The material on which this diagram was based was reported in Jenkins, *et al.* (1958).

We should emphasize that the SD represents only a partial approach to the analysis of meaning. Osgood, Suci, and Tannenbaum (1957) readily acknowledge the limitations of their procedure and caution that semantic space for concepts in general is multidimensional. Nevertheless, for a great many words, the single dimension of evaluation accounts for a substantial portion of the meaning.

REFERENCES

ANDERSON, H. and ANDERSON, G. (Eds.), *An introduction to projective techniques.* Englewood Cliffs, New Jersey: Prentice-Hall, 1951.

BOUSFIELD, W. A., WHITMARSH, G. A., and DANICK, J. J. Partial response identities in verbal generalization. *Psychological Reports,* 1958, 4, 703–713.

BROEN, W. E. Response disorganization and breadth of observation in schizophrenia. *Psychological Review,* 1966, 73, 579–585.

BUGELSKI, B. R. *The psychology of learning.* New York: Holt, 1956.

CARROLL, J. B. *Language and thought.* Englewood Cliffs, New Jersey: Prentice-Hall, 1964.

COFER, C. N. and FOLEY, J. P. Mediated generalization in the interpretation of verbal behavior. I: Prologomena. *Psychological Review,* 1952, 49, 513–540.

CREELMAN, M. *The experimental investigation of meaning.* New York: Springer Publishing Company, 1966.

ELKIN, D. G. The characteristics of conditioned reflexes to a complex verbal stimulus. *Vop. Pskhol.,* 1955, 1, 79–89.* This citation and all subsequent starred items are included in the bibliography of the 1961 Razran article in *Psychological Review.*

FEATHER, B. Semantic generalization of classically conditioned responses. *Psychological Bulletin,* 1965, 63, 425–441.

FRIES, C. C. Meaning and linguistic analysis. *Language*, 1954, 30, 57–68.

GLAZE, J. A. The association value of nonsense syllables. *Journal of Genetic Psychology*, 1928, 35, 255–267.

HORTON, D. L. and KJELDERGAARD, P. M. An experimental analysis of associative factors in mediated generalization. *Psychological Monographs*, 1961, 75, Whole No. 515.

HULL, C. L. Quantitative aspects of the evolution of concepts: an experimental study. *Psychological Monographs*, 1920, 28, No. 123.

KAPUSTNIK, O. P. The interrelation between direct conditioned stimuli and their verbal symbols.* (In Razran, 1961)

KELLER, M. Mediated generalization: The generalization of a conditioned galvanic skin response established to a pictured object. *American Journal of Psychology*, 1943, 56, 438–448.

KENT, G. H. and ROSANOFF, A. J. A study of association in insanity. *American Journal of Insanity*, 1910, 67, 37–96.

KOTLIAREVSKY, L. I. Cardio-vascular conditioned reflexes to direct and to verbal stimuli. *Fiziol. Zh. S.S.S.R.*, 1936.* (In Razran, 1961)

LAFFAL, J. *Pathological and normal language.* New York: Atherton Press, 1965.

LURIA, A. R. and VINOGRADOVA, O. S. An objective investigation of the dynamics of semantic systems. *British Journal of General Psychology*, 1959, 50, 89–105.

MILLER, G. A. Some preliminaries to psycholinguistics. *American Psychologist*, 1965, 20, 15–20.

MINK, W. D. Semantic generalization as related to word association. *Psychological Reports*, 1963, 12, 59–67.

NOBLE, C. An analysis of meaning. *Psychological Review*, 1952, 59, 421–430.

OSGOOD, C. E. *Method and theory in experimental psychology.* New York: Oxford University Press, 1953.

OSGOOD, C. E. On understanding and creating sentences. *American Psychologist*, 1963, 18, 735–751.

OSGOOD, C. E., SUCI, J. S., and TANNENBAUM, P. H. *The measurement of meaning.* Urbana, Illinois: University of Illinois Press, 1957.

PAVLOV, I. P. *Conditioned reflexes.* London: Oxford University Press, 1927.

RAZRAN, G. H. S. Salivating and thinking in different languages. *Journal of Psychology*, 1935, 1, 145–151.

RAZRAN, G. H. S. A quantitative study of meaning by a conditioned salivary technique (semantic conditioning). *Science*, 1939, 90, 89–90.

RAZRAN, G. H. S. Semantic and phonetographic generalizations of salivary conditioning to verbal stimuli. *Journal of Experimental Psychology*, 1949, 39, 642–652.

RAZRAN, G. H. S. Experimental semantics. *Transactions of the New York Academy of Science*, 1952, 14, 171–177.

RAZRAN, G. H. S. The observable unconscious and the inferable unconscious in current Soviet psychophysiology: Interoceptive conditioning, semantic conditioning, and the orienting reflex. *Psychological Review*, 1961, 68, 81–147.

RIESS, B. F. Semantic conditioning involving the galvanic skin response. *Journal of Experimental Psychology*, 1940, 26, 238–240.

RIESS, B. F. Genetic changes in semantic conditioning. *Journal of Experimental Psychology*, 1946, 36, 143–152.

SAPORTA, S. Linguistics and communication. In L. Thayer (ed.), *Communication, theory and research*. Springfield, Illinois: Charles C. Thomas, 1967.

SHVARTS, L. A. The problems of words as conditioned stimuli. *Byull. eksp. Biol. Med.*, 1954, 38, 15–18.* (In Razran, 1961)

SHVARTS, L. A. Conditioned reflexes to verbal stimuli. *Vop. Psikhol.*, 1960, 6, 86–98.* (In Razran, 1961)

TITCHENER, E. B. *A beginner's psychology*. New York: The MacMillan Co., 1915.

VINOGRADOVA, O. S. and EYSLER, N. A. The manifestations of verbal connections in recording vascular reactions. *Vop. Psikhol.*, 1959, 2, 101–116.* (In Razran, 1961)

VOLKOVA, V. D. On certain characteristics of the form of conditioned reflexes to speech stimuli in children. *Fiziol. Zh. S.S.S.R.*, 1953, 39, 540–548.* (In Razran, 1961)

CHAPTER 6

Bilingualism

The reasons for which languages are taught in schools and universities are sometimes absurd. The means which are used are sometimes violent, out of date, or immoral, and hurt the feelings of most learners. The standard of teachers and textbooks is poor. These seem to be the real dangers of multilingualism, which in itself belongs—if thorough enough—to the great achievements of the human mind.

Veroboj Vildomec[*]

Whether all languages sprang from a common origin or emanated simultaneously from a variety of sources is a question for which no answer will ever be supplied. We do know, however, that, through some process or other of differentiation, language has come to assume approximately 1,500 different forms. To this large number should be added hundreds of dialects within various languages, some of which are almost as mutually unintelligible as separate language systems.

Because of movements of populations through migration and conquest, and in more recent historical periods through immigration, colonization, and annexations of territory, groups of people speaking different languages have been thrown together in daily contact and communication. The coexistence of two languages within the same political unit or geographic region has given rise to the phenomenon of bilingualism, the

---

[*] *Multilingualism* Leyden: A. W. Sythoff, 1963, p. 240.

extent of which is probably greater today than ever before in history because of a greater mixture of populations and easier means of communication in the contemporary world.

Contact and convergence between different languages and cultures result in a sociological situation in which an individual learns elements from more than one linguistic and cultural system. Linguists refer to this learning situation as *language contact* and to the particular learning process as *bilingualization*. Linguistic change resulting from such contact is called *interference*.

It is evident from these considerations that bilingualism could be studied from the linguistic, the sociocultural and the psychological points of view, depending on the major interests of the investigator. In actual fact, such a convenient division of scientific labor is rarely encountered, because it is difficult to investigate one set of variables to the exclusion of the others. This will be quite evident as we sample some of the variety and diversity of research in bilingualism. First, however, we must take up a number of basic issues in the study of bilingualism.

CONCEPTIONS OF BILINGUALISM

Although the popular conception of the bilingual person is that of an individual with native-like proficiency in more than one language, such a definition of bilingualism would be unacceptable to most language specialists. Among the latter we find considerably less than unanimity of opinion with regard to the definition of bilingualism. At one end of the spectrum we might put Lee's (1932) characterization of the student as bilingual with one relative in the home who was a native speaker of a foreign language; at the other end we could locate Haugen's (1952) specification of the minimal qualification for bilingual status as the ability of the speaker to produce complete meaningful utterances in two or more languages. Diebold (1961) has recommended the abandonment of the lower criterion of bilingualism and has proposed the term "incipient bilingualism" to include the study of those individuals who do not use the second language but who, upon testing, show some comprehension as a result of contact with language-using models. In most psychological studies on bilingualism the degree of proficiency in the two languages is operationally defined in terms of length of exposure to the two languages, number of years studied, relative dominance of one language system, etc. In general the factor of proficiency is treated as a variable. Some tests of dominance or bilingual balance will be considered later.

It is interesting to note that even the question of *degree* of bilingualism is anything but a simple and straightforward matter. As Mackey (1962) has pointed out, gauging the degree of bilingualism in an individual or group is a complex process that involves phonological, grammatical, graphic, lexical and semantic issues. Furthermore, an individual's command of these aspects must be assessed in relation to speaking, listening, reading and writing. Thus, a person may have a more perfect command of the grammar of Language A than of Language B, but his reading vocabulary in the latter may be larger than in the former. None of the studies reviewed in this chapter has made use of such an elaborate and detailed analytical model in the determination of degree of bilingualism.

For the sake of convenience, throughout the present discussion, we shall adopt Weinreich's (1953) definition and consider bilingualism "the practice of alternately using two languages" (p. 1). The persons involved in such practice will be referred to as bilinguals.

THEORETICAL CONSIDERATIONS

As Haugen (1952) points out, in becoming bilingual, an individual "must set up a competing system that covers the same or similar ground and serves the same or similar purpose as his primary system." According to Weinreich (1953), "A comprehensive psychological theory of bilingualism ought therefore to account for both the effectively separated use of the two languages and for interference of the languages with one another" (p. 71). How are we to think of these coexistent systems? Are they best understood as one code or two? Should they be schematized as overlapping or discrete?

Weinreich identifies three possible types of bilingualism, in each of which the relation between signifier and signified is different. In the first type, interlingual translations such as *casa* and *house* are treated as separate signifiers with separate significates. Thus there are conceived to

be two parallel systems: *casa*   + *house*   .

The second type of bilingualism is that in which the individual may possess one set of significates with two signifiers:

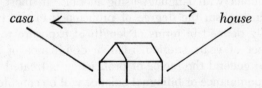

The third type is a variant of the second. Here the speaker learns his second language with the help of the first language. Thus: *casa* → *house*

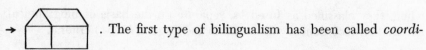 . The first type of bilingualism has been called *coordinate bilingualism*. The second and third types have generally not been distinguished in the psychological analyses of the problem; they have received the name *compound bilingualism*. Ervin and Osgood (1954) have analyzed these two hypothetical types of bilingualism. In their terminology the compound language system is characterized by having two sets of linguistic signs and two sets of linguistic responses which come to be associated through the same set of representational mediation processes (meaning):

$$
\begin{array}{ccc}
S_A & \!\!\!\!\!\diagdown\; r_{m_1} \text{————————} s_{m_1} \diagup\!\!\!\! & R_A \\
S_B & \diagup r_{m_2} \text{————————} s_{m_2} \diagdown & R_B
\end{array}
$$

This is a parallel to Weinreich's types two and three. In contrast to this form of bilingualism is the coordinate system in which each linguistic sign has its own set of mediational (meaning) responses. Thus:

$$
\begin{array}{ccc}
S_A \text{———} r_{m_1} \text{————————} s_{m_1} \text{———} & R_A \\
S_B \text{———} r_{m_2} \text{————————} s_{m_2} \text{———} & R_B
\end{array}
$$

The former type of bilingualism is presumed to develop from the indirect method of language learning typical of educational settings; the latter is the supposed product of learning two languages in settings that are physically and culturally more distinct.

Lambert, Havelka and Crosby (1958) explain the distinction by relating the acquisition of a second language to principles derived from paired-associate learning and transfer. In the study of retroactive inhibition the subject first learns r_1 to S_1. When he later learns R_2 to S_1, interference between the two responses is the typical result. An analogous learning problem confronts the bilingual when, for example, the symbols "church" and "eglise" are both associated with the same event in the environment (Lambert, Havelka and Crosby, 1958). One way to minimize interference is to increase the distinctiveness of the two learning tasks. Thus, S_1 is no longer associated with two responses R_1 and R_2; now there are two functional stimuli: $S_1 \rightarrow R_1$ and $S_2 \rightarrow R_2$. In the Lambert, *et al.*, terminology the distinction is between *fused* (compound) and *separate* (coordinate) bilingualism.

Lambert, Havelka and Crosby (1958) attempted to measure predicted performance differences of their Montreal French-English bilinguals whom they classified as fused vs. separate on the basis of biographical material, in accordance with the Ervin and Osgood (1954) criteria.

> Acquisition contexts were considered separated when one language was learned exclusively in the home and the other exclusively outside the home, when one parent consistently used one language and the other parent a different language, or when one language was acquired in a particular national or cultural setting distinct from that in which the second was acquired. Acquisition was considered fused when both parents used both languages indiscriminately, when both languages were used interchangeably inside and outside the home, or when an individual acquired his second language in a school system stressing vocabulary drill and translation and where the first or native language was used as the method of instruction (p. 239).

In those cases where the second language was acquired in a fused context but the subject had used the acquired language either exclusively or primarily for at least one year, he was also classed as separate. They also required that all subjects be balanced bilinguals. The measurement of dominance (or its opposite, bilingual balance) was based on methods developed by Lambert (1955) and Lambert, Havelka and Gardner (1959). In the former study, reaction time (speed with which the subject followed directions printed in either language) was found to correlate highly with degree of experience with the second language and relative verbosity in the two languages. In the later study this measure was also found to correlate significantly with facility in word completion, comparative recognition thresholds, detection of embedded words, speed of reading, response set to pronounce words such as *silence, important,* in either French or English. (It did not correlate with speed of translation.) Based on this selection procedure, Lambert, *et al.*, obtained 23 separated and 9 fused bilinguals. The separated bilinguals were further subdivided into 15 bicultural and 8 unicultural. These subjects rated *house, drink, poor, me* and their French translations on the semantic differential. In accordance with the hypothesis, separated bilinguals with bicultural backgrounds showed a significantly greater difference in meanings of translated nouns than fused bilinguals.

Another test of the hypothesis involved the learning of 20 common English words by the anticipation method, to a criterion of 8 correct responses. This was followed by three trials on a 20-item nonsense syllable list. Finally retention of the original list was tested. This was

compared to a similar list of words when three trials of French translations were interposed between learning and retention. It was found that
the fused bilinguals benefited from the interpolation of the French
translations.

For the separated bilinguals—both unicultural and bicultural—the
translations had the same effect as interpolated nonsense syllables. Finally, it was predicted that fused bilinguals should have greater facility
in switching from one language to another. Each subject was asked to
translate 20 French and 20 English words and speed of translation was
measured. On this test there was no difference between the two groups.

Lambert and Fillenbaum (1959) assigned bilingual aphasics to fused
versus separated groups according to their language learning experiences. They found that:

> Bilingual aphasics who learned their languages in a coordi-
> nate fashion are more likely to lose the use of only one of their
> two languages if they become aphasic whereas compound
> bilinguals show a more general language deficit affecting their
> two languages when they become aphasic (Lambert 1963, b,
> p. 119).

In a later study employing balanced fused and separated French-English bilinguals, Jakobovits and Lambert (1961) tested semantic satiation
effects. In an initial session subjects rated the words to be tested on the
semantic differential. Later subjects repeated a word for 15 seconds
and then rated either the same word, the translation of that word or an
unassociated word in the same language or in the different language.
The investigators hypothesized that for fused bilinguals there would be a
greater cross-satiation effect, so that repetition of a French word would
result in a decrease in the intensity with which its translation was rated
on various semantic differential scales. In general this prediction was
substantiated.

Two of the findings reported by Jakobovits and Miron bear further
discussion. One result in their study was that bilinguals in general were
not especially prone to semantic satiation effects. Another was that under
the different word-control/different language condition the compound
bilingual group showed a significant satiation effect, whereas intensity
ratings increased in the coordinate group (though not significantly). The
authors consider the cross-satiation and the different word-control/
different language conditions to be examples of language switching situations. The authors suggest that compound bilinguals, in order to use
their two languages efficiently, have had to inhibit other language re-

sponses while using one of their languages. This inhibition of mediators comes to make language switching difficult. Coordinate bilinguals, on the other hand, from the nature of their system, have no need for such inhibitory checks and therefore repetitive elicitation of mediators may actually "excite" the mediators of translated equivalents. Predictions from these hypotheses were only partially supported.

What is important about the Jakobovits and Lambert view is that it reflects an attempt to improve upon the Ervin and Osgood (1954) analysis of language switching. According to Ervin and Osgood, it should be facilitative to decode from a foreign language in the compound bilingual since both S_A and S_B have the same mediators. Encoding the foreign form should be hampered by direct response competition. On the other hand, decoding from one language to another in the coordinate system should be more difficult since it must be based on similarity between S_{m_1} and S_{m_2} or perhaps it may be achieved by a learned connection between $S_{m_1 \rightarrow m_2 \rightarrow} S_{m_2}$. Theoretically, encoding should suffer less from response competition in the coordinate bilingual. With practice in translation from A to B in the coordinate bilingual, S_A may come to elicit $r_{m_2} \rightarrow s_m \rightarrow R_B$ without $r_{m_1} \rightarrow s_{m_1}$ occurring. Or, s_{m_1} may elicit R_B directly (as in the compound system). Clearly this schema does not explain why the different word-control/different language condition showed satiation effects in the compound bilingual and some (though not statistically significant) sensitization effects for the coordinates.

In a study of learning and recall in bilinguals, Ervin (1961, b) found support for the notion of covert language responses which may inhibit or facilitate recall depending upon the language of the learning and recall task. In her study of Italian-English bilinguals, she found that:

> 1. pictures easier to name in the bilingual person's more fluent language were recalled better, regardless of language of learning;
> 2. the worst condition of recall represented a situation in which learning had occurred in the dominant language and recall was conducted in the other language; and
> 3. pictures easier to name in the bilingual's less fluent language were recalled equally well in either language but learning in the subordinate language was superior.

The differences seem to substantiate her hypotheses:

> 1. there are covert Rs in the language of easier naming, when overt language is restricted;

2. covert responses in the same language as the overt R strengthen recall in that language;

3. spontaneous translation is more probable into the dominant language. (Ervin, 1961b, p. 451).

The Lambert, Havelka and Gardner (1959) argument that a more balanced bilingual should require similar amounts of time to translate from one language into the other seems to be a correlative hypothesis to Ervin's assumptions. However, Lambert, *et al.* (1959), found no correlation between degree of bilingual balance and comparative speed of translation. About half their subjects showed greater speed in reading one language and translation into the other language. Triesman (1965) has reported similar results. Certainly the process of translation is a poorly understood phenomenon.

ENCODING PROCESSES AND CODE SWITCHING

It is the mark of a fluent bilingual individual that he manages to keep his language generating essentially unilingual. Observations have pointed to some major organizing principle as yet unidentified by research which underlies the psychological separation of the bilingual's two languages. It may be that experiences are coded once, in common, and each of the bilingual's languages draws from this experience; or, it may be that events are coded separately in the language in which they are experienced. Kolers (1963) has given these respective interpretations the designations of *shared hypothesis* and *separate hypothesis*. In a test of these hypotheses, Kolers performed a word-association experiment with three groups of bilinguals. Subjects who were native speakers of German, Spanish and Thai, respectively, and bilingual in English as the second language, were given word-association tasks involving: English to English, Native Language to Native Language, English to Native Language and Native Language to English. There were five semantic categories of words.

Results showed that the proportions of shared responses did not vary significantly on interlingual versus intralingual tasks, nor did they vary with the frequency of the stimulus word. Kolers states that if the meaning of words were stored in common in some supralinguistic or linguistically neutral form he would expect to find a higher proportion of shared responses—especially since his subjects could be classified as compound bilinguals. Furthermore, the pattern of associations was uncorrelated with method of learning the language, years of residence in an English-speaking context or age of onset of second-language learning. On the basis of this data, Kolers disagrees with the notion that language acquisition context determines forever linguistic performance. Kolers' (1963, p. 299) statement bears quoting:

> An alternative suggestion is that after a certain level of language skill is reached, irrespective of how the second language was learned, the two groups of subjects converge in the way purely linguistic factors affect their encoding of experience.

As Lambert (1963) reminds us, learning a foreign language is not only learning a new form of speech, it requires a cultural and sociological shift as well. Subjects probably do converge, but whether the semantic differential or word-association tasks are appropriate measures of the convergence is open to question.

Another interesting finding in the Kolers experiment is that although the percentage of shared associates did not vary with frequency of the stimulus word, it did vary with the kind of "semantic space" occupied by the stimulus word. Thus, there were more shared associates to concrete words than to more abstract words. Kolers relates this to the more precise associations that could be built to a concrete word through manipulation of the referent. This would seem to imply that concrete words elicit a smaller variety of high associate responses.

In another study of interlingual word associations, Lambert and Moore (1966) compared American and French monolinguals with Canadian monolinguals and bilinguals in their word-association responses to the Kent-Rosanoff. This was an intralingual task that differed from Kolers' task, which measured both inter- and intra-lingual associations. Lambert and Moore measured the degree of equivalence of primary responses and degree of overlap of all responses. The result which is of most interest in the present context is that the percentage of equivalent responses and degree of overlap changed in accordance with the language and culture. French norms from France were thus more distant from Canadian bilinguals responding in French than were English responses from monolingual English Canadians. However, the responses of the monolingual French Canadians are the closest to the bilingual Canadian in French. Bilinguals in English were equally distant from both English and French Canadian monolinguals and slightly more like Americans than English Canadian.

Lambert and Moore's (1966) emphasis in their interpretation of the data is strikingly different from that of Kolers. They stress the modification of response stereotypy as bilinguals change the language of the response. According to the authors, this indicates that in becoming bilingual, people can learn to rely on subtle features of the two languages and that associational response diversity may be one of the features of the languages learned that aids in keeping the two languages functionally separate. In general, they interpret associational responses as connotative meaning networks, parts of which may be activated when their appropriate stimulus words are either decoded or about to be encoded.

Dalrymple (1967) used a modified version of the Stroop test to measure interlingual interference. In the usual form, the subject is presented with color names written in a nonmatching color and must name the color of the ink as quickly as possible. In the bilingual version of the test the color word is written in one language and the subject has to name the color of the ink in the other language. He found that intralingual interference was no greater than the usual interlingual interference, and concluded from this that when the bilingual is operating in one language the other is not necessarily blocked or switched off. Perception of a word may actually prime all words associatively connected, independent of language. This is reminiscent of the Jakobovits and Lambert (1961) explanation of the sensitization effects in their coordinate bilinguals. Dalrymple suggests further that the distinction between the subject's languages is a formal one and that from a psycholinguistic standpoint he should be considered as possessing a single language system. From this point of view, then, interference should be related to the degree of semantic similarity between interfering and response words, whether or not these are of the same language. One might question whether the evidence from this study is adequate to support such a conclusion. If the system is really so well integrated, how are the languages kept separate?

Kolers (1965) has asked whether language may be considered a code like any other. The distinction he makes between language and other codes is that language is not only a set of categories, but also includes rules for the joining of categories. To test the difference between language and an arbitrary code he developed unilingual lists of monosyllable words printed either in all red, all black, mixed red and black or both red and black. Analogous lists were either all English, all French, mixed French and English or in both French and English. The lists were presented once, at the rate of one word per second, after which the subject had 2 minutes to write down the words recalled. The lists were 70-items long, and analysis was done on the 50 interior items (i.e., minus the first 10 and the last 10 items) to eliminate confusion from primacy and recency effects. Recall for the unicodal and unilingual lists was similar, but recall for the mixed code list (red or black) was only half that of the mixed language list. The conclusion was that language cannot be considered an arbitrary code.

A more recent study bears directly on this issue. Nott and Lambert (1968) studied the organization of memory in bilinguals by analyzing free recall for categoried and noncategoried lists of both unilingual and bilingual (French and English) composition. The subjects were divided into three groups: Balance Bilingual, French Dominant or English Dominant. Each subject received all list types: French noncategory, French category, English noncategory, English category, Bilingual noncategory, Bilingual category. There were three categoried conditions: (1) *implicit condition,* words in random order; (2) *explicit condition,* category names given in advance; (3) *blocked condition,* category names given in advance and items blocked according to category.

According to the results, dominant bilinguals recalled fewer words from "category" lists in their weaker language and from bilingual category lists, but showed no differences between languages with noncategory lists. Two questions were raised in the discussion of these results. Why was recall of the weaker language list poorer than recall of the stronger list only in the categoried condition? Even giving the names of the categories in advance and blocking them on the list did not bring performance to the stronger language level. The authors offered the suggestion that decoding in a weaker language takes more time. The intriguing implication is that the form of category storage is somehow different from storage of noncategory lists and that this difference is attested to by the difference in performance characteristics for weaker and stronger languages.

The other problem raised in this experiment is that the bilingual categoried list was more difficult than the unilingual categoried condition, even for balanced bilinguals. There was a significant number of translation errors (recall in opposite language) in the bilingual categoried list, but not in the bilingual noncategoried list. Again, even blocking the category in the list and giving category names in advance did not equalize performance in the bilingual vs. unilingual condition. To explain this the authors suggest that, at least in the categoried condition, the words are stored as "meanings" which must be tagged with the word of a particular language for the bilingual condition. This means searching category storage and putting the language tag to it.

There is an obvious need for clarification of the relations among meaning, synonymity and association in the literature on bilingualism. When we vary "D," as in the Lambert, Havelka and Crosby (1958) study, what else are we varying? Is it an artifact, perhaps, that unicultural coordinate bilinguals have "D" ratings similar to those of compound bilinguals, but show effects of interpolated synonyms similar to those found among bicultural coordinate bilinguals who have greater "D" ratings for those synonyms?

There are no conclusive answers to questions of unicodalism or bicodalism as a function of task; of mediation via semantic content or through other associative factors; of the relation of transfer effects in language-switching situations to speed of translation. With respect to the distinction between compound and coordinate bilingualism, for what tasks does language acquisition method significantly influence future performance? While there is some evidence that transfer effects differ (Lambert, Havelka and Crosby, 1958), other findings (Kolers, 1963) seem to indicate that the distinction does not hold for free association tasks. A closer analysis of what Haugen (1952) calls "these ragged margins of linguistic behavior" may shed further light on not only the phenomena of bilingualism, but on the nature of language in general.

BILINGUALISM AND INTELLIGENCE

Thus far our discussion of bilingualism has been addressed primarily to issues of a theoretical and scientific nature. We turn now to a consideration of further issues with respect to bilingualism that have pragmatic implications. Living in an essentially monolingual culture[1] like that of the United States, it is easy to lose sight of the fact that bilingualism is a way of life for people in many countries. For these people, such questions as the possible adverse effects of bilingualism upon intellectual development are matters of intense concern.

Research on bilingualism in relation to intelligence has been carried on for nearly half a century. Saer (in Saer, Smith and Hughes, 1924) using a Welsh version of the Stanford-Binet, found that rural bilingual children were consistently inferior in IQ to rural monolingual children over an age span of 7 to 11 years. Comparable differences were not found when urban bilingual and monolingual children were compared. In his interpretation of these results, Saer stressed the "mental confusion" that he saw resulting from the introduction of a second language before the child achieved mastery of the mother tongue.

The years that followed Saer's report have produced a great many

---

[1] This characterization does not disregard the obvious fact that various groups in the United States with a common national origin (e.g., Mexican Americans) possess a distinct spoken and written language, in addition to English. Moreover, as we shall try to show in a later section (Chapter 10, Urban Language: A Negro Problem), certain groups with a common subcultural identity can be identified on the basis of common usage of a dialectical variant of spoken American English.

studies of bilingualism and intelligence, but results have been extremely equivocal and contradictory. Peal and Lambert (1962) have commented:

> A large proportion of investigators have concluded from their studies that bilingualism has a detrimental effect on intellectual functioning. The bilingual child is described as being hampered in his performance on intelligence tests in comparison with the monolingual child. A smaller proportion of the investigations have found little or no influence of bilingualism on intelligence, in that no significant difference between bilinguals and monolinguals on tests of intelligence was apparent (p. 1).

Of the investigations that Peal and Lambert reviewed, only two yielded results which suggested that bilingualism could have favorable consequences for intellectual development.

It is not difficult to find reasons for these contradictory research findings, beginning with divergent definitions of bilingualism itself (Darcy, 1963). Other major sources of difference have included:

1. Lack of precision in the determination of degree of bilingualism;

2. Differences in the type of intelligence tests used;

3. A general failure to isolate bilingualism as a variable from educational retardation, socioeconomic and cultural conditions, emotional concomitants or any combination of these factors.

One of the most carefully conceived and executed studies of the influence of bilingualism upon linguistic and arithmetical attainments was reported by Macnamara (1966). The study was conducted with students in national (i.e., public) schools in the Republic of Ireland and involved a comparison of children from English-speaking homes who had been taught in Irish with similar children who had been taught in Engish. The comparison extended over English, Irish and arithmetic, as measured by a series of standardized tests; and extensive precautions were taken to eliminate bias in sampling.

The author noted some significant differences between his study and research reported by previous investigators.

> The bilingual situation that has been studied most frequently in the past is that of immigrants to the U.S.A. who are

in process of losing the language of their country of origin and acquiring English. Such people almost invariably require English in order to conduct their affairs and converse with their friends and acquaintances. Their children, too, have enormous incentives to become competent in English, for it is the language of the school and of the society in which they live.

The Irish situation is quite different. The incentives put forward for learning Irish are cultural and political only, and they do not appear to inspire any sense of urgency in the majority of Irish people. Their children live in an English-speaking environment and depend for their knowledge of Irish almost entirely on their teachers. Thus, unlike bilingual children in the U.S.A., Irish children are asked to acquire a second language which is not the language of the world they live in (p. 135).

Given these considerations, it is not surprising that Macnamara found substantial retardation in both English and arithmetic among his bilingual subjects; and for the children living in Irish-speaking districts, the attainments in English and arithmetic were poorest of all. Macnamara concludes:

For many of these children, the adult world, in Ireland or in England, will be an English-speaking one; and they appear to be ill-equipped indeed for life in it (p. 138).

REFERENCES

ARSENIAN, S. *Bilingualism and mental development*. New York: Columbia University Press, 1937.

ARSENIAN, S. Bilingualism in the post-war world. *Psychological Bulletin*, 1945, 42, 65–86.

DARCY, N. T. Bilingualism and the measurement of intelligence: review of a decade of research. *Journal of Genetic Psychology*, 1963, 103, 259–282.

DALRYMPLE, A. E. C. Interlingual interference in a color-naming task. *Psychonomic Science*, 1967, 8, 167–168.

DIEBOLD, A. R., Jr. Incipient bilingualism. *Language*, 1961, 37, 97–112.

ERVIN, S. M. Semantic shift in bilingualism. *American Journal of Psychology*, 1961a, 74, 233–241.

ERVIN, S. M. Learning and recall in bilinguals. *American Journal of Psychology*, 1961b, 74, 446–451.

ERVIN, S. M. Language and TAT content in bilinguals. *Journal of Abnormal and Social Psychology*, 1964, 68, 500–507.

ERVIN, S. M. and OSGOOD, C. E. Second language learning and bilingualism. In C. E. Osgood and T. A. Sebeok (Eds.), *Psycholinguistics. Journal of Abnormal and Social Psychology Supplement*, 1954, 139–146.

HAUGEN, E. Problems in bilingualism. *Lingua*, 1952, 2, 271–290.

JAKOBOVITS, L. and LAMBERT, W. E. Semantic satiation among bilinguals. *Journal of Experimental Psychology*, 1961, 62, 576–582.

KOLERS, P. A. Interlingual word associations. *Journal of verbal learning and verbal behavior*, 1963, 2, 291–300.

KOLERS, P. A. Bilingualism and bicodalism. *Language and Speech*, 1965, 122–126.

LAMBERT, W. E. Measurement of the linguistic dominance of bilinguals. *Journal of Abnormal and Social Psychology*, 1955, 50, 197–200.

LAMBERT, W. E., HAVELKA, J., and CROSBY, C. The influence of language-acquisition contexts on bilingualism. *Journal of Abnormal and Social Psychology*, 1958, 56, 239–244.

LAMBERT, W. E. and FILLENBAUM, S. A pilot study of aphasia among bilinguals. *Canadian Journal of Psychology*, 1959, 13, 28–34.

LAMBERT, W. E., HAVELKA, J. and GARDNER, R. Linguistic manifestations of bilingualism. *Journal of Personality*, 1959, 72, 77–82.

LAMBERT, W. E. Psychological approaches to the study of languages I. On learning, thinking, and human abilities. *Modern Language Journal*, 1963, 27, 51–62.

LAMBERT, W. E., and MOORE, N. Word association responses: comparison of American and French monolinguals with Canadian monolinguals and bilinguals. *Journal of Personality and Social Psychology*, 1966, 3, 313–320.

LEE, L. E. *A study to determine whether bilingual pupils of high school grade are handicapped in their study of history because of vocabulary difficulties.* Rutgers University, Unpublished M.Ed. thesis, 1932.

MACKEY, W. F. Bilingual interference: analysis and measurement. *Journal of Communication*, 1965, 15, 239–249.

MACNAMARA, J. *Bilingualism and primary education.* Edinburgh: Edinburgh University Press, 1966.

NOTT, R. and LAMBERT, W. E. Organization of memory in bilinguals. Paper presented at Eastern Psychological Association Convention, 39th Annual Meeting, Washington, D.C., 1968.

PEAL, E. and LAMBERT, W. E. The relation of bilingualism to intelligence. *Psychological Monographs*, 1962, 76, No. 546.

SAER, D. J., SMITH, F. and HUGHES, J. *The bilingual problem.* Wrexham, England: Hughes and Son, 1924.

TRIESMAN, A. M. The effects of redundancy and familiarity on translating and repeating back a foreign and native language. *British Journal of Psychology*, 1965, 56, 369–379.

VILDOMEC, V. *Multilingualism.* Netherlands: A. W. Sythoff-Leyden, 1963.

WEINREICH, U. *Languages in contact.* New York: Linguistic Circle of New York, 1953.

CHAPTER 7

Sound Symbolism in Language

Hermogenes. I should explain to you, Socrates, that our friend Cratylus has been arguing about names; he says that they are natural and not conventional; not a portion of the human voice which men agree to use; but that there is a truth or correctness in them, which is the same for Hellenes as barbarians.

Cratylus: *The Dialogues of Plato*

THE EXISTENCE of sound symbolism in language—a phenomenon in which the affective component of meaning exceeds the referential component in a particular utterance—has long been a well-documented intuition on the part of linguists and psychologists. Only within the past several decades, however, have psychologists systematically explored the role of such symbolism in the reactions of language users to verbal stimuli. In this chapter we shall survey some of the empirical studies that have attempted to examine sound symbolism, both within single languages and as a universal linguistic phenomenon.

Examples of sound symbolism abound in many natural languages. Markel (1961), for example, recognized a common connotation in many English words that begin with a *gl-* cluster: *glad, glance, glass, gleam, glimpse, glitter, globe, glove* and *glow*. Bolinger (1950) analyzed even the residues in the following two series: *glitter, glow, glare; flitter, flow, flare*. Thus, /gl/ indicates "phenomena of light," /fl/ "phenomena of movement," /itr/ "intermittent," /ow/ "steady," and /r/ "intense." Numerous examples of the same sort may also be found in German, as in the initial cluster gr-, indicating "sinister, eerie": *grässlich, grauen, grausig, Greuel, greulich, gruselig.*

Sound symbolism is not specific to Indo-European languages. Arabic, for instance, is a language that is especially rich in this phenomenon; its lexicon contains extensive, complex networks of connotative relationships connected by means of the sound symbolism implicit in root radicals. To take but a single illustration, many words containing *gh*ayn (no close English approximation possible) as the first radical connote "concealment, darkness, obscurity." Thus, we have: *gh*aaba (to set, as the sun), *gh*aara (to seep into the ground), *gh*abasa (to become dark), *gh*abana (to hoodwink, gyp), *gh*ataa (to cover, conceal), *gh*atasa (to immerse, submerge), *gh*amma (to cloud over), *gh*ilaaf (covering, book jacket), and so on, for many more words.

Although examples from just the few languages mentioned above could be multiplied many times over, and the list of languages which display this phenomenon could be lengthened indefinitely, these illustrations should suffice to convey the extent of sound patternings and affective meanings in natural languages.

The term used to characterize this phenomenon has undergone several changes since its inception (credited by Bolinger in 1950 to A. H. Tolman in 1887). In the first empirical analysis of sound symbolism, Sapir (1929) used the term *phonetic symbolism* to refer to the expressive component of symbolism in sounds. Most psychologists have adopted this term, and some have even extended its usage in order to distinguish between phonetic symbolism (the theory that given sounds have affective meanings in a language) and *universal phonetic symbolism* (the theory that given sounds have the same affective meanings in all languages). Linguists, however, have adopted other terms for the same general phenomenon, according to various schools of thought and individual preferences. Bolinger (1950) used the term *phonestheme* but credited it to Householder, who in turn borrowed it from Firth. Markel (1961), however, substituted the term *psychomorph*, on the grounds that the latter term better related the unit of analysis with other linguistic units. He thus defined the psychomorph as "a non-morphemic unit of one or more phonemes for which a connotative meaning can be established, but this connotative meaning may not accompany all occurrences of the unit" (p. 86). In the present review, we shall retain the terms that were used by the original authors.

Empirical analyses of phonetic symbolism have generally been of two types, classified according to methodology and identified by Taylor (1963) as word matching or analytical. In the former type of methodology the subject is presented with pairs (usually antonymic) of words in two languages, at least one of which is unknown to the subject. He is then asked to match corresponding members of the pairs in the two languages, and significantly correct guessing is assumed to indicate the operation of some type of phonetic symbolism cues. Methodologies of the second type have been widely variable, but the subject is generally asked to judge sounds of nonsense words along one or more dimensions of connotative meaning (e.g., size, roundness, movement and so on). All remaining studies of phonetic symbolism can generally be described as a combination of the above two methodologies.

WORD-MATCHING EXPERIMENTS

In an experiment whose methodology has become the classical paradigm of phonetic symbolism experiments, Tsuru and Fries (1933) presented 36 pairs of Japanese words to 57 subjects, then asked the subjects to match the words to those of equivalent English pairs. No levels of significance of correct guessing were given, but 69 percent of the guesses were reported to be correct. In another study using the word-matching methodology, Brown, Black and Horowitz (1955) presented 21 pairs of antonyms of sensory continua to 86 subjects. The pairs were presented audio-visually in three languages (Hindi, Czech and Chinese), and the subjects were asked to match English meanings to each stimulus word. The experimenters found significantly better than chance guessing for all three languages but reported no better guessing of words of the Indo-European languages than that of Chinese words. In order to explain this correct guessing the experimenters accepted the theory of a "physiognomic language," composed of universal, unlearned intersensory connections—a sort of universal synesthesia. They postulated that the origin of speech could have been in the arbitrary association of sounds and meanings but then progressed toward phonetic symbolism, so that a given speech form survived only if it were "representational." Brown, et al. (1955), concluded that "in evolution of languages, speech forms have been selected for symbolism and that we are moving toward a golden millennium of physiognomic speech" (p. 393).

Using a methodology similar to that of the above investigators, Maltzmann, Morisett and Brooks (1956) presented 65 subjects with 25 stimulus words and 25 pairs of response words in English, Japanese and Croatian. The experimenters found that the English-Japanese and English-Croatian pairs were matched well above chance but that the Japanese-Croatian pairs were not. The experimenters argued that phonetic symbolism did not explain their results so that the ability to match foreign words must be based upon a complex sort of learning process, probably involving mediated generalization (since English words had to be involved in the association).

In an experiment designed partially to reconcile the above findings, Blackbill and Little (1957) recognized that the conclusion of universal phonetic symbolism as stated by Brown, *et al.* (1955), was simply not susceptible to rigorous testing in its most general form. They therefore tried to delimit the phenomenon under the study by determining (1) the accuracy of guessing as affected by the mode of presentation, as audio, visual or both, (2) the accuracy of guessing from a random sample of a determinate population, and (3) several specific stimulus characteristics which cause accurate guessing. Using lists of 50 words each in Hebrew, Japanese, Chinese and English, the experimenters presented 240 subjects in six experimental groups with word pairs and asked if each pair had the same or different meanings. They used three methods of presentation (auditory only, auditory and visual and visual only) and two forms of presentation (one word of the pair in English, or both words of the pair foreign). They found significantly above chance guessing of word pairs involving English-Hebrew, Japanese-Chinese and Japanese-Hebrew; pairs involving Chinese-Hebrew, however, were guessed at a significantly below chance level. Moreover, they found an interaction effect in the experimental manipulations in that visual presentation improved guesses in the English-foreign-pairs condition but not in the foreign-pairs condition. The experimenters concluded that the universal phonetic symbolism phenomenon cannot apply for all words of all languages. They admitted, however, that their positive findings raise interesting questions for possible language typologies. Finally, the authors asserted that inter-subject agreement could have been elevated by certain stimulus characteristics of the word pairs. Among the most frequent such characteristics (obtained by post-hoc inspection of the data), the experimenters listed word length, vowel constituents (especially back vs. front), consonant constituents (especially by method of articulation), hyphenation and spacing, and connotation. Two tests yielded a "potency ranking" of these characteristics in the order connotation, vowels, length, spacing and consonants.

Brown and Nuttall (1959) noted that, although the above three studies purportedly measured the same phenomenon with essentially the same methodologies, important procedural differences among them could possibly explain the differences in the results and in the consequent interpretations. The authors claimed that at least three areas of methodologies differed in this regard: (1) in the form of presentation, Brown, *et al.* (1955), used only the English-foreign-pairs (E-F-P) condition; Maltzmann, *et al.* (1956), used only the Foreign-foreign (F-F) condition; and, although Brackbill and Little (1957) used both the above conditions, they required the subjects to match only on a same-different (S-D) basis; (2) in the method of presentation, Brown, *et al.* (1955), used audio-visual means (and visual only for a small control group); Maltzmann, *et al.* (1957), used visual means only; and Brackbill and Little used all three possible means but reported no significant differences; and (3) in the selection of the word list, each group of experimenters followed their own criteria of simplicity and availability. In an experimental test of the effects of the above differences, Brown and Nuttall varied the form of presentation of word pairs in English, Chinese and Hindi, using an audio-visual presentation of their original word list (even while acknowledging the criticisms of Brackbill and Little [1957] in this regard). The experimenters found that in all conditions and in all languages, correct guesses were made at a level significantly above chance; but guesses made in the E-F-P condition were best. Differences between the other conditions were not significant, and differences between languages in the same condition were not significant. The experimenters concluded that the phenomenon of universal phonetic symbolism is sensitive to the form of presentation because only the E-F-P condition allows subjects to determine the appropriate semantic contrast involved in a word pair and to guess correctly. The authors therefore reformulated Brown's original phonetic symbolism theory into one requiring a referent continuum:

> Antonyms naming opposite ends of sensible referent continua (in languages with which the subject is unfamiliar) contrast with one another on appropriate phonetic dimensions often enough to make possible better than chance matches with equivalent terms in the subject's native language. This condition, if it exists, need not be explained by a myth about the origin of speech in physiognomic representation. It is possible that in the history of languages, antonyms evolve toward phonetic contrasts appropriate to this semantic contrast and that pairs so contrasting sound 'right' to native speakers and so have a superior prospect for survival (Brown and Nuttall, 1959, p. 445).

At the same time the authors admitted they were uncertain of which sensible continua to use in their word pairs and postulated the use of only those of magnitude and those associated with them (e.g., "heavy-light," "slow-fast," "dark-bright," etc.).

In a direct test of the above hypothesis, Weiss (1963) asked whether only antonym pairs (providing a meaning dimension) would work in the E-F-P condition, or whether non-antonym pairs would work as well. He presented 394 subjects with English-Hindi and English-Chinese word pairs which were either antonyms or mixed pairs (i.e., words on different dimensions). He reported highly significant correct guessing for all pairs but no significant differences between the experimental conditions so that the use of antonym pairs did not increase correct guessing. Moreover, the subjects reported about the same degree of difficulty of guessing in both conditions, whereas Brown and Nuttall (1959) predicted that the subjects should have more difficulty in guessing non-antonymic pairs (i.e., pairs without marked dimension of meaning). On the basis of this data, Weiss concluded that the meaning dimension described by Brown and Nuttall (1959) is unnecessary for accurate guessing, but that a meaningful context—represented by the English words—provides a necessary orientation for the subject in order to direct his attention to the appropriate phonetic elements. That is, the presence of an English word in a test pair provides a category of experiences which the subject must use to find the appropriate meaning of a sound sequence to that "to the extent that sound-sense relations congruent with the subject's experiences have found their way into all natural languages, correct guessing is likely to occur" (Weiss, 1963, p. 106). Weiss (1966) elaborated upon this statement following another experiment in which 318 subjects matched the Japanese equivalent of one of a pair of English stimulus words for 28 word sets. Again, the words were nonantonymic but sensation-related. From his results of significantly correct guessing, Weiss concluded that his previous theory had been supported. He therefore postulated the following sequence of events to be an appropriate process of phonetic symbolism: (1) experiences are assimilated as categories, some of which are bipolar ("large-small") and others of which are not ("hoarse," "vibrating"), (2) many experiences are accompanied by more or less characteristic sets of sounds, (3) consistent pairings of the sounds and experiences are learned and associated with the above categories, (4) conversely, the experiences and categories are hierarchically associated with the sounds, (5) when the subject is presented with an unmeaningful sound sequence, he attributes these learned associations to it, (6) the sounds associated with meaning categories are incorporated into words denoting those categories, (7) some meaning categories are shared by different language groups, and (8) some sounds associated with those categories are associated universally. Step (6) explains the phenomenon of phonetic symbolism, while steps (7) and (8) explain universal phonetic symbolism.

ANALYTICAL EXPERIMENTS

In the first published empirical study of phonetic symbolism, Sapir (1929) performed three experiments to determine the existence and extent of phonetic symbolism in English. His experiments took the form of analytical experiments in that he tested the connoted symbolic magnitude values of different consonants and vowels. In the first such experiment Sapir presented the subjects with pairs of CVC nonsense syllables differing by a single character and asked the subjects to rate the syllables on a relative magnitude scale. For example, the subjects were told that "mal" and "mil" meant "table" and asked which word designated the larger table. The experimenter reported only percentages of responses, but over 75 percent of the subjects consistently favored *a* as being larger than *i*. In a second experiment, Sapir presented 500 subjects with 100 word pairs, each pair representing a different contrast, listed in the following groups of contrasts: (1) tongue height of vowels, (2) lip rounding of vowels, (3) fronting of unrounded vowels, (4) voicedness in consonants, and (5) stops vs. spirants or fricatives. Results of the experiment were not given completely but were reported to be "as expected," and "symbolic discriminations run encouragingly parallel to the objective ones based upon phonetic considerations" (Sapir, 1929, p. 233). In the last of the set of experiments, Sapir presented the subjects with a nonsense word having an arbitrary meaning as a starting point. The word was then systematically varied by a single feature at a time, and the subject was asked to describe the change in meaning accompanying the change in form. (The procedure was spontaneous, almost free association.) Again, no quantitative results were given, but partial lists of responses were included with the comment that many subjects consistently responded to phonetic cues for many presentations. Sapir presented a kinesthetic explanation for the above phenomena, relating the psychological feeling of magnitude for a given phoneme to the kinesthetic feeling of the size of the oral cavity. For example, a high forward tongue pronouncing *i* produces a narrow resonance cavity, while a low, slightly retracted tongue pronouncing *a* produces a larger resonance chamber; this difference is transferred to the sounds themselves. Thus, reasoned Sapir, at least some phonetic symbolism must be universal.

Newman (1933) reported data taken from the same set of experiments performed with Sapir. In his first experiment Newman presented 100 word pairs of the type used in Sapir's first study to 60 subjects in three age groups (the independent variables were the ages of the subjects and the grammatical categories of the referents). Using Thurstone scaling methods, Newman derived a "Symbolic Magnitude Scale" for eight vowels (i, e, ε, ä, a, u, o, ɔ). He found that the grammatical category of the referent had no effect upon the scaling and that younger subjects (aged 9–13) had essentially the same subjective patterns as the older subjects (aged 16 up) but that they discriminated less well and less consistently. He found that these symbolic magnitude judgments were due to three mechanical factors: (1) the kinesthetic factor of the articulatory position of the tongue (front-back), (2) the acoustic factor of the characteristic frequency (high-low), and (3) the kinesthetic factor of the oral cavity size (small-large). Using the same methodology and scaling procedure in a second experiment, Newman asked the subjects to rate words varying nine vowels and 15 consonants along two scales, large-small and dark-bright. He found that similarities existed between the two scales, but where the magnitude scale was patterned on the three factors of the first experiment plus vowel quantity, the brightness scale was patterned exclusively on articulatory and frequency bases. From the two experiments Newman concluded that phonetic elements actually are patterned on a non-linguistic scale, due to certain mechanical factors rather than to linguistic associations.

The work of Sapir (1929) also stimulated the research of Bentley and Varon (1933), who tested the relationships of nonsense syllables to different combinations of the following categories: size, angularity, foolishness, endurance, liquidity, sentimental attachment, motion, noisiness, solidarity and strength. (Scales were sometimes formed from the antonymic adjective of each category.) The experimenters used only three highly trained observers for most of their experiments, rather than a population of naive subjects. In the first experiment ("methodology" in their terminology), the experimenters presented 40 series of CVC syllables and asked the observers to free-associate with each stimulus in order to see if the *a* and *i* components of certain of the words would provoke words denoting magnitude in the direction predicted by Sapir (1929) and by Newman (1933). This effect was not found. Using the second methodology, the experimenters presented 50 CVC syllables and asked their observers to rate the degree of relation of each word to each of the ten scales listed above. Results were presented only in terms of fractional parts of agreement, but it was found that there was little agreement in the positive reports (i.e., high degree of relationship between sounds and scales) and much agreement of negative reports (i.e., little or no relation between sounds and scales). In the third method, 30 subjects were asked to pick which word of 20 CVC pairs was more closely related to five category words. Most relationships were reported as only "slight." In the fourth method the experimenters presented 26 subjects with 36 word pairs and three category words with their opposites (to form scales). Asked to give the relation of the pairs to the category if it existed, most subjects gave fairly consistent results (e.g., *a* was reported as larger and softer than *i*), but again results were barely quantitative. In all of the preceding experiments the subjects were allowed to state the degree of the relationship of the word to the scale (category), whereas Sapir (1929) and Newman (1933) used a forced-choice technique not allowing for gradations. As a result, Bentley and Varon (1933) found that many of the scales they used were not applicable to the stimuli. Finally, the investigators tested the theories of Sapir and Newman concerning the kinesthetic origin of phonetic symbolism. They presented 327 subjects with five pairs of sounds, three of which were vocal and two of which were instrumental. Three response scales were used, but only one scale was applied to each pair of sounds. The experimenters interpreted the substantial intersubject agreement they found with all stimulus pairs to mean that visual perception of the stimulus production alone produced essentially identical cues to those of phonetic symbolism so that linguistic reference was unnecessary. They therefore held the concept of phonetic symbolism as superfluous to the most economical explanation of the data.

In a procedural variation of the standard analytical technique, Davis (1961) cross-culturally compared abstract drawings with the nonsense words "uloomu" and "takete" (modified from an earlier related experiment by Kohler). The experimenter found that both African children speaking only Kitongwe (a Bantu dialect) and monolingual English-speaking children matched "takete" to a predominantly angular drawing and "uloomu" to a predominantly round drawing with significantly better than chance frequency. Davis therefore concluded that a phenomenon of universal phonetic symbolism provided the proper cues for correct matching in both groups.

Beginning with the intuitive impression that certain words in English sharing an initial consonant cluster also share an element of connotative meaning, Markel (1961) derived a procedure designed to yield a qualitative and quantitative connotation profile of given sound sequences. Using 15 scales from the Semantic Differential of Osgood, Suci and Tannenbaum (1957), Markel presented 103 subjects with five word pairs formed from the consonant clusters *gl, fl, sm, sp* and *st* and the syllabics /-ah/ and /-iy/ (established in previous phonetic symbolism experiments to have opposite meanings along several dimensions). The experimenter assumed that if the difference score in ratings of a given word pair along a given dimension was not significant, then the relative constancy was due to the consonant cluster and that dimension served to characterize that cluster connotatively. Moreover, ratings exceeding a certain amount characterized that cluster as being "quite" applicable in that dimension. Thus, Markel produced connotative profiles for the clusters he tested, varying both in amount and in kind.

In a series of experiments involving cross-cultural experimentation, Taylor and Taylor (1962) reported highly damning evidence against the theory of universal phonetic symbolism, while supporting the theory of phonetic symbolism within a single language. The experimenters first formed CVC nonsense syllables of six consonants and three vowels to test interaction effects of the phonetic environment upon the phonetic symbolism phenomenon. No significant effects were found. In the second experiment four consonants and vowels were used to form CVC patterns in order to test the effects of syllable length, number of syllables and stress position in two-syllable words. An effect of the number of letters was found upon the size connotation (i.e., longer words were perceived as larger), but not of the number of syllables *per se* (i.e., only because polysyllabic words are generally longer than monosyllabic words); moreover, no significant effect of stress position on phonetic symbolism was found. In their final experiment Taylor and Taylor presented nearly-monolingual subjects of four different native languages (English, Korean, Japanese and Tamil) with the same CVC words of the second experiment and asked the subjects to rate the words on five-point scales along four dimensions (size, movement, warmth and pleasantness). The experimenters found significant phonetic symbolism effects in all languages, but the symbolism was not the same for the different languages. For example, initial *t* and *p* were regarded as very small in English but as very big in Korean, and initial *d* was regarded as very big in Japanese but very small in Tamil. The investigators thus concluded that the phenomenon of phonetic symbolism surely exists in natural languages, but it is not universal. Interpreting these data in a later article, Taylor (1963) hypothesized that a major variable of phonetic symbolism must be the language habits of the speakers of a given language. These habits force the association of a specific sound or sound sequence with a generalized meaning. For example, English speakers habitually associate an initial *g* with bigness, simply because many words in English connoting bigness begin with *g*. For the same reason, argued Taylor, an initial *d* is associated with bigness in Japanese (from "debu," fat; "dekkai," huge; "daikibo," on grand scale; and so on). Taylor claimed that this hypothesis explained not only why speakers associate certain sounds with certain meanings but also why the associations differ for speakers of different languages. In a discussion of the implications of this hypothesis, the author proposed the use of the experimental method of Taylor and

Taylor (1962) as a typological index of genetic relatedness of languages, because similarity of language habits should imply genetic relatedness. Advertisers and PR men could use the effects of phonetic symbolism to give names to products which would connote the product itself, thereby presumably increasing the saliency of the item for the consumer; for example, she suggested the name "kor" for a cool beverage for English speakers. The experimenter did admit, however, that such a proposal should first be subjected to validity studies.

In a blistering attack on Taylor's arguments, Weiss (1964a) pointed out that Taylor's criticisms of earlier research in phonetic symbolism were the result of biases and selective reporting. Thus, she reported negative results of previous studies (e.g., Maltzmann, *et al.*, 1956, and Brackbill and Little, 1957) without considering the critical procedural differences reported by Brown and Nuttall (1959). Moreover, she was biased in speaking of "spurious positive findings" of earlier research without considering "spurious negative findings." Moreover, the language-habits theory of Taylor came under attack on three points: (1) the theory begs the question of why certain unrelated words in a language which share a connotation also share structural components, (2) the theory fails to explain why only initial consonants are associated with meanings, and (3) in examples of the application of the theory, only those words which supported the theory were given while those that failed to support it were selectively ignored. Weiss therefore suggested that a theory of phonetic symbolism use sound and semantic hierarchies, rather than isomorphic relations between single sounds and single meanings. Such a theory, of course, is that proposed by Weiss (1963, 1964, 1966) explained in the previous section.

Using a variation of the picture-matching methodology of Davis (1961), Weiss (1964b) demonstrated the effects of meaningfulness of referent categories upon the phonetic symbolism response. With the dimensions of magnitude, brightness and angularity, he established four experimental conditions, each containing 22 subjects: (1) the match of meaningless nonsense-word pairs to nonsense-picture pairs representing the above dimensions, (2) the match of the same nonsense-word pairs with meaningful referent objects presented verbally, (3) the match of "high meaningfulness" (by pretest) nonsense-word pairs with the above picture pairs, and (4) the match of "high meaningfulness" nonsense words to the above referent objects. All nonsense words were in a CVCV canonical form, employing the same phonetic contrasts. The experimenter found that all four groups matched words to pictures or objects at significantly greater than chance frequencies. Moreover, the referents condition—predicted to provide greater referent meaningfulness than the picture condition—raised the scores of both high and low-meaningfulness nonsense words, but it affected the three dimensions differentially. Weiss concluded that the results generally supported his hypothesis that referent meaningfulness aids the matching response. Thus, his theory of experiential sharing with a narrowed referent gained additional support (i.e., intersubject agreement is higher when meaningful referents are provided because they reduce the possible number of bases for judgment).

The most recent analytical experiment in phonetic symbolism examined the effects of oral-gesture cues on the phonetic symbolism response. Vetter and Tennant (1967) subvocally presented 60 subjects with the stimulus words "oho" and "iti" and asked the subjects to identify the larger referent. The subjects guessed in the expected direction at better than chance frequency. In a second experiment, the experimenters presented 40 subjects with pairs of nonsense syllables such as the ones used by Sapir (1929). Two experimental conditions, vocal and nonvocal, were used. Again, the subjects in both conditions correctly ranked the *a* and *i* elements at highly significant levels. Vetter and Tennant interpreted these results to suggest that cues derived from the perception of mouth articulations produce responses similar to those cues of phonetic symbolism. Future experiments in phonetic symbolism, therefore, must impose stricter controls upon the stimuli used in order to eliminate extraneous variables.

CONCLUSION

The many studies presented in the preceding section of this chapter found varying, even conflicting results. The phenomenon of universal phonetic symbolism has been seriously challenged by the cross-cultural study of Taylor and Taylor (1962), although other such studies are needed in order to substantiate this claim. The phenomenon of language-specific phonetic symbolisms, however, has received wide empirical support. In view of these conclusions, the next step in the study of phonetic symbolism is the systematic examination of the patterns of connotative meaning of the sounds in a large sample of natural languages. Such an analysis might reveal trends and universals of sound symbolism not yet identified by psycholinguistic investigation.

REFERENCES

BENTLEY, M. and VARON, E. J. An accessory study of "phonetic symbolism." *American Journal of Psychology*, 1933, 45, 76–86.

BOLINGER, D. L. Rime, assonance, and morpheme analysis. *Word*, 1950, 6, 117–136.

BRACKBILL, Y. and LITTLE, K. B. Factors determining the guessing of meanings of foreign words. *Journal of Abnormal and Social Psychology*, 1957, 54, 312–318.

BROWN, R. W., BLACK, A. H., and HOROWITZ, A. E. Phonetic symbolism in natural languages. *Journal of Abnormal and Social Psychology*, 1955, 50, 388–393.

BROWN, R. W., and NUTTALL, R. Method in phonetic symbolism experiments. *Journal of Abnormal and Social Psychology*, 1959, 59, 441–445.

DAVIS, R. The fitness of names to drawings. A cross-cultural study in Tanganyika. *British Journal of Psychology*, 1961, 52, 259–268.

MALTZMANN, I., MORISETT, L., JR., and BROOKS, L. O. An investigation of phonetic symbolism. *Journal of Abnormal and Social Psychology*, 1956, 53, 249–251.

MARKEL, N. Connotative meanings of several initial consonant clusters in English. *Georgetown University Monograph Series on Languages and Linguistics*, 1961, 14, 81–87.

NEWMAN, S. S. Further experiments in phonetic symbolism. *American Journal of Psychology*, 1933, 45, 53–75.

OSGOOD, C. E., SUCI, G. J., and TANNENBAUM, P. H. *The measurement of meaning*, Urbana, Illinois: University of Illinois Press, 1957.

SAPIR, E. A study in phonetic symbolism. *Journal of Experimental Psychology*, 1929, 12, 225–239.

TAYLOR, I. K. Phonetic symbolism re-examined. *Psychological Bulletin*, 1963, 60, 200–209.

TAYLOR, I. K., and TAYLOR, M. M. Phonetic symbolism in four unrelated languages. *Canadian Journal of Psychology*, 1962, 16, 344–356.

TSURU, S., and FRIES, H. A problem in meaning. *Journal of General Psychology*, 1962, 16, 344–356.

VETTER, H. J., and TENNANT, J. A. Oral-gesture cues in sound symbolism. *Perceptual and Motor Skills*, 1967, 24, 54.

WEISS, J. H. Role of "meaningfulness" versus meaning dimensions in guessing the meanings of foreign words. *Journal of Abnormal and Social Psychology*, 1963, 66, 541–546.

WEISS, J. H. Phonetic symbolism re-examined. *Psychological Bulletin*, 1964a, 61, 454–458.

WEISS, J. H. The role of stimulus meaningfulness in the phonetic symbolism response. *Journal of General Psychology*, 1964b, 70, 255–263.

WEISS, J. H. A study of the ability of English speakers to guess the meanings of nonantonym foreign words. *Journal of General Psychology*, 1966, 74, 97–106.

CHAPTER 8

The Vocal Expression of Emotion

Oh that my words were colours! But their tints
May serve perhaps as outlines or slight hints.

Byron: *Don Juan*

As JOEL DAVITZ POINTS OUT in his introduction to *The Communication of Emotional Meaning* (1964), it has always been important for the clinician to be sensitive, to empathize, to understand and to be intuitively responsive to his patients' feelings and emotions. He cannot be content with the general, denotative meanings of words; he must search out their affective significance. For the psychiatrist and clinical psychologist, this has always been a vague sixth sense he has had to acquire and refine. There have been few general principles that have been experimentally validated upon which the clinician could base his judgments of emotional meaning.

Recently, however, the expression of emotion by the voice has been the subject of much experimental investigation. Research in this area began during the 1920's and 1930's and, following a temporary decline during World War II, picked up again in the 1950's and 1960's. (It should be noted that there has been a good deal of repetition of previous work.) Investigation has generally taken two forms: (1) the study of manifest verbal content, and (2) studies of vocal but nonverbal content or modes of communication. Carl Rogers is considered to be one of the pioneers in the systematic study of the former. Snyder (1947), Auld and Murray (1955) and Pool (1959) have also centered their efforts on content analysis. Many experimenters, however, have found that the most useful indicators of emotional meaning are to be sought in the nonlexical area. They have found that the more important aspect of affective communication is *how* something is said, rather than *what* is said. Davitz states that his experimenters discovered "emotional meanings were communicated nonverbally far beyond chance expectation" and that "emotional meanings can be communicated reliably by content-free speech." Thus, vocal communication—verbal and content-free speech—carries "information about the soundmaker's emotions, no matter how carefully he tries to hide them behind the acoustic symbols he emits" (Ostwald, 1963). The voice can be viewed as a "primary resonator of emotions and, therefore, provides a medium for the quantitative analysis of emotional states" (Alpert, Kurtzberg and Friedhoff, 1963).

Normal human speech consists of two simultaneous sets of cues. The first is the articulated sound patterns which form words, phrases and sentences. These are characterized as a rapidly changing succession of stimuli presenting semantically meaningful material. The second set of cues includes the discriminable qualitative features of the voice itself. It is this set of cues which is most relevant to the study of the vocal expression of emotion. Soskin and Kauffman (1961) describe this second set of cues as the *carrier* on which articulated sounds are superimposed. Within this carrier may be the major cues to emotional disposition.

Ostwald (1963) gives a graphic illustration of the distinction between carrier and semantic content. A psychiatrist asked a woman patient undergoing psychotherapy how she felt. With a tremulous voice and an anguished expression, she replied that she felt fine. There is a glaring discrepancy here between the denotative meaning of "feeling fine" and the emotive meaning inferred from the nonverbal acoustic sign (tremulous voice) or the cues conveyed by the anguished expression. We must assume that the emotional import of the patient's utterance which is transmitted nonverbally alters dramatically the meaning of the words themselves.

Before reviewing some of the studies that have been conducted on the vocal expression of emotion, it is necessary to devote some preliminary discussion to theoretical accounts of emotion. The term emotion has been used in relation to many different psychological states and forms of behavior. Because it has been given so many diverse meanings, a brief glimpse at some representative views on emotion may help clarify some of the more complex issues involved in the vocal expression of emotion.

THEORIES OF EMOTION

Theories of emotion can be roughly divided into three approaches: (1) those which emphasize purely physiological processes; (2) those which stress physiological factors plus awareness of change by the organism; and (3) those which attempt to interrelate physiological and cognitive factors. In developing their theories of emotion, most investigators have considered emotion from one or the other of two viewpoints: either the situation produces some physiological change which is then interpreted as an emotion, or the situation precipitates an emotional response which in turn produces a physiological change within the organism.

A rather classical example of the first approach, which relies heavily on physiological processes, was presented by McDougall. He describes a "primary" emotion as "the affective operation of any one of the principal instincts" (Smith, 1922, p. 17). According to Smith, McDougall uses the term instinct as that which is

> . . . constituted by innate constructional details of the organism, such that, confronted by a particular situation, it tends to react in a particular way. The particularity of this emotion is, therefore, precisely proportional to that of the reaction, dependent in turn upon the situation and the organism (Smith, 1922, p. 22).

For McDougall the differences between different "emotions" are simply a matter of the different kinds of endosomatic sensations concerned, their different intensities and the different proportions in which they are present. Even though emotions are varied, McDougall feels that the changes induced by like conditions in like individuals are sufficiently similar to warrant description of their corresponding emotions by the same name. Hence, in so far as individuals are alike and in so far as the situations they encounter are similar, they will react similarly and experience similar emotions.

McDougall's "primary" emotions and their appropriate instinctive responses are as follows: (Ruckmick, 1936).

Emotion	Instinctive Responses
Fear	Flight
Disgust	Repulsion
Wonder	Curiosity
Anger	Pugnacity
Subjection	Self-abasement
Elation	Self-display
Tender emotion	Parental

[From] these seven primary emotions together with feelings of pleasure and pain (and perhaps also feelings of excitement and depression) are compounded all, or almost all, the affective states that are popularly recognized as emotions, and for which common speech has definite names (Ruckmick, 1936, p. 125).

McDougall expands this list further to include some fourteen primary emotional qualities and their parallel instinctive responses.

According to the James-Lange theory of emotion, physiological reactions precede cognitive responses. "Bodily changes follow directly the perception of the exciting fact, and our feeling of the same changes as they occur is the emotion" (Smith, 1922, p. 17).

Smith in his outlook on emotions combines McDougall's and the James-Lange theory in the following definition.

> Emotion is the effect produced in consciousness by the endosomatic adjustments elicited in the organism by the stimulus applied to it, or, more generally, by the situation which it encounters. It is thus associated in the most intimate possible manner with the reaction corresponding to that situation on stimulus, and may thus be correctly described as 'the affective aspect of the operation of an instinct' (1922, p. 24).

Unlike the aforementioned investigators, Krech and Crutchfield (1958, p. 230) introduce awareness as part of the emotion. They treat emotion as a multi-dimensional term with the implication that physiological changes follow cognitive responses.

> In its broadest psychological meaning, the term emotion refers to a stirred-up state of the organism, reflected in three quite different ways:
> 1. emotional experience, e.g., the person feels angry;
> 2. emotional behavior, e.g., he curses and attacks his tormentor;
> 3. physiological changes in the body, e.g., the blood rushes to the face, the heart beats faster, etc. These three aspects are intimately related.

Emotional experience is then further classified into four "dimensions," (1) intensity of feeling, (2) level of tension, (3) hedonic tone and (4) degree of complexity.

Like Krech and Crutchfield, Eisenson, Auer and Irwin (1963, p. 69), emphasize the awareness of a physiological change by the organism, but unlike them, they perceive the physiological reaction as preceding the cognitive. They refer to emotion as:

> . . . a component of a complex reaction that an individual undergoes in a given situation. The component emotion is characterized by:
> 1. a marked change in the internal state of the organism;
> 2. awareness of the change; and
> 3. behavior indicative in an attempt to adjust to the given situation.

DeRivera (1962) presents a "decision theory of emotions." He states that:

> . . . emotions arise when an animal decides how it wishes to interact with some object in its environment. Thus, emotions do not arise without a conflict—a decision to make, but they are basically functional, i.e., without making the decision the animal would not be able to act (DeRivera, 1962).

The animal must make a series of six independent decisions which determine how the animal should act. Decisions include such choices as to extend or contract and to be attracted or repulsed by the object. When four other decisions are added, various combinations are available which permit the specification of ninety-six different emotions. Unlike Darwin, DeRivera does not emphasize the involuntary aspects of emotional expression, but rather a series of decisions which the animal must make before it can act.

Schachter and Singer (1962) emphasize the interaction of cognitive and physiological factors in defining emotional states. They note that, although various emotional states differ in regard to the overall level of physiological arousal or activation of the organism, there are subjective differences in emotional response patterns that, nevertheless, have the same level of activation. Thus, subjectively different emotional states may be associated with similar physiological reactions (Schachter and Singer, 1962). Happiness and anger may have relatively similar levels of activation, yet they are subjectively different. The differences in these emotional states are explained in terms of the individual's cognitive interpretation of the situation in which he experiences the state of activation. Hence, emotions are determined partly as a function of how a situation is viewed perceptually by the subject; and consideration of activity level as well as cognitive variables is necessary to determine the specific emotional response.

Many investigators tend to view emotions as disruptive and disorganizing forces which impair rather than help the individual in his efforts at adjustment. Exponents of this viewpoint argue that emotional responses are characterized by predominantly random, excessive and largely useless motor as well as verbal behavior. As Dockeray (1933, p. 620) puts it:

> . . . emotion may be considered the opposite of attentive or organized behavior. There are segments of the total behavior which are largely organized, such as certain glandular and visceral reactions, but the total picture is that of disorganization.

Zipf (1965), in equating emotion with physical energy, also adheres to this disorganizational viewpoint of emotion. For example, a static state of material organization is potential energy since its general direction is toward disintegration. The more rapidly and extensively the disorganization takes place, the more intense the accompanying energy. Thus in equating emotions with physical energy he suggests that as we proceed from the less complex to the more complex in the totality of our being, emotion is "emitted." The more rapidly and the more extensively the change takes place, the more intense is the concomitant emotion. Without change in organization, there is no emotion. Without emotion, no change. Thus he considers the two concomitant with the possibility of a causal relationship implied.

A related view of emotional behavior emphasizes the reorganization of response patterns. The individual reorganizes his response patterns by meeting new situations in terms of his background of experience or with a modified response pattern. This concept of emotional behavior, according to Eisenson, et al. (1963), may explain the more intense emotions such as fear, anger and rage, but not the less intense and hedonistically more pleasant emotions such as joy or the unpleasant emotions of sadness and grief.

What are we to make of this welter of conflicting viewpoints? Surely the reader must find himself completely dismayed. It must be emphasized, however, that theoretical disputes in psychology have never been a bar to research. On the contrary, some of our most significant advances in psychological science have originated within the sharpest controversies. Actually, the approach of Schachter and Singer (1962) which we described very briefly above has claims to be considered a major attempt at a theoretical synthesis. It is an approach which takes into consideration both the physiological and cognitive aspects in determining the emotional response.

Schachter, it will be recalled, observes that various emotional states seem to differ in terms of the organism's gross level of physiological arousal or activation. But differences in activation alone do not account for subjective differences in emotional states. For example, joy and anger might both be accompanied by relatively high levels of activation, so that subjectively different emotional states are associated with similar physiological responses. Thus, some other factor must account for an emotional state being labeled "joy" or "anger." This, Schachter attributes to the individual's cognitive interpretation of the situation in which he experiences the state of activation.

EXPLORATIONS OF ACOUSTIC PHENOMENA

Descriptive schemas and terminologies of various kinds have been devised by people who study, or in some way deal with, acoustic phenomena as a means of communicating verbally about sounds. Musicians speak of intonation, timbre and tempo; acousticians talk of noise, decibels and frequencies; linguists use terms like inflection, stress and pitch levels; and voice therapists describe hoarseness, registers and melody (Barbara, 1958). One would welcome an exercise in comparative philology that sought to determine which words from the various disciplines actually refer to the same acoustic phenomena.

Trager (1965) identifies the acoustic phenomena which accompany language by the term *paralanguage*. Paralanguage is divided into *voice set* as background for, and *voice qualities* and *vocalizations* as accompaniments of, language proper.

Voice set involves the physiological and physical peculiarities that result in the patterned identification of individuals as members of a societal group, persons of a certain age, sex, state of health, body build, etc.

Voice qualities are speech events such as pitch range, vocal lip control, glottis control, pitch control, articulation control, rhythm control, resonance and tempo. These can be identified on the following gradients:

1. pitch range

        spread $\begin{cases} \text{upward} \\ \text{downward} \end{cases}$

    narrowed $\begin{cases} \text{above} \\ \text{below} \end{cases}$

2. vocal lip control

rasp $\begin{cases} \text{heavy (hoarseness)} \\ \text{plain} \end{cases}$

openness $\begin{cases} \text{slight} \\ \text{full} \end{cases}$

3. glottis control

voicing $\begin{cases} \text{over} \\ \text{under} \end{cases}$

breathiness $\begin{cases} \text{slight} \\ \text{heavy} \end{cases}$

4. pitch control

$\begin{cases} \text{sharp transition} \\ \text{smooth transition} \end{cases}$

5. articulation control

$\begin{cases} \text{forceful} \\ \text{relaxed} \end{cases}$

6. rhythm control

$\begin{cases} \text{smooth} \\ \text{jerky} \end{cases}$

7. resonance

$\begin{cases} \text{resonant} \\ \text{thin} \end{cases}$

8. tempo

$\begin{cases} \text{increased} \\ \text{decreased} \end{cases}$

In contrast with voice set and voice qualities, which are overall or background characteristics of the voice, the vocalizations are actual specifically identifiable sounds or aspects of sounds. Trager divided vocalizations into three types: *vocal characteristics, vocal qualifiers* and *vocal segregates.*

Vocal characteristics include such items as laughing, crying, yelling, whispering, moaning, groaning, etc. Vocal qualifiers are divided into three kinds: those of *intensity, pitch height* and *extent.* Within each of these is a dichotomy.

Intensity $\begin{cases} \text{overloud} \\ \text{oversoft} \end{cases}$ somewhat considerably very much

Pitch height $\begin{cases} \text{overhigh} \\ \text{overlow} \end{cases}$ slightly appreciably greatly

Extent $\qquad \left\{ \begin{array}{l} \text{drawl} \\ \text{clipping} \end{array} \right\} \quad \begin{array}{l} \text{slight} \\ \text{noticeable} \\ \text{extreme} \end{array}$

Vocal segregates are those sounds that do not seem to fit into ordinary phonological frames in a language. They seem to be identical with the actual linguistic sounds in the language being studied, but do not appear in the kinds of sequences that can be called words. These include such items as the English "uh-uh" for negation, "uh-huh" for affirmation, and the "uh" of hesitation.

Dittman and Wynne (1961) have investigated Trager's paralinguistic system. Excerpts of psychotherapeutic interviews of varying emotional tone and excerpts from an unrehearsed conversation from a radio broadcast were coded according to Trager's system. The authors noted that:

> The linguistic phenomena proved to be highly reliable, while the paralinguistic did not, but the reliable linguistic codings were independent of the emotive expressions in the different interviews of the individual differences among the speakers represented by the interviews and the radio program (p. 203).

They found a variability in the agreement between interviews in many categories. This suggests that Trager's system lacks reliability. In addition, the vocal characterizers and vocal segregates occurred too infrequently within the sample to permit a reliability check.

Dittman and Wynne explained their results in terms of the fundamental difference between the type of systematization that can be used for linguistic phenomena and that which can be used for vocal communications other than language. "The difference lies in the fact that language is made of discrete elements, while emotional communication in speech consists of continuous phenomena that have more complex interrelations" (Dittman and Wynne, 1961, p. 203). Many experimenters, including Osser (1964) and Piddington (1963), agree with Trager that these emotional factors of speech are best described as continua. Moreover, Dittman and Wynne state that not enough research has been done yet to tell if "they are describable in present-absent terms; it may be that emotional communication is always present in speech" (1961, p. 203).

Another investigator (Ostwald, 1963) distinguishes between *qualitative attributes, visualization of sound* and *acoustic measurement.*

Qualitative attributes may be defined with respect to a system of complex interactions between the auditor and the sound inputs, i.e., they represent a combination of sensory and interpretative reactions on the part of the listener toward the particular sound in question. Qualitative attributes are subdivided into seven categories, each of which constitutes a gradient. The categories are: *rhythmicity, intensity, pitch, tone, speed, shape* and *orderliness.*

Rhythmicity designates properties of sound that are defined in terms of the continuum: *rhythmic—————————irregular.* This is one of the most fundamental characteristics of the sounds produced by living creatures. An example would be the human heart-beat.

Intensity designates properties of sound that are identified with reference to the continuum: *loud—————————soft.* The upper extreme of this continuum (circa 120 decibels) is marked by the appearance of pain as an accompaniment to auditory sensation. The lower end of the continuum (approaching 0 decibels) marks the physiological threshold of hearing.

Pitch identifies the characteristics of sound defined along the gradient: *high-pitched—————————low-pitched.* Pitch is basically a function of the frequency of sound vibrations that reach the ear. However, it is rather difficult to specify the extremities of the pitch continuum, for judgments of pitch are influenced by the operation of other aspects of the acoustic stimulus. For purposes of general discussion, we may consider the audible frequency range as lying between 20 cycles per second (for the low end) and 20,000 cycles per second (for the high end). It should be noted that age is a significant variable; the hearing range is greater in children than in adults.

Tone is defined with respect to the continuum: *tonal————————— noisy.* Tonal sounds are composed of single vibratory frequencies or contain a number of vibratory frequencies which are multiples of one another. At the opposite end of the continuum is noise, which is composed of many vibratory frequencies that overlap and mingle with one another, producing extremely complex wave-forms (Beranek, 1954).

Speed is defined along the continuum: *fast—————————slow.* As in the case of pitch, intensity and tone, physiological limitations of the hearing apparatus determine the capability to perceive the speed of an acoustic stimulus. At the slow end of the continuum, attention lapses after approximately .8 second. Consequently, when the impulse rate drops below one sound per second, the attention of the auditor must be sustained by additional cues. At the fast end of the spectrum, there is a merging of successive impulses to produce the impression of a steady sound.

Shape refers to the attributes of sound as defined with respect to the continuum: *impulsive—————————reverberant.* Shape is a property that is related to the onset, growth, steady-state, duration, decay and termination of an individual sound. A pistol shot, for example, has a sudden beginning, rapid rise to peak intensity and quick decay to silence. The subjective experience is that of an abrupt, crashing sound. At the reverberant end of the spectrum, there is a gradual bginning of the sound, a slow growth into a steady pattern, the maintenance of a semitonal quality (depending on the characteristics of the noisemaker and its environment), and a slow decay to silence.

Orderliness is defined along the gradient: *compact——————— expanded*. A sound is said to be compact when its single constituents form a recognizable and orderly configuration. At the expanded end of the continuum, sounds are lacking in tone, organized intensity and rhythm; they are experienced as monotonous and dissonant. Unlike rhythmicity, an auditory experience that seems to be biologically determined, orderliness varies as a function of individual differences in learning. For instance, a foreign language sounds unintelligible and chaotic before one has learned to recognize its intrinsic patterns or order.

Visualization, as represented by a system such as the International Phonetic Alphabet, represents another way of dealing with sound. The phonetic alphabet consists of a series of diagrammatic sketches, as it were, of individual speech sounds. It does a more accurate job of depicting speech sounds than does our conventional alphabet, but it is much less precise than acoustic measurement.

Acoustic measurement, as Ostwald (1963) points out, is one of the most scientific methods available for dealing with sounds. Through the use of acoustic filters, analogous in their function to chemical filters, it is possible to separate sounds into their frequency components. Filters of varying fineness permit the study of different-sized spectrum bands in terms of their energy levels (Scott, 1957). Band-pass filters are of two kinds: fixed and adjustable. Fixed band-pass filters divide the sound spectrum into equal-sized bands (e.g., octaves, half-octaves) from 20 cycles per second to 20,000 cycles per second. Adjustable band-pass filters permit the measurement of sound energy levels at points anywhere across the frequency spectrum. The amount of energy passed by each filter can be measured by a meter or depicted visually by means of the sound spectrograph.

SPEECH

Ostwald classifies speech into *denotative speech* and *emotive speech*. Denotative speech is defined as that portion of verbal behavior which can be understood by reference to vocabulary, grammar and other formal rules of language. Emotive speech starts with transcendental words and phrases capable of rapid fluctuations in meaning and goes on to the borderland of linguistics.

The view of Eisenson, Auer and Irwin (1963), on speech and emotion is in accordance with Ostwald's definition of emotive speech, as Eisenson states that the more intense the feeling, the more difficult it is for the state to be verbalized. According to Eisenson et al., strong emotive speech is characterized by vividness. In general, the more emotionally charged the language, the less definite the meanings of the individual words.

Diversification of content characterizes the verbal utterances of persons in a state of heightened affect. The verbal flow of such speakers contains more words and a greater variety of words than do the utter-

TABLE 8.1

ANALYSIS OF SPEECH CHARACTERISTICS OF 40 PATIENTS WITH AFFECTIVE DISORDERS
(After Newman and Mather, 1938)

	Depression	Mania
Articulatory movements	lax	vigorous
Pitch range	narrow	wide
Pitch changes	stepwise; infrequent	gliding; frequent
Emphatic accents	absent or rare	frequent
Pauses	hesitating	accented
Resonance	nasal	oral
Level of style	colloquial	elevated
Syntactic elaboration	meager	rich
Syntactic techniques	limited	diversified
Initiation of response	slow	quick
Length of response	short	long

ances of persons with lowered affect, including the mildly and more severely depressed, which contain few words and tend to include verbal repetition. These observations are consistent with the findings of Zipf on his studies on the relationship between emotional states and articulateness of meaning (Zipf, 1965). Whatmough also agrees. "A relationship between frequencies and affectivity is demonstrable. Low frequency goes with high affectivity . . ." (Whatmough, 1956, p. 212).

Newman and Mather (1938) in their study of persons with affective disorders, found that patients in heightened states spoke with high diversification of content, while patients in low affective states spoke with low diversification of content. Other characteristics of the utterances of persons with affective disorders are summarized in Table 8.1 (Newman and Mather, 1938).

Davitz (1964) classified speech as conveying information in vocal and verbal modes—the vocal mode being the acoustic attributes of speech, and the verbal the content of the speech. The meaning of a sample of speech, including its emotional meaning, is a function of what is said and how it is said, the interaction of verbal and vocal aspects of the total message. Davitz ties in these two modes with Schachter's theory of emotion; and although the evidence is not clear-cut, it is suggested that perhaps the verbal aspect of speech primarily reflects the cognitive determinatus of emotional states, while the vocal aspects are a function of the speaker's state of activation.

Some indirect support for this view is provided by the results of Davitz's research (discussed in detail later) concerned with vocal correlates of emotional expressions. Briefly, these findings indicate that subjective active feelings tend to be communicated by a loud voice, with relatively high pitch, flaring timbre and fast rate of speech. In contrast, subjectively passive feelings are communicated by a relatively softer voice, with relatively lower pitch, more resonant timbre and slower rate of speech. Therefore, assuming that subjective activity parallels physiological activation, the vocal aspects of speech might well reflect the level of activation associated with particular emotional states.

It would be unreasonable to assume a one-to-one relation between physiological activation and subjective activity. The social situation must be considered as well as the various social conventions influencing patterns of communication. Nevertheless, other things being equal, a person in a highly activated state probably tends to behave in ways which involve a relatively high degree of energy expenditure. Thus the activation dimension of emotional states is reflected to some extent in the form of behaviors which communicate emotional meanings.

EMOTIONAL MEANING AND VOCAL EXPRESSIONS

To investigate the communication of emotional meaning by vocal expression three major techniques have been used to eliminate or control the verbal information conveyed by speech. In some studies, speakers attempt to express feelings merely by reciting the alphabet or counting, for example from 1–9, assuming that neither letters nor numerals carry meaning relevant to emotional communication (Davitz and Davitz, 1959,a, Dusenberry and Knower, 1939). Other researchers have utilized standard verbal content that presumably is emotionally neutral; speakers recite the same few sentences while trying to express different feelings, so that whatever emotional meaning is communicated depends upon vocal rather than verbal cues (Fairbanks and Pronovost, 1939; Pollack, *et al.*, 1960). In recent years, a number of studies have capitalized on electronic filtering techniques which substantially decrease the verbal content of tape recorded utterances without destroying the simultaneous emotional communication carried by certain vocal characteristics of speech (Soskin and Kauffman, 1961; Starkweather, 1956).

Ruckmick (1936) reviewed some earlier studies made on the relationship of vocal expressions to emotions. These visualized and analyzed changes in pitch and in intensity of voice, in its vibrato and in its general pattern, through photographic recordings. The recordings were of dramatic and conversational performances, by competent speech performers. The results generally indicated that there were definite tendencies for heightened feelings to find vocal expression at the higher end of the performer's pitch range, and for neutral and depressed states to be expressed at the lower end of the pitch range.

In a series of studies by Pronovost and Fairbanks (1939), the relationship of pitch to simulated emotion is reported, along with an analysis of the pitch characteristics of key affective states. Results are shown in Table 8.2.

TABLE 8.2

PITCH CHARACTERISTICS OF KEY AFFECTIVE STATES (After Pronovost and Fairbanks, 1939)

Simulated Emotion	Median Pitch Level	Total Pitch Range	Inflectional Range	Pitch Change
Contempt	low	wide	moderate	moderate
Anger	high	wide	widest	most rapid
Fear	highest	widest	moderate	moderate
Grief	low	narrow	narrowest	slowest
Indifference	lowest	narrowest	moderate	moderate

Both Ruckmick's survey and the Pronovost and Fairbanks studies uphold the common observation that happy and angry persons who give voice to their feelings do so at higher pitch levels than sad or "indifferent" persons. Skinner (1935), on the other hand, believed that force was a more reliable index than pitch for differentiating the vocal reactions of happiness and sadness. He found that vocal expressions in happy states are characterized by an increase in the use of force while the same are characterized by a reduction in sad states.

In the Davitz and Davitz study (1959,a), the investigators instructed each of eight speakers to express 10 different feelings by reciting parts of the alphabet. These vocal expressions were tape recorded and the recordings were played to 30 judges, who were given a list of 10 feelings and asked to identify the emotional meaning conveyed by each expression. Like all other studies in the area, Davitz found that on the average, feelings were communicated far beyond chance expectation. However, speakers varied markedly in the accuracy with which their vocal expressions were recognized; one speaker's expressions were identified correctly in only 23 percent of the cases, while another speaker communicated accurately well over 50 percent of the time. Listeners, too, showed a wide range of difference, varying in accuracy from 20 percent to nearly 50 percent correct. And finally, as most other studies have reported, feelings clearly differed in the accuracy with which they were communicated; anger, for example, was communicated accurately over 63 percent of the time, while pride was identified correctly in only 20 percent of the cases.

Differences in the ease on accuracy of communicating various feelings have been reported in several studies. Pfaff (1953) found that out of nine categories of feeling which he investigated, joy and hate were most accurately communicated, while shame and love were the most difficult to recognize. These kinds of differences are consistently mentioned in the literature, but only one relatively minor study has focused specifically on an attempt to account for this phenomenon. Beginning with the observation that identifying an emotional expression is essentially a problem in discrimination, Davitz and Davitz (1959b) reasoned that subjective similarity of the feelings portrayed should be inversely related to the ease of discriminating among expressions of these feelings. Thus, it would seem reasonable to expect greater difficulty in discriminating between anger and impatience than between anger and sadness. The results of their research generally support this position, though the data demonstrate that subjective similarity among feelings accounts for only a small part of the variance in accuracy of communication. Davitz and Davitz also report that given expressions of two similar feelings, such as anger and impatience, the subjectively stronger of the two feelings is communicated more accurately. Beyond these preliminary findings, the literature provides no answer to the question of why various feelings are communicated with differential accuracy.

The research has not been especially productive in defining the vocal cues which convey specific emotional meanings. Undoubtedly this is partly a function of the complex technical difficulties involved in establishing measures of vocal characteristics (Scott, 1958; Dittman and Wynne, 1961).

The result of an early study by Dusenberry and Knower (1939) suggest that the sequential pattern of speech provides important cues for recognition of emotional meaning. Testing this hypothesis in a later, more carefully designed study, Knower (1941) compared recordings of vocal expressions played backwards with those played in normal sequence. He found that the reversed expressions were recognized beyond chance expectation, but the accuracy of the judgments was greatly impaired. He therefore concluded that the sequential pattern of speech was a significant aspect of emotional expression, but subsequent research has by and large failed to follow up this lead in defining the particular sequences of vocal cues which are associated with the communication of various meanings.

If the sequence of cues is an important component of speech which carries emotional meaning, the next step in research would seem to be specifying the vocal characteristics which are involved in this sequential pattern. Two studies suggest that rate, pitch and the time of pauses in a vocal utterance are consistently related to the meanings expressed. Fairbanks and Hoaglin (1941) reported that feelings such as anger, grief and contempt may be differentiated in terms of rate, ratio of pause time to phonation time and aspects of pitch such as range and rate of range. For example, anger tends to be expressed by a relatively fast rate; grief, by a high ratio of pause to phonation time; and fear, by relatively high pitch.

Despite these findings, feelings apparently can be communicated accurately even with marked reduction in the range and specificity of the vocal stimulus. Knower (1941), for example, found that even when speakers whispered, which eliminates the fundamental frequency of the normal voice, the accuracy of listeners was four times that expected by chance. Pollack, Rubenstein and Horowitz (1960) also reported that the emotional meanings expressed by samples of whispered speech played under increasing signal-to-noise ratios were identified at above chance levels. Perhaps even more striking, Pollack, et al., found that emotional communication was possible with speech samples as short as 60 milliseconds.

Thus, regardless of the technique used, all studies of adults thus far reported agree that emotional meaning can be communicated accurately by vocal expression. Also the research to date offers a few, limited clues about vocal characteristics of emotional expression, but these clues have not been consistently helpful in identifying speech correlates of particular emotional states.

Dimitrovsky (1962) centered her study on the development of sensitivity to vocal communication of emotion during childhood. Her subjects were children aging from five to twelve. They were asked to identify vocal expressions of four categories of emotional meaning: love, happiness, sadness and anger. The subjects heard tapes and were then asked to point to one of four stick figure drawings representing the above four categories. The subjects were, in addition, given a test of verbal intelligence. Dimitrovsky found that with age, the ability to correctly identify the emotional meaning of vocal expression increased—as was to be expected. Yet, there was no marked consistent difference in the pattern of correct and incorrect responses made by the subjects at the various age levels from five to twelve. In addition, she found that "children at all age levels favored the emotions with negative valence, giving the responses 'sad' and 'angry' more often than the responses 'happy' and 'loving'" (Dimitrovsky, 1962). From this, she concluded that "the tendency to respond in terms of negative emotional meaning appears to be peculiarly characteristic of children" (Dimitrovsky, 1962).

One might question the above conclusions on the grounds that perhaps negative emotions are simply easier to identify—considering the experimenter's statement that "expressions of sadness were most frequently identified." This was followed in frequency by expressions of anger. It seems then that children, rather than *favoring* emotions with negative content, perhaps only found them easier to identify. One also wishes that she had followed this study with a similar experiment with adults to determine if they, too, identified the negative emotions more frequently. Data of this kind could permit some evaluation of her statement that the tendency to respond in terms of negative emotional meaning is peculiarly characteristic of children.

Undoubtedly a major problem in this area is the technical difficulty involved in describing speech. A promising line of research is suggested by Hargreaves and Starkweather (Davitz, 1963), who have used spectrographic records of speech to identify vocal qualities relevant to emotional communication.

Studies using electromechanical methods of analyzing speech would surely be an important step toward defining the vocal cues of emotion. But, in addition to studies of this sort, it is also imperative to investigate the auditory cues which can be discriminated by listeners, rather then by electronic devices; for in the final analysis, the cues heard and perceived by listeners must carry the emotional meanings conveyed in interpersonal, vocal communication.

Research focused on factors related to accuracy in recognition of vocal expressions of emotion is rather limited. There are nonetheless a few studies whose results suggest some correlates of sensitivity to vocal expression.

Gates (1927) noted that both age and intelligence of children were positively correlated with accuracy of identification of emotional expression in one speaker. Dimitrovsky (1962) also found that girls were more accurate than boys as judges of vocal expression of feeling. This raises the question of sex differences in the ability to perceive and express emotional meaning. Levy (1962) found no significant sex differences in either ability. Her original hypothesis was that women show greater accuracy in these abilities than men, yet this contention was not supported by the experimental evidence. Dusenberry and Knower (1939) found that women in their sample were superior to men in the accuracy of their judgments, but the difference was not statistically significant. Pfaff (1954) reported a difference significant beyond the .001 level in the direction of greater accuracy for college women in comparison with an equivalent sample of men. But Fay and Middleton (1940), on the other hand, failed to find reliable differences in sensitivity between men and women. Thus, the studies concerned with sex differences in ability to recognize vocal expressions of emotion present, on the whole, a confusing and contradictory picture.

Beldoch's (1961) research dealt with the interrelation among various modes of emotional communication. He poses the question, "Is there a general factor of sensitivity, or are people sensitive to one mode of expression without being especially sensitive to other modes?" The study presented to the subjects tape recorded speech selections of male and female speakers reciting neutral paragraphs in an attempt to communicate various emotional states. In addition, subjects were given musical selections and opaque projections of abstract art. A 300-item adjective check list, a questionnaire which elicited background information on the subject's attitudes toward, and experiences of, the various media, a self-report scale of sensitivity to other peoples' emotional expressions and a vocabulary test, comprise the materials used in the experiment.

> Significant intercorrelations were obtained among the ability to identify the expression of feeling in all three media. Vocabulary scores also correlated significantly with ability in all three modes and with the total score . . . Background training or current interest in the arts did not contribute to success with any of the instruments. None of the adjectives on the check list discriminated between high and low scorers on the sensitivity measures, but self-reported sensitivity did distinguish between groups—the high scorers described themselves as more sensitive than the low scorers (Beldoch, 1961).

He concludes that the abilities in the "discursive and non-discursive modes have some common variance" but that they are independent of each other in many ways.

Levitt (1962) reached similar conclusions in his investigation of the relationship between vocal and facial emotional expressive abilities. He examined the "comparative communication efficiency of the vocal, facial and combined vocal-facial modes." He determined that feelings were communicated more effectively by the facial than the vocal mode: "Vocal-facial communication, while superior to vocal communication, was not more effective than facial communication alone." Like Beldoch, Levitt discussed his results in terms of a general factor underlying the communication of feeling. Levitt states that:

> . . . since the experimental data showed that only a small part of the variance in emotional communication could be accounted for by a general factor, it was postulated that there were also specific factors involved in specific aspects or modes of communicating different feelings (Levitt, 1962).

Beldoch and Levitt thus arrive at similar conclusions.

The two studies suggest possibilities for further research in this particular aspect of emotional communication. It would be interesting to investigate the relationship, if any, between the ability to judge facial expressions and the ability to perceive emotion in abstract art, as well as correlations between the ability to judge vocal recordings and musical selections.

Levy (1962) studied the "relationship between the ability to express and to perceive vocal communications of feeling." The variables investigated were:

1. Expression, or ability to express feelings vocally to others.

2. Other-perception, or the ability to identify feelings expressed vocally by others.

3. Self-perception, or the ability to identify one's own vocal expression of feeling.

She found that the three variables are positively intercorrelated. These results add support to the ancient admonition, "Know thyself." Before one can attempt to understand others, he must first know himself.

The methods used for a great majority of the studies cited above employ human judges. These studies based on subjective judgments have been extremely valuable, but recent developments in instrumentation have had the advantage of being both objective and easily quantifiable.

A number of studies have used electronic filtering techniques which decrease the verbal content of the utterances without destroying the emotional communication of the vocal characteristics of speech. Among these studies is one by Kramer (1963). Paragraphs were read and taped by American actors who tried to portray five different emotions. Japanese actors, in Japanese, also tried to portray the same emotions. Listeners made judgments of the emotions presented from normal recordings of the test passage in English, recordings in filtered English and recordings in Japanese. Kramer concludes that:

> . . . the over-all percentage of correct matches was approximately the same for normal and filtered recordings of portrayals by the American actors. The previous literature has assumed that the only difference in judgment between normal and filtered speech was due to the absence of words in the latter. Present study shows that this is not true; knowledge of how a person judges normal speech permits no prediction of how he will judge filtered speech (Kramer, 1963).

Kramer also found that the judges were able to match emotions correctly with those that were portrayed in Japanese, though not all emotions were as easy for Americans to recognize in Japanese. This study shows not only the type of thing that can be done with electronic equipment, but also indicates the interest that has been shown recently in cross-cultural studies in this area.

John Bowman Adams, for example, conducted a study "On Expressive Communcation in an Egyptian Village" (1964). In this village, friendliness, hostility and other emotional attitudes were determined by "meanings conveyed by subtle qualities of tone, pitch and melody." Content had little to do with expressive communication, since content was often rote. In addition, Adams discovered that the "presentational meanings" in one culture differ greatly in another. For example, "the speech melody and rhythm that connote 'sincerity' in Egypt usually seems to an American to sound 'cross' or 'belligerent' " (Adams, 1964).

THE WORK OF DAVITZ AND ASSOCIATES

In a study by Davitz (1964), an attempt was made to identify the perceptual and cognitive processes likely to be involved in recognizing the emotional meaning of a vocal expression.

Beginning with the vocal expression itself, it seems obvious that emotional meaning must be conveyed by auditory cues of vocal expressions. Therefore, in order to understand the meanings expressed, it was assumed that the listener must first be able to discriminate the auditory cues which carry these meanings.

Hearing the vocal cues of expression might be necessary for understanding, but it did not seem a sufficient basis for identifying the meanings expressed. In one pattern or another, the nonverbal characteristics of speech, tone, timbre, inflection, etc., combine to represent symbolically a specific emotional meaning, and though the exact pattern of cues associated with various meanings cannot be defined with great precision, it is obvious that these patterns of interrelated vocal characteristics are complex, symbolic stimuli. Therefore, to respond appropriately to these stimuli, to "understand" and identify the meanings expressed by these complex, nonverbal symbols, a listener presumably must have the cognitive ability to deal with abstract symbols, to perceive and meaningfully organize numerous, subtle, nonverbal characteristics which comprise a vocal symbol with emotional meaning.

Having perceived and somehow organized the vocal stimulus, a listener is required to interpret its emotional meaning. Although there is no explicit, standardized dictionary defining emotions in terms of vocal cues, reliable communication would seem unlikely without at least some implicit knowledge, on the listener's part, of the more or less conventional vocal cues of emotional meaning.

Since the subjects were required to name or label the feeling expressed involving some sort of verbal ability, it was reasoned that verbal ability would be likely to be associated with the ability to identify emotional meanings.

The subjects were 61 graduate students and the following variables were measured for each subject:

1. ability to make auditory discriminations;
2. abstract symbolic ability;
3. knowledge of vocal characteristics of emotional expression;
4. verbal intelligence;
5. ability to identify vocal expressions of emotional meaning.

Under auditory discrimination, the following four dimensions were tested:

1. pitch;
2. loudness;
3. time;
4. timbre.

The ability to identify vocal expressions of emotional meaning was measured by a 45 item tape recording of expressions of 8 different emotional meanings plus 5 non-emotional or neutral items. Using a content-standard technique, speakers expressed each of the following emotional meanings: affection, anger, boredom, cheerfulness, impatience, joy, sadness and satisfaction (see Table 8.3., Davitz, 1964).

The study of perceptual and cognitive correlates yielded positive results. Each of the four variables (pitch, loudness, time, timbre) was found to be positively related to a measure of ability to identify vocal expressions of emotional meaning, and a multiple correlation of .60 was obtained between a combination of all four variables and the measure of emotional sensibility. The results of this study support the view that emotional sensitivity can be conceputalized in terms of complex stimuli, intervening perceptual and symbolic processes and subsequent verbal responses.

Another study (Davitz, 1964) investigated some of the auditory cues associated with vocal expressions of emotional meaning. To explore this problem, two sets of variables were selected: one which was concerned with dimensions of emotional meaning, a second concerned with auditory characteristics of speech. The variables involved in emotional meaning were based on the research of Osgood, Suci and Tannenbaum (1958), which yielded three aspects of emotional meaning: (1) *valence*, (2) *strength*, (3) *activity*. The speech variables used included: (1) loudness, (2) pitch, (3) timbre and (4) rate of speed. The study considered the relation between each of the three variables of emotional meaning and each of the four speech variables.

TABLE 8.3

CHARACTERISTICS OF VOCAL EXPRESSIONS CONTAINED IN THE TEST OF EMOTIONAL SENSITIVITY
(After Davitz, 1964)

Feeling	Loud-ness	Pitch	Timbre	Rate	Inflection	Rhythm	Enunciation
Affection	soft	low	resonant	slow	steady & slight upward	regular	slurred
Anger	loud	high	blaring	fast	irregular up & down	irregular	clipped
Boredom	mod. to low	mod. to low	moderate resonant	mod. slow	monotone or grad. falling	...	somewhat slurred
Cheerfulness	mod. high	mod. high	moderate blaring	mod. fast	up & down	regular	
Impatience	normal	norm. mod. high	moderate blaring	mod. fast	slight upward	...	somewhat clipped
Joy	loud	high	moderate blaring	fast	upward	regular	...
Sadness	soft	low	resonant	slow	downward	irreg. pauses	slurred
Satisfaction	normal	norm.	somewhat resonant	norm.	slight upward	regular	somewhat slurred

Four female and three male speakers each expressed 14 different feelings by content-standard speech. In terms of content, the same two sentences were embedded in 14 different paragraphs, each paragraph designed to express one of the 14 emotions. The speakers read each paragraph expressing the feeling with which it was concerned plus a non-emotional paragraph. These readings were tape recorded and the two sentences of each paragraph were spliced so as to provide a recording of different emotional expressions with standard content.

The 14 feelings expressed were: admiration, affection, amusement, anger, boredom, cheerfulness, despair, disgust, dislike, fear, impatience, joy, satisfaction and surprise. The recordings of all seven speakers were judged by 20 persons who were given the list of 14 feelings and asked to identify the feeling expressed, using the non-emotional reading of each speaker as a base.

A final tape, consisting of the reading of each feeling identified most frequently for male speakers and for female speakers, plus the non-emotional reading by each of these speakers, was played to a second set of 20 judges who were asked to rate each expression on four 7-point scales:

1. loudness (loud _____ soft)
2. pitch (high _____ low)
3. timbre (blaring _____ resonant)
4. rate of speech (fast _____ slow)

These were also rated using the non-emotional recording of the speakers as a base line. The recordings were rated on 9 scales of the Semantic Differential by a third set of 20 judges. Each of the three dimensions was represented by 3 scales:

valence by 1. good _____ bad
         2. pleasant _____ unpleasant
         3. beautiful _____ ugly
strength by 1. strong _____ weak
         2. large _____ small
         3. heavy _____ light
activity by 1. fast _____ slow
         2. active _____ passive
         3. sharp _____ dull

The data were analyzed by correlating each of the dimensions of emotional meaning with each of the vocal characteristics of speech. The correlation of activity with each auditory variable was statistically significant.

These data plus those collected in another study by Davitz on erroneous judgments of vocal expressions of feeling support the generalization that loudness, pitch, timbre and rate of speech are a function of the subjectively rated activity level of the emotion communicated. Presumably valence and strength are communicated by other, perhaps more subtle and complex, auditory cues.

CONCLUDING REMARKS

In the studies we have reviewed, the form and content of emotional expressions have been treated separately. That is, the studies have involved vocal expressions with standardized content, controlling the information conveyed by the verbal aspects of the message, or the content has been analyzed only in regard to the relative amount of diversification. But since in normal conversation meanings are communicated both vocally and verbally, an important problem for further research is the interaction of these components of speech in determining meaning.

REFERENCES

ADAMS, J. B. On expressive communication in an Egyptian village. In Hymes, D. (Ed.) *Language in culture and society.* New York: Harper & Row, 1965.

ALPERT, M., KURTZBERG, R. L., and FRIEDHOFF, A. J. Transient voice changes associated with emotional stimuli. *Archives of General Psychiatry,* 1963, 8, 362–365.

AULD, F. and MURRAY, E. J. Content-analysis studies of psychotherapy. *Psychological Bulletin,* 1955, 52, 377–395.

BERANEK, L. *Acoustics.* New York: McGraw-Hill, 1954.

BARBARA, D. A. (Ed.) *Your speech reveals your personality.* Springfield, Illinois: Charles C. Thomas, 1958.

BEKESY, G. VON. *Experiments in hearing.* New York: McGraw-Hill, 1960.

BELDOCH, M. The ability to identify expressions of feeling in vocal, graphic, and musical communication. *Dissertation Abstracts,* 1961, 22, 1246.

CARROLL, R. P. *Emotion.* Washington, D.C.: The Daylion Company, 1937.

DAVITZ, J. R. *The communication of emotional meaning.* New York: McGraw-Hill, 1964.

DAVITZ, J. R. and DAVITZ, L. The communication of feelings by content-free speech. *Journal of Communication,* 1959a, 9, 6–13.

DAVITZ, J. R. and DAVITZ, L. Correlates of accuracy in the communication of feelings. *Journal of Communication,* 1959b, 9, 110–117.

DERIVERA, J. H. A decision theory of the emotions. *Dissertation Abstracts,* 1962, 23, 296–297.

DIMITROVSKY, L. S. The ability to identify the emotional meaning of vocal expression at successive age levels. *Dissertation Abstracts,* 1962, 24, 2983.

DITTMAN, A. T. and WYNNE, C. Linguistic techniques and the analysis of emotionality in interviews. *Journal of Abnormal and Social Psychology,* 1961, 63, 201–204.

DOCKERAY, F. C. Emotions as disorganized response. *Psychological Bulletin,* 1933, 30.

DUSENBERRY, D. and KNOWER, F. H. Experimental studies of the symbolism of action and voice. I. A study of the specificity of meaning in facial expression. *Quarterly Journal of Speech,* 1938, 424–435.

DUSENBERRY, D. and KNOWER, F. H. Experimental studies of the symbolism of action and voice. II. A study of the specificity of meaning in abstract tonal symbols. *Quarterly Journal of Speech,* 1939, 25, 67–75.

EISENSON, J., AUER, J. J., and IRWIN, J. V. *The psychology of communication.* New York: Appleton-Century-Crofts, 1963.

FAIRBANKS, G. and HOAGLIN, L. W. An experimental study of the durational characteristics of the voice during expressions of emotions. *Speech Monographs,* 1941, 8, 85–90.

FAY, P. J. and MIDDLETON, W. C. The ability to judge the rested or tired condition of a speaker from his voice as transmitted over a public address system. *Journal of Applied Psychology,* 1940, 24, 645–650.

GATES, G. S. The role of the auditory element in the interpretation of emotions. *Psychological Bulletin,* 1927, 24, 175 (Abstract).

KNAPP, P. H. (Ed.) *Expressions of emotions in man.* New York: International University Press, 1963.

KNOWER, F. H. Studies in the symbolism of voice and action. V. The use of behavioral and tonal symbols as tests of speaking achievement. *Journal of Applied Psychology,* 1945, 29, 229–235.

KNOWER, F. H. Analysis of some experimental variations of simulated vocal expressions of the emotions. *Journal of Social Psychology,* 1941, 14, 369–372.

KRAMER, E. R. Elimination of verbal cues in judgments of emotion from voice. *Journal of Abnormal and Social Psychology,* 1964, 68, 390–396.

KRAMER, E. R. Judgment of portrayed emotion from normal English, filtered English, and Japanese speech. *Dissertation Abstracts,* 1963, 24, 1699–1700.

KRECH, D. and CRUTCHFIELD, R. S. *Elements of psychology.* New York: Alfred A. Knopf, 1958.

LEVITT, E. A. The relationship between vocal and facial emotional communicative abilities. *Dissertation Abstracts,* 1962, 23, 1783.

LEVY, P. K. The relationship between the ability to express and to perceive vocal communication of feeling. *Dissertation Abstracts,* 1962, 22, 4082–4083.

LICKLIDER, J. C. R. Basic correlates of the auditory stimulus. In Stevens, S.S. (Ed.), *Handbook of experimental psychology.* New York: John Wiley and Sons, 1951.

NEWMAN, S. and MATHER, V. G. Analysis of spoken language of patients with affective disorders. *American Journal of Psychology*, 1938, 94, 913–942.

OSSER, H. A. A distinctive feature analysis of the vocal communication of emotion. *Dissertation Abstracts*, 1964, 25, 3708.

OSTWALD, P. F. *Soundmaking: The acoustic communication of emotion.* Springfield, Illinois: Charles C. Thomas, 1963.

PFAFF, P. L. An experimental study of the communication of feeling without contextual material. *Speech Monographs*, 1954, 21, 155–156. (Abstract)

PIDDINGTON, R. *The psychology of laughter.* New York: Gamut Press, 1963.

POLLACK, I., RUBENSTEIN, H., and HOROWITZ, A. Communication of verbal modes of expression. *Language and Speech*, 1960, 3, 121–130.

POOL, I. Content analysis. In Knapp, P. H. (Ed.) *Expressions of emotions in man.* New York: International University Press, 1963.

PRONOVOST, W., and FAIRBANKS, G. An experimental study of the pitch characteristics of the voice during the expression of emotion. *Speech Monographs*, 1939, 6, 87–104.

RUCKMICK, C. A. *The psychology of feeling and emotion.* New York: McGraw-Hill, 1936.

SCHACHTER, S. and SINGER, J. Cognitive, social and physiological determinants of emotional states. *Psychological Review*, 1962, 69, 379–399.

SCOTT, H. H. Noise measuring techniques. *Handbook of noise control.* Harris, C. (Ed.). New York: McGraw-Hill, 1957.

SCOTT, W. C. M. Noise, speech and technique. *International Journal of Psychoanalysis*, 1958, 39, 108–111.

SKINNER, E. R. A calibrated recording and analysis of the pitch, force, and quality of vocal tones expressing happiness and sadness; and a determination of the pitch and force of the subject. Concepts of ordinary soft and loud tones. *Speech Monographs*, 1935, 2, 81–137.

SMITH, W. W. *The measurement of emotion.* New York: Harcourt, Brace and World, 1922.

SNYDER, W. In Knapp, P. H. (Ed), *Expressions of emotions in man.* New York: International University Press, 1963.

SOSKIN, W. F. and KAUFFMAN, P. E. Judgment of emotion in word-free voice samples. *Journal of Communication*, 1961, 11, 73–80.

STARKWEATHER, J. A. The communication value of content-free speech. *American Journal of Psychology*, 1956, 69, 121–123.

TRAGER, G. L. Paralanguage: a first approximation. In Hymes, D. (Ed.), *Language in culture and society.* New York: Harper & Row Publishers, 1965.

WHATMOUGH, J. *Language.* New York: St. Martin's Press, 1956.

ZIPF, G. R. *The psycho-biology of language.* Cambridge, Mass.: The MIT Press, 1965.

CHAPTER 9

Pronouns of Address as Indicators of Social Change

. . . taunt him with the license of ink;
if thou *thou'st* him some thrice, it shall
not be amiss.

Shakespeare: *Twelfth Night,* Act III, Sc. 2

LINGUISTIC BEHAVIOR—just as any other category of social behavior —is structured and governed by certain rules. Brown (1965) points out the significance of social norms in relation to culture and language. Social norms constitute the expectancies and regularities of much social activity—the guides to behavior that define what is appropriate and what is inappropriate. A norm specifies who does what in which situation, or, in linguistic behavior, who *says* what in which situation. These social norms are applied only to socially recognized classes of people and not to individuals. Therefore, in discussing norms which shape linguistic behavior, it is only appropriate to speak of groups and classes within groups; the individual's idiosyncrasies are relatively unimportant.

Since language is such an important part of culture, when the culture and its norms change so does the language. As customs or regularities in behavior change and develop, there are similar changes in linguistic customs. One example of the implicit rules governing language behavior and their relation to the overall culture is the manner in which one individual addresses another. It will readily be seen that these linguistic rules change simultaneously with an alteration of cultural beliefs and ideologies. This chapter will concentrate on the interaction of culture and language with focus on the idea previously identified as the *linguistic relativity hypothesis,* that language to some degree directs cognitions and aids in defining situations. Further, it possesses the capability of operating as a force to initiate cultural change as well as being modified by changes in other cultural dimensions (Hoijer, 1965; Silverberg, 1940).

The proper manner in which to address a person is important in any culture. Studies have shown that there is a strong correlation between the pronouns of address used and certain aspects of the social structure. Through the use of pronouns of address one may indicate one's attitude, social class and in general the relationship of the speaker to the listener. Any changes in the status system should be mirrored in the language (Hymes, 1965; Finkenstaedt, 1964; Brown, 1958).

Brown and Gilman (1960) state that the forms of address always follow rules which are understood by the whole society. The most significant of these rules are those concerned with the interpersonal relationship, the relationship between the speaker and the person addressed. The pronoun form chosen for address serves to relate the members of the society with the other members. There are two basic rules of address that work in relating one person to another. These are the rules pertaining to the dimensions of solidarity and status or power. These two dimensions have been found to regulate a large amount of social interaction. In solidarity there is a perceived similarity among members which produces liking; this liking stimulates increased interaction and more perceived liking which in turn produces more liking and solidarity. On the other hand, status points out the differences between members rather than the similarities. It identifies in an interpersonal situation who has more power over the other, that is, who can control the behavior of the other.

As implied above, the forms of address are related to the type of interpersonal relation. Some pronouns of address will show liking, while another will show status distinctions. To understand the forms of address, Brown and Gilman (1960) introduced what they call the T and V forms of address. In the early Latin culture there were two accepted forms of address: "tu" for the singular and "vos" for the plural. The emperor at that time took over the pronoun "vos," which was formerly plural, to be used by others in addressing him. The authors suggest that plurality is a "natural metaphor" for social power. It expresses the greatness of the individual. Numerous rulers since have used the plural when speaking of themselves: for instance, the British monarchs' use of "we."

Moreover, in the Middle Ages the Germans changed the use of "ihr" from the second person plural to a singular of reverence. Later, "er," the third person singular, was chosen as the pronoun of reverence since "ihr" was overused in that everyone began saying it to everyone else just to be polite. Still a third choice was made to indicate reverence. This was "sie," the third person plural. "Ihr" is an example of plurality as a metaphor of power. "Er" indicates social distance for one addresses a person as if he is not present. Plurality and social distance are both exemplified in the use of "sie."

After a while, the Latin plural "vos" was also used in addressing other high-status people besides the emperor. "Tu" was used to address persons of lower status. Brown classifies such pronouns as the Latin "vos" and the German "sie" as a V form of address. The V form is used to connote respect and dignity. The Latin "tu" and German "du" are T forms of address. The T indicates inferiority and subordination.

Sometime in the medieval period a set of rules developed which has been termed the asymmetrical status norm. An even greater distinction of the use of T and V forms came about. The person with higher status or power was addressed differently than the person of lower status or power. The superior individual says T and receives V, a form of deference, from the inferior person (Brown and Gilman, 1960; Brown, 1965; Schlauch, 1942; Silverberg, 1940).

Examples of the preceding may be: the nobleman says T to the commoner and receives V; the parent says T to the child and receives V; the same modes of address existed for the master and the servant. However, the pronominal address between equals was reciprocal. One received and gave the same form. A member of the upper class would both give and receive the V form while the lower classes exchanged the T form.

So far the rules for using the pronouns of address are primarily based on status. The solidarity dimension was added when the rules differentiating the address among equals came into being. The rules became increasingly complicated. T began to be used by both the upper and lower status persons in addressing their equals to indicate intimacy; the V came into use among equals to indicate formality.

This solidarity semantic, which did not develop until some time after the status norm, has grown considerably and is still growing. In many cultures the solidarity norm has suppressed the status norm to a great extent.

As stated, people of both class levels began to use the mutual T and mutual V. The mutual T was used for brothers and sisters, lovers and close friends and the mutual V was used between strangers and new acquaintances. Now the use of each pronoun of address could be interpreted in two ways. When the use of T was symmetrical, it expressed intimacy but when it was non-symmetrical it was an indication of condescension. In a like manner, formality was expressed by V when it was reciprocal, but deference was stated when it was non-reciprocal.

As the complexities of the rules of address multiplied, conflict arose. Simplification and change were needed. Adherents of the "Strong" Linguistic Relativity Hypothesis would probably maintain that the change in culture came after the resolution of the linguistic conflict. Followers of the "Weak" Linguistic Relativity Hypothesis, on the other hand, may insist that the linguistic change followed the cultural change. Arguments over which came first are obviously rather sterile. It is enough to say that when there is a shift in the situation where one normally says T and V, a linguistic norm has been modified. This may be used as linguistic evidence for sociocultural change.

The solution of the conflict was the suppression of the status norm and the supremacy of the solidarity norm. One can explain this specific choice of dealing with the conflict by reviewing the cultural changes going on at the time. The non-reciprocal status norm is associated with a relatively static social status situation. That is, the power and status of an individual are likely to be ascribed at birth, and there is little hope of change in this category. As societies evolved in the direction of open-class systems, there occurred an introduction of more egalitarian ideology. The suppression of the status norm eliminates at least from pronominal usage any distinctions of inter-personal relationship even though status distinctions may be expressed by other linguistics means. Moreover, the number of relationships thought cohesive enough to use the mutual T is increasing and the number calling for the mutual V is decreasing. For example, many cultures in the last century have witnessed a change in the use of the pronouns of address in the parent-child relationship. The parents, the superiors, used to give the T and receive the V from their children. Now it is more common for them to exchange the mutual T in a show of intimacy and solidarity.

The preceding is true for many European languages as well as for the American language. In France it would be considered quite rude to say T to a waiter although according to the past status norm it would have been correct since there is actually quite a difference in status. However, today's ideology requires him to deny this asymmetry of status. This is very much in keeping with the ideals of the United States and the norms of its democratic society. American English has attempted the suppression of the status norm, at least in regard to its manifestation in pronominal address, to an even greater extent. While most countries still retain a choice in the pronouns of address, as the Spanish "tu" and "usted," American English has only the pronoun of address, "you." In this one pronominal respect English may be said to be classless. "You" is addressed to a superior, inferior or equal. Also, "you" is used with the stranger or friend. Americans tend to view the Germans as snobbish when they use pronouns to indicate exclusiveness as in addressing a stranger with "sie" and a child with "du" (Schlauch, 1942).

While the non-reciprocal patterns for pronouns has been generally abandoned in Europe, there can still be detected inequality of status in one area of usage. In many cultures dyads begin with the mutual V and as intimacy increases it is exchanged for the mutual T. The shift from V to T can be functional in a "rites de passage" sense. In Germany the child in past years was called "du" until adolescence when he was called "sie." All his child-like tendencies were associated with his "du" personality and his acquired social behaviors with his "sie" personality. The change from "du" to "sie" was the mark of acceptance into the society (Silverberg, 1940).

Brown and Gilman (1960) supply the example of the graduate student in the American culture becoming a member of the university faculty. The title "Dr." is now inappropriate in addressing his new colleagues, but to call them immediately by their first name would seem impertinent. During the period of transition and adjustment, the new faculty member may use the pronoun of address "you" which does not indicate status of any sort.

Most of the research concerning the pronouns of address has been done in a European or American cultural context. However, some researchers have examined pronominal usage in Oriental cultures. Howell (1965) has analyzed a series of "Blondie" cartoon strips in a Korean-language newspaper. He suggests that, in the absence of an authority relationship, interaction between Koreans tends to be characterized by symmetrical patterns of either polite/honorific or familiar forms, depending on whether or not the people involved enjoy a solidarity relationship. Yoshida (1964) has presented examples of how asymmetries in terms of address have been disappearing with successive breaches of social class barriers in a Japanese agricultural community.

As a generalization, one might say that the rules and possible choices for pronominal address in most Oriental societies tend to be more elaborate than those found in Western culture.

The norms of pronominal address provide an interesting instance of how culture can be studied through the use of linguistic materials.

Prospects for further research in this area are extremely stimulating. Among the topics awaiting attention are the investigation of first person pronominal usage and the question of how the use of verbs and adjectives is related to the cultural beliefs and ideologies of those who employ similar and dissimilar forms.

REFERENCES

BOAS, F. Linguistics and ethnology. In D. Hymes (Ed.), *Language in culture and society*. New York: Harper and Row, Publishers, 1965.

BROWN, R. W. *Language, thought and culture*. Ann Arbor: University of Michigan Press, 1958.

BROWN, R. and GILMAN, A. The pronouns of power and solidarity. In T. A. Sebeok (Ed.), *Style in language*. Cambridge, Massachusetts: MIT Press, 1960.

BROWN, R. *Social psychology*. New York: The Free Press, 1965.

BROWN, R. and FORD, M. Address in American English. In D. Hymes (Ed.), *Language in culture and society*. New York: Harper and Row, Publishers, 1965.

CHASE, S. *Power of words*. New York: Harcourt, Brace and World, 1954.

EVANS-PRITCHARD, E. E. Nuer modes of address. In D. Hymes (Ed.), *Language in culture and society*. New York: Harper and Row, Publishers, 1965.

FINKENSTAEDT, T. You and thou. Reviewed by Simon Potter, *Modern Language Review*, 1964, 59, 88–89.

FIRTH, J. R. On sociological linguistics. In D. Hymes (Ed.), *Language in culture and society*. New York: Harper and Row, Publishers, 1965.

GOODENOUGH, W. H. Cultural anthropology. In D. Hymes (Ed.), *Language in culture and society*. New York: Harper and Row, Publishers, 1965.

HOIJER, H. Language and culture. *American Anthropological Association Memoirs*, 1954, 79, 1–105.

HOIJER, H. Linguistics and cultural change. In D. Hymes (Ed.), *Language in culture and society*. New York: Harper and Row, Publishers, 1965.

HOWELL, R. W. Linguistic status markers in Korean. *The Kroeber Anthropological Society Papers*, 1965, 55, 91–97.

SCHLAUCH, M. *The gift of tongues*. New York: Modern Age Books, 1942.

SILVERBERG, W. V. On the psychological significance of Du and Sie. *Psychoanalytic Quarterly*, 1940, 9, 509–525.

YOSHIDA, T. Social conflict and cohesion in a Japanese rural community. *Ethnology*, 1964, 3, 219–231.

CHAPTER 10

Urban Language: A Negro Problem

"din teacher start checkin' de boys, see which one had i'. An' one boy name Bill
Bailey had a whole pocketful of i'. An' teach' say I'ma tell dis to de princiba too dat
chu go 'round' stealin' school prope'ty. He say I ain' steal school prope'ty. My
muvver pay for dis whin she pay for de tax. She say, your muvah ain' pay for dis.
Dis b'long to de school,' an' she start talkin' all lat ov' ol' junk an' waster half de
peri'd. Din we start talkin' 'bout light, how, speed o' light an' na speed o' soun' an' all
'a' kinna stuff."

from The Washington Post*

MANY PEOPLE OF MINORITY GROUPS—Negroes, Puerto Ricans, American Indians, those of Mexican or South American extraction and poor
whites living in secluded mountain regions—speak a dialect or language
that differs from standard American English. These people may find that,
regardless of their other skills or abilities, many vocational and social
opportunities are denied them because of their speech. It seems particularly ironic that native-born American Negroes, for example, are con-
fronted with a language barrier in the land of their birth. The situation is
far from new, but it did not become a problem until recently, when the
Negro finally acquired a visible presence in his own country. Now that
the Negro is insisting that he be incorporated and made part of the

---

* Peggy Thomson. Washington's Second Language. *The Washington Post,*
POTOMAC, Sunday, June 11, 1967.

mainstream of American society, these language differences become a
pressing problem for the schools.

Equal educational opportunities—which means better education for
Negroes—has long been a major objective of civil rights groups. However, little attention had been given to the type of linguistic education
that should be sought for urban schools. Recently, the Center for Applied Linguistics in Washington, D. C., addressed itself to this matter. As
stated in their request to the Carnegie Foundation for funds to support
the Urban Language Study and Materials Development Project
(ULSMDP):

> The English used by most socio-economically disadvan-
> taged Negroes in the U.S. severely limits their ability to
> participate equally in the economic and social opportunities
> enjoyed by the majority of Americans (October, 1966).

In addition to the Urban Language Study Project, many articles have
been written characterizing the speech of the American Negro as a
dialect with its own rules and systematic grammar. The problem within
the schools, however, as well as in the nation at large, is that the
possession by the Negro of his own distinctive language is recognized by
only a few teachers and administrators.

Teachers must first be made aware that Negro children enter the
classroom learning situation with a complete language system of their
own. This language system has structure and coherence; it is not just a
haphazard arrangement of bad grammar, sloppy speech habits or random mistakes due to lack of proper instruction, all of which were
attributed to it in the past. Nor is the Negro child using an inferior
language pattern or substandard dialect. This long-held value judgment
has no place in linguistics and certainly should have no place in the
teaching of language skills.

Since there is such a low level of difference between standard and
nonstandard English, teachers often acquire the conviction that Negro
students simply have a low aptitude for learning "correct" forms. This is
not the case. The student in the classroom is being exposed to a new and
different language, without recognizing that he possesses, and encounters interference from, a complete language system of his own. There is
not even a name for the language spoken by many Negroes, which is
why such inaccurate terms as "dialect" and "nonstandard" must be used.

McDavid (in Shuy, 1964) cites the case of Warren, Ohio, to illustrate
the independence and persistence of the Negro speech pattern as a fully
defined dialect—a distinct linguistic system with a grammar of its own

which is as systematic as the grammar of standard English. McDavid maintains that this town of about fifty thousand is not large enough for educational segregation to have any particular effect on the quality of English teaching in the high schools. Yet the Negro graduates from Warren High who usually did well on their College Boards, in their compositions showed all of the grammatical features associated with uneducated Negro speech, especially errors with regard to inflectional endings on verbs and nouns. McDavid concluded that although the schools were not segregated, other social contacts were, since these grammatical forms would not have persisted if whites and Negroes lived together as equals.

Not until recently has there been a narrowly focused study of the history of the Negro dialect. Many of the studies that had been performed up until this time used such widely focused techniques (primarily those techniques associated with the Linguistic Atlas procedure) that the Negro was but lightly touched upon. Such studies tended to confirm the idea that the speech of Negroes is nearly identical to that of whites. Now there is evidence that North American nonstandard Negro dialects are related to English-based Creole and Pidgin English from the Carribbean and West Africa, and go all the way back to the days of the slave trade.

To define the Negro dialect and distinguish it from the standard American spoken by many educated whites and Negroes in urban centers, one has to isolate the dialect features of a particular socio-economic stratum of that particular ethnic group. One must ascertain the characteristics of the speech behavior of uneducated Negroes and how this speech compares with that of educated Negroes as well as both educated and uneducated whites.

Several features of Negro dialect are readily distinguishable in comparison with standard English.

1. The zero copula (omission of the verb 'to be'):
    'He out.'
    'She over there.'
2. Possession indicated without the use of a possessive morpheme:
    'The lady hat.'
    'The man car.'
3. Use of the verb 'be' as a time extension auxiliary:
    'He be busy.' (He is habitually busy.)
    'He busy.' (He is busy at this particular moment.)
4. Lack of agreement between subject and verb:

'Mr. Gibson have a dog.'
'He do?'
'I goes.'
'They eats.'

5. The addition of /s/ in cases where the form of the noun
is already plural and the omission of the possessive /s/ in
instances where its use is required to form the plural in
standard English:
'The childrens.'
'The mens.'
'The boy wagon.'

A grammatical phenomenon often encountered in Negro dialect is
similar to the forms "voici" and "voila" in French. These *presentatives*, as
they are called, are used to call the attention of the listener to the
existence or presence of something. The dialect of urban areas such as
Washington, D.C., shows presentatives in at least its child version. The
forms "There go the book," and "Here go the book on the table" mean
"There is the book" and "Here is the book on the table." The teacher who
speaks and understands only Standard English might complain: "But I
don't see the book *going* anywhere."

Negro nonstandard and white standard speech also differ considerably
with respect to phonological considerations. Among the more prominent
differences that might be mentioned are:

1. The quality of richness of Negro vowel sounds;
2. The tendency on the part of Negroes to nasalize certain
vowel sounds, to the extent that the following consonants are
almost completely dropped; and
3. The characteristically more lax pronunciation of nearly
all consonants.

The lilt and stress variations in Negro speech give an overall effect of
softness and lushness. One discredited theory attributed this phenomenon to the configuration of the Negro skull, with its wide nasal orifices
and enlarged sinuses. A more plausible line of thought suggests that it is
a carryover from guttural African dialects, although this interpretation
has not been systematically validated.

The African Influence Hypothesis has a number of interesting variants
and some presumptive evidence for its support. It has been noted, for
example, that most of the natives brought to the New World as slaves
were members of tribes that spoke some version of Bantu (Bena, Kongo,

Suto, Swahili, Teke, etc.). Thus they shared a common linguistic background. This language contains a great many more guttural consonants and nasal vowels than does the English language. One theory suggests that, rather than being completely influenced by white colonial speech, the Negro may have contributed to, and been responsible for, a number of Southern dialect variations. For example, the extreme nasalization of Negro speech has no apparent basis in any British dialect, whereas extreme nasalization is nearly universal in the many-branched African language. Also, both the Southern and Negro dialects have unstable /eh/ and /ay/ and /oh/ and /aw/ sounds, pairs of which belong to a single phoneme in the Zulu African dialect. The American Negro, therefore, may say "behd" or "bayd" for *bed;* he may say "mehk" or "mayk" for *make,* with complete interchangeability.

In addition, the substitution of /b/ for /v/ may be accounted for in American Negro speech by the fact that there is no /v/ in the African language. Moreover, the most persistent vestigial remnant found in the Negro dialect is the Negro pronunciation of /h/. The African language features a peculiar pronunciation which is followed by a /k/ or velar sound, the same roughened sound that is found in Southern white and Negro pronunciations of /k/ and /g/, which tend to sound equivalent to /ky/ and /gy/, as in "kyawd" (card) and "gyawden" (garden).

Finally, it should be noted that the wide vocal range of Negro dialect —from guttural to falsetto—in comparison with which standard English is almost a monotone, has an unmistakable resemblance to African dialects. Most African languages use varying tonal levels to convey semantic variation. Zulu, for example, uses nine such tonal changes.

We should also mention Negro slang, a topic that is apart from the matter of dialect, but one which is almost equally important in the study of Negro urban speech patterns. In-group language is extremely significant in the preservation of racial identity. Because of its connotating values, it inculcates feelings of pride and belongingness. It expresses the group's unique experiences and positive self-concepts. Such experiences do, after all, require a particular language form which sets it apart from other languages, even as the group's identity and unique experiences set it apart from other groups.

The trauma of non-acceptance, linguistically and socially, causes the dialect of the Negro to be a liability in the midst of the majority culture. At the same time, dialect and slang are important both psychologically to its speakers and as a means of survival within the group. Ethnic-based slang is part of the unique pattern of Negro social behavior. Too often it tends to be confused with dialect. The distinction is readily illustrated by an example or two of each:

Slang: He didn't dig his vines.
Dialect: He ain' like his clothes.
Standard: He didn't like his clothes.
Slang: She's a phat chick.
Dialect: She a pretty girl.
Standard: She's a pretty girl.

Slang is readily identified by its characteristic use of picturesque and colorful figures and patterns: "That skinky broad is a Mississippi bama" (That ugly girl is a rustic from Mississippi), "He really tightened up on his enjoys" (He stopped doing those things which gave him enjoyment), "The Hawk is really talking" (It's very windy today).

Slang, then, is a deliberate lexical substitution, whereas dialect is a pattern of different linguistic forms which the speaker is unaware he is using and often does not recognize as different, especially when he is as socially isolated as the Negro ghetto-dweller. Slang, moreover, is jealously guarded by those who use it. It is speech that is very carefully manipulated, yet which changes very rapidly. Oddly enough, those who speak a radically nonstandard form of dialect do not use slang as much as those who have a relatively firm grasp of the standard dialect.

The features which we identified as characteristic of Negro dialect are not found universally in the speech of American Negroes, but their occurrence is primarily restricted to Negro speech. Some Negroes may never use any of these dialect features; many others use some of them in special styles. For example, a person may have a public style which is mostly free of specific Negro dialect features and, in addition, an "in-group" ethnic style in which the same speaker uses Negro dialect features, especially pronunciation and paralinguistic features plus current "in-group" slang. Many educated Negroes exhibit this dialect-switching ability.[1] The bidialectic's reply when questioned about his dialect switching ability is often that the non-ethnic style is his normal dialect while the ethnic dialect is only a special put-on style. But one might ask: If a person knows two dialects equally well and each of them is appropriate in a different situation, which can be said to be that person's "normal" dialect?

Phonological and paralinguistic features are markers of the Negro dialect. Research suggests that the non-standard dialect is relatively

---

[1] *See* Labov (in Shuy, 1964). Labov studied the difference between casual and formal speech. He found that dialect-switching was more prevalent where greater pressures toward social mobility existed. The studies were done in New York City and were completed in 1964.

uniform among Negroes of low socio-economic status throughout the U.S. and differs from comparable dialects spoken by whites.

If the data supports the theory that the non-standard speech of Negroes in any particular part of the country is structurally closer to the non-standard speech of Negroes in other parts of the country than to the non-standard speech of local whites, there would be a resultant direct effect on the way remedial language materials should be organized and distributed. From the literature thus far, this theory is close to being adequately supported. The problem with the data up to this point is the fact that the term dialect in the U.S. is used in conjunction with so-called "wide-meshed" linguistic screening procedures. Such methods, as we pointed out earlier, do not focus on the Negro. More finely calibrated procedures are employed by the Urban Language Study project in Washington, D.C. Data on the Negro dialect are compiled in two ways: (1) close attention is paid to syntactic structures, and (2) younger informants (14 years and under) are used. The latter represents a refinement over earlier studies to the extent that older informants, as adults, do a larger amount of code switching.

The Urban Language Study of the Center for Applied Linguistics was initiated in the latter part of 1965 (with the aid of a grant from the Ford Foundation). The staff consists of eight linguists, one anthropologist and one sociologist. The objective of the study is to provide teaching materials for standard English as a second dialect for "culturally disadvantaged" Negroes of the lower socio-economic stratum. The basis for their materials will be linguistically valid analyses of the standard and nonstandard dialects. The staff plans to test the materials in selected D.C. schools and to revise them according to the recommendations of teachers using them.

One of the main contributions of the study is to give evidence and publicity to the concept of a Negro dialect. The development of teaching materials is invaluable but could only be attempted after the Negro speech is recognized as an autonomous system. Other studies are also being done in Washington, D.C., on the existence and effects of the Negro dialect.[2]

After the recognition of the Negro dialect by teachers is accomplished, the problem arises as to how standard English should be taught. Although there is a certain amount of debate in the literature, it is gener-

---

[2] Other studies currently in progress or recently completed in the District of Columbia include a project on "Psychological Correlates of Dialectolalia" conducted by the Speech Department of Howard University, and George Washington University's Department of Education study on language facility and dialect formation in children.

ally proposed that early in his educational experience, the Negro child should be taught English as a foreign language or more precisely, utilizing foreign language techniques.

William Stewart, in a paper presented at a conference sponsored by the Illinois Institute of Technology and the National Council of Teachers of English in 1964, uses the term "quasi-foreign language." He describes the teaching situation where although the structural correspondences between the language of the learner and the language being taught (as the vocabularies) may be so close that the learner could be considered to already have a native command of the language being taught, there would still be enough difference between the two systems (as the grammars) to necessitate the use of foreign language techniques. The main problem in implementing this type of contrastive technique is the lack of awareness of teachers and their resistance to giving up pattern practice and principal parts drill.

Many teachers are unaware of the complexity of language and of the language user. One must consider the dignity of the individual. In this respect learning new language habits should be construed as adding new habits to the old while valuing the differences between the two systems.[3] One must *use* rather than attack the language which the learner speaks every day. Cresswell (in Shuy, 1964) says that this contrastive method is the best one primarily because it can be used naturally. In their social relations with peers, and in their desire to be part of various social groups, language learners "compare their own patterns with those of a group to which they belong, isolate the differences and adopt the patterns of the sought for group" (p. 68). Instruction can be based on this same natural procedure, with the students identifying and establishing the differences between their own dialect and standard English.

Repetition and practice alone are not effective. The student does not hear what is not available to him in his own dialect. He has to be able to become attentive to the elements of speech being learned. He is ordinarily passive in the learning situation; usually he lacks motivation. While he knows that he is learning standard English because it will be important to him in the future, he is really only paying lip service to the

---

[3] Linguists are still divided on the question of what teachers should do about a "substandard" dialect. Some argue to eliminate those features which interfere with standard English and thus "hamper upward mobility." Others argue that the non-standard features can be retained but used only in socially appropriate contexts. The question essentially is whether the Negro should be made bidialectical or to maintain the older goal of trying to impose standard English and totally eradicate the nonstandard dialect. As studies have shown, this cannot be done in the classroom alone, but can only be accomplished within the life situation as a whole.

importance of language learning. Use of foreign language methods to teach standard English encourages the change from passive to active participation.

There are many problems in teaching standard English as a foreign language. Teachers recognize a foreign language as an autonomous system with rules and status of its own. However, with the "quasi-foreign language," the linguistic system is considered inferior. Traditional grammars do not exist for the Negro dialect to use in the contrastive procedures. Teachers and students themselves tend to regard the cases in which the learner's speech differs from standard English as a departure from a system rather than as a conformity to another entire linguistic system. Because the two systems are so close in appearance, they are not likely to be aware of the interference from one system to the other.

Once teachers recognize the Negro dialect as a separate linguistic system, another problem arises. In trying to stress awareness of the Negro speech as a dialect system of its own, one must be cautioned not to draw so much attention to the Negro student's distinctive pattern of speech that he overcompensates and creates an affected air of speech snobbery. In recognizing the Negro dialect as a separate grammatical system, another type of difficulty can arise. Most classroom teachers are aware that the grammar of the slum Negro is a major problem. However, most teachers do not know what to do about the problem. When they start to talk about the Negro pattern of speech as distinguished from the speech of whites, they are treated to sermons on the evils of discrimination. This can be quite silly; the mere mention of Negro language characteristics can hardly be considered discrimination. The distinctive linguistic features of Negro dialect must be openly discussed, otherwise there is a genuine danger that discrimination will be perpetuated.

It must also be recognized that many of the factors that influence speech are unconscious. Problems in learning English have been treated as purely structural problems but there is growing evidence that dialect is associated with disparate social values. An example is cited of the southern Negro students who strongly reject the standard dialect of the local educated whites preferring a more "northern" standard dialect even if it is structurally more remote from their own dialect than is the local white standard.

Research on the Negro linguistic system has not been extensive due to racist connotations. Respect for the feelings of Negroes has also discouraged research. Many Negroes, especially educated Negroes, are sensitive about too much concentration on distinctively Negro behavior, especially that identified as lower-class Negro behavior. The resistance is due to feelings of insecurity and the conviction that this kind of data tends to promote the stereotyped image of the Negro American. The racial association of dialect traits combines with the usual linguistic problems characteristic of "quasi-foreign language" relationships to produce what is undoubtedly one of the most difficult and demanding problems that urban public school systems may ever be called upon to face.

Ralph Ellison made two important points with reference to the attitudes of deprived Negro children in a September 1963 speech delivered at a conference sponsored by Educational Services Incorporated. First, he stated that human beings cling to the language which makes it possible for them to control chaos and to survive in the situations in which they find themselves. Second, he maintains that the way to teach new forms or patterns of language is not to attempt to eliminate the old forms, "but to build upon them while at the same time valuing them in a way which is consonant with the desire for dignity that is in each of us." For example, in changing the teaching procedures in accordance with the spirit of Ellison's recommendations, instead of telling the child of the Negro ghetto that he must give up his "bad grammar," the linguistically sophisticated teacher would encourage the child to acquire a second grammar in addition to his own, without weighting one at the expense of the other.

Segregation is perpetuated at least in part by the non-standard language patterns of the American Negro. It is obvious that one of the mainstays of *de facto* segregation will have been removed when every Negro citizen is provided assistance in attaining sufficient command of standard English to fulfill his potentialities in terms of social and occupational opportunities.

It is generally conceded in the professional literature that before any language habits can be changed, students must acquire the ability to perceive significant contrasts between their own dialect and the standard language system. Serious objections are raised, however, to the use of terms like "foreign language teaching" in relation to the teaching of standard English on the grounds that such nomenclature is misleading or inaccurate and may prove offensive to certain groups. Better research and terminology are sorely needed in this field of linguistic research. More studies are needed with better screening procedures and more inclusive samples.

Today we are facing an entirely new dimension in language teaching. What remains is the vital necessity for communication among interested groups and the importance of making the results of research more widely known.

REFERENCES

DILLARD, J. L. *The Urban Language Study of the Center for Applied Linguistics. The Linguistic Reporter*. Washington, D.C.: Center for Applied Linguistics, 1964.

FERGUSON, C. *A proposal to the Carnegie Foundation for support of the Urban Language Study and Materials Development Program*. Washington, D.C., 1965.

GUMPERZ, J. and HYMES, D. (Eds.), *The ethnography of communication. The American Anthropologist*, 1964, 66. Special Publication (1–186).

HAYES, A. S. (Ed.), *Recommendations of the work conference on literacy*. Washington, D.C.: Center for Applied Linguistics, 1964.

HAYES, A. New directions in foreign language teaching. *Modern Language Journal*, 1965, 49, 281–293.

KRIEDLER, C. The influence of linguistics in school grammar. *Linguistic Reporter*. Washington, D.C.: Center for Applied Linguistics, 1966.

SHUY, R. (Ed.), *Social dialects and language learning*. Champaign: Illinois Institute of Technology, 1964.

STEWART, W. Observations on the problems of defining the Negro dialect. *Conference on the language component in the training of teachers of English and reading: Views and problems*. Washington, D.C.: Center for Applied Linguistics, 1966.

STEWART, W. *Clearinghouse for social dialect studies*. Washington, D.C.: Center for Applied Linguistics, 1966.

STEWART, W. *Non-standard speech and the teaching of English*. Washington, D.C.: Center for Applied Linguistics, 1964.

CHAPTER 11

Special Language: The Psychedelic Subculture

Drug language is as much a sign of "belongingness" and "togetherness" as it is a device for communicating the content of an experience. No wonder a person with LSD senses futility in talking with non-users; to the latter, the words are neither signals for sympathy, nor are they understood as affirmations that one is a particular kind of a person or a fellow member of an important in-group.

Richard Blum: Utopiates*

SOMETHING AKIN to "culture shock" occurs upon entering a group of LSD users. There is a removal or distortion of many familiar cues; other cues are substituted which are novel and strange. How widespread and common are such cues among LSD users? By what means—these cues and others—do members of the LSD movement communicate with one another?

According to the definition of "mind-manifesting" drug use, LSD users are a part of the psychedelic movement. Recent research has disclosed that various life styles (Cheek, 1966) accompany various objectives of LSD use: sexual, mystical, religious, self-therapy, kicks. A "novelty,"

"adjunct," or "regular" usage, then, may serve to distinguish groups within the newly forming psychedelic movement. Individually purposeful groups, therefore, depict different aspects and intensities of the larger LSD culture. Becker (1966) suggests this culture is in the process of becoming standardized. Institutionalization for drug use is becoming normative with regard to dosage, frequency, effects to be expected, similar definitions of the subjective LSD experience and emergency criteria.

Even before such culture (or combination of subcultures) reaches consensus, however, certain aspects of behavior and appearance may be identified as characteristic of drug users, or "hippies." Acording to *Ramparts* magazine, a monthly San Francisco publication, "[H]ippies are many things, but most prominently the bearded and beaded inhabitants of the Haight-Ashbury, a little psychedelic city-state edging Golden Gate Park" (Feb., 1967). While it is important to use self definitions when examining a group, this description presupposes a limited locale for psychedelics even though it does denote the concentration of an "established" community life style that exists in one area and for one type of LSD use.

The subject is broader, however, and may be identified by reference to groups across the northwest, midwest and northeastern United States, in particular. Looking beyond artifacts of clothing and appearance—similar to characteristics of the aging Bohemian groups popularized in the last fifteen years—LSD users anywhere may be more accurately identified by their language and their social communication.

LSD use is learned behavior transmitted through communication channels and social contexts already established; then it is discussed and evaluated among LSD users in verbal and non-verbal gestures quite distinct from that of the larger society. The social heritage of LSD use consists of the ways of acting, believing and speaking. The language of any given "society" is part of its social heritage, passed from old members to new ones. Just as the novice must learn customs and traditions of a group's behavior, so an LSD user must learn which words go with which objects and situations, word-order, pronunciation and the numerous nuances of meanings. In fact, older members have linguistic standards to which the newcomer must conform. While different individuals may set unique stamps of combination and meaning upon established ways of speaking, nevertheless there is a common core to all these individual treatments. Language is a group product which, like every other part of the LSD social heritage, must be learned.

With respect to the argot associated with LSD use, it is appropriate to designate contextual terms and phrases, presently being coined by psychedelic users themselves, as a "special language." Such a structured jargon refers to the outcome of a common tendency to adapt a language (English) to the functions of a particular group (Lindesmith and Strauss, 1949). And it is through this very language that insights from LSD use are formulated as knowledge and transmitted to and shared with others in the culture, thus becoming a social rather than merely an individual possession. That a special language *does* exist may be seen when a person who is "outside" the hippie culture is made acutely aware of being a stranger to the ways of that group solely upon encountering its distinctive vocabulary.

Within the psychedelic language the highest lexical frequency exists for reference to the mind-manifesting experience, e.g., turned on, high, trip, good scene, grooving, lifted off, freakout, doing a thing, and spaced out. Language seems to carry the history and interests of these people as well as features of their environment which group members feel to be important. As Lindesmith and Strauss (1949) have noted, "Words employed by people designate, refer to and select aspects of the world relevant to their lives." It has often been pointed out that the Eskimos functionally utilize many different words for snow to distinguish its various properties. Similarly, LSD users find it of practical importance to differentiate between the beginning (lift-off), midway highlight (clear white light) and completion (reentry) of an LSD experience.

Words also differentiate between the psychedelic experience resulting from marijuana (getting stoned) and from LSD (on a high). The concept of getting "turned on" refers to *any* mind-expanding experience, but is usually used only after the substance has been acknowledged. It is interesting that only one word, "acid," is the absolute substitute for LSD-25, but it is further delineated qualitatively as "Sandoz acid," "pharmaceutical" or "a cube," the latter being the least descriptive.

Such language is not only a group product and the embodiment of group interests; it is the necessary medium without which most human groups could not exist. There must be a certain amount of understanding, agreement and shared knowledge as to common processes in collective behavior, and language makes possible the continuity of activities as well as their conceptual bases in time and space. Thus a hippie from the west coast can talk with and understand a hippie from the east coast.

Expressive verbal behavior is also important to LSD users—as important in some instances for reassurance as is the representative language aforementioned for descriptive purposes. Although hippies deny engaging in "social small talk," they often *do* expect one another to talk whether or not he feels he has anything new to add.

Such "social ritual" is evident for instance, when the speaker seeks any kind of *friendly* response,—or, as Simmel calls it "Talks for the sake of talking." Making conversation, moreover, gives evidence of good will and sociability, *when it is* couched in psychedelic terms. For example: "Man, it's a beautiful day—the wind comes in layers and the greens and blues all around are laced with lavender." (Male speakers, interestingly enough.) The expected reply, which is what confirms the definition of the situation (I am speaking to you in this situation), is the reassurance that the remark was understood in appropriate terms: "Groovy. I'm into it too." The reply is interpreted to mean that the second speaker feels similar sensations regarding the wind—perhaps the same, once they have been so verbalized—and is experiencing color changes as well, paralleling the first speaker's remark. Without the second speaker's appreciation, (for both the sensations and the fact that the first speaker would initiate the conversation in this manner) rapport would not be as well established—or not be established at all if the two people are not well known to each other.

Friendships are often, in fact, formed on the basis of use, and frequency of use, of the special language.

Showing an appreciation for the retained depth of such mind-expanding experiences can additionally affirm a unity of aims and purposes in LSD use. That is, two persons using LSD for spiritual ends or self-therapy would be more likely to entertain such a conversation (illustrating a similar definition of both the past subjective and present daytime experiences), than would a person experimenting with LSD for kicks talking to a self-therapist user. In fact, it may be most general of all that, as Rose (1956) quotes Georg Simmel:

> In purely sociable conversation, the topic is merely the indispensable medium through which the lively exchange of speech itself unfolds its attractions . . . For conversation to remain satisfied with mere form it cannot allow any content to become significant in its own right . . . [Talk] thus is the fulfillment of a relation that wants to be nothing but relation —in which, that is, what usually is the mere form of interaction becomes its self-sufficient content.

And yet, one technique for achieving group organization and solidarity is by the very use of the special language of LSD groups. Phrases such as "that's a groove" (connoting a good feeling); "I really got into something last night" (had a deep ego-involvement during a psychedelic experience); and "I'm gonna do my thing" (have an LSD experience) are descriptive of the psychedelic movement and are meant to connote the characteristically more subjective—almost internally or physiologically so—sensations, evaluations and reactions.

Such communication is deliberately utilized with selective audiences, and it appears that the drug-users reserve it for people they know will understand the significance of the symbology, i.e., have had a psychedelic experience or are generally in the company of those who have had one. In this way a special language gives an immediate identification between two people and provides cues, as well, for possibly related attitudes. The use of this particular jargon indicates a link with the national psychedelic movement which is unmistakable. It can be a means of identification without full disclosure. Additionally, the "small talk" most drug users claim to abhor is often a functional method of letting jargon "slip" to indicate usage of psychedelics indirectly in a conversation with a stranger.

A final note on the subjective experience and its link with communication seems in order. The LSD experience employs conversation prior to, during and following the activity. The social setting in which communication occurs always affects it to some degree and in various ways. More precisely, communication is affected by how individuals in the particular social setting define the situation. Thus, a person may consider a "trip" to be a "bum" one, having for him an unpleasant interpretation of the events which transpired. Even a social scientist in his research must remember that, as Merton (1957) comments, "Men respond not only to the objective features of a situation, but also, and at times primarily, to the meaning this situation has for them." In the case of a bad trip, a crowded room full of laughing, dancing people may bring about memories of past wall-flower situations to a particular user, intensified beyond his tolerance from the effects of the drug.

Behavior is ordinarily not a simple response to environmental stimulation but constitutes a succession of adjustments to interpretations of what is occurring. In the case of a psychedelic experience, moods and interaction patterns shift rapidly, sometimes intensifying, sometimes mitigating the subjective experience—but all such shifts modifying the individual's perspective to a certain degree. A person orients himself to the context (subjective, if under LSD) in which he finds himself, ascertains his interests, and then proceeds to react to the situation. "When men share common understandings, then, they also have common expectations . . ." Shibutani (1961). The extent to which behavior under LSD can be organized in terms of group norms, i.e., that not everyone will have the same feelings of pleasure or displeasure at the same time, is revealed by the emotional and verbal dispositions manifested in standardized situations at other times. It is communication that provides opportunities for acknowledging such consensus in interpreting and accepting definitions of the subjective experience. Observation of persons during a trip will in no way prepare one to undergo the same experience without having first discussed it verbally. "Words," as Rose (1956) suggests, "permit men to relate their behavior to each other to a much greater extent than do non-verbal symbols."

A person's conception of reality (even under LSD) is largely, therefore, a social process—the product of group participation, conversation and shared meanings. Users of drugs, like all other people, approach their daily world and/or subjective experiences through expectations learned as participants in organized groups, and a person's conception of either of these environments is something that is constructed. Meanings are essentially what people in a given universe of discourse agree that they are through time-tested behavioral response. What people generally call "reality" is a working orientation over which there is a high degree of consensus. In fact, if during an experience any one person panics, the others will immediately begin overloading him with conversation. The discussion is an effort by the group to distract the tense person's thoughts, reassure him that the situation is not rare or abnormal and reconfirm that he is in the same situation as they, and for them it is valued as good. The consensus of such persuasion is usually that mechanism which allays anxiety—purely by its *re*definition of the situation as necessary or normal for an LSD experience (Becker, 1966). As Shibutani also says:

> The definition of the situation is a reconstruction from sensory experiences; it arises from selecting what is pertinent and bringing to bear upon it memories of other events thought to be relevant (1961).

Each time a person enters a new social setting, e.g., having an LSD experience, he is introduced into a new communication channel. "People who communicate develop an appreciation of one another's tastes, interests and outlook upon life" (Shibutani, 1961). In particular, an LSD user's outlook is both shaped and limited by the communication networks in which he becomes involved. It would be fruitful for future research to perform quantitative surveys (perhaps employing measures similar to Bales' small group analyses) recording the number of people with whom any one user interacts directly during a trip; the length of time spent; overt reactions to such interaction; and activities and preoccupations of a person while he remains alone or aloof from others tripping with him. When compared—even qualitatively—with this same person's communication chains while not under the influence of a drug, it would be interesting to see if verbalization increases or decreases as a result of LSD use, both during and following a trip. Other particular questions for study would be to investigate the amount of verbal interaction between two strangers who trip together for the first time (assuming they are within a group setting), the amount of influence other members of the session have upon their initial meeting during the experience, and the resultant interaction between the two as a result of LSD use.

While there are innumerable questions raised concerning the effects of LSD use upon behavior, it remains important that research be defined in terms of either the viewpoint of the user or from the perspective of the observer—for definitions of the situation from these respective vantage points will be distinctively different.

BEGINNING A PSYCHEDELIC DICTIONARY

Acid:	LSD-25, lysergic acid diethylamide
Acidhead:	A regular LSD taker
Acid test:	A term coined by the Kesey group in San Francisco to label a rock-and-roll dance performed to multiple sound and light effects.
Bag:	A particular interest area; temporary fetish.
Bananas:	A preparation for smoking made from the inside of banana peel skins which is baked at 400° for approximately 2 hours on a cookie pan. It is not certain whether the effect is mind-manifesting (psychedelic), or simply to be useful for 'kicks.'
Bum trip:	Also known as a 'bummer.' A bad LSD experience.
Busted:	To be arrested.
Cap:	Capsule, often used as 'a cap of LSD.'
Cubehead:	A regular LSD user. Sugar cubes are one form of blackmarket LSD.
Diggers, The:	A group serving as 'the Salvation Army' of Haight-Ashbury, giving out free food and clothing to anyone.

DMT: Dimethyltryptamine: a short-acting psy-
                chedelic that is injected or smoked. Lasts
                for approximately one hour. Sensations are
                more intense, and usually more visual than
                LSD-25.

Downs: mood resulting from taking depressants.

Drop a Cap: Swallow a capsule of LSD.

Ego games: Intellectual or social interaction imagined
                by the self while having a psychedelic ex-
                perience; also, intellectual or social maneu-
                vers directed towards an individual during
                a psychedelic experience.

Feds: Federal agents in Narcotics; FBI represent-
                atives.

Flip: Go psychotic.

Freakout: A bad LSD experience. Also, complete ego
                loss (but requires a bad experience first).

Grass: Marijuana. Also known as 'boo,' 'gage,' 'tee.'

Great or Clear
White Light: Complete ego-loss under psychedelic ex-
                perience; relates to the visual aspects of
                transcendental experiences during one stage
                of which conceptual vision may be seen as
                all-encompassing white light.

Grateful Dead,
The: A West Coast rock-and-roll group under
                the entrepreneurial aegis of Owsley Stan-
                ley.

Groove: Also, groovy, 'it's a groove,' 'I'm in a
                groove,' or 'I grooved with it.' Having plea-
                surable connotations, i.e., 'the experience
                was good; this feels good to me.'

Guide: A person who 'baby-sits' for the psychedelic
                user during a session.

Guru: A person who acts as one's teacher and
                guide in matters of fundamental intellec-
                tual concern (to prepare for or help one
                through a psychedelic experience).

"H":   Heroin. Also known as 'smack.'

Head: User of any one of the psychedelic drugs. Also, used locally to connote a 'good' person, i.e., praise for someone with a similar liberal attitude or who is generally liked.

Heat: Law enforcement pressure.

High: A state of euphoria or extreme pleasure which may or may not be induced chemically. Locally indicates a euphoric state induced by LSD to distinguish it from reaction of marijuana.

Hooka: Turkish water pipe, usually for smoking hashish.

IFIF: The International Federation for Internal Freedom, created in 1962 by the original Harvard Research group for work not affiliated with the University.

Joint: Also known as a stick. Marijuana cigarettes. Archaic: reefer.

Karma: Fate. The force generated by a person's actions that is held in Hinduism and Buddhism to be the motive power for the round of rebirths and deaths endured by him until he has achieved spiritual liberation and freed himself from the effects of such force.

Lift off: Also, get off, get high: the initial sense of feeling a psychedelic drug begin to affect the mind.

Lightning: Achieving the clear white light.

Mandala: A graphic mystic symbol of the universe that is typically in the form of a circle enclosing a square and often bearing symmetrically arranged representations of deities. It is usually chiefly in Hinduism and Buddhism as an aid in meditation. Also, when in the form of a square, known as a 'God's Eye.'

Mic: Microgram. A thousandth of a milligram. LSD dosages are usually between 100 and 1500 micrograms for individual trips.

Mg: Milligram. A thousandth of a gram. Dealers usually receive these quantities for distribution.

Narc: Narcotics officer. Also known as 'The Man.'

Nirvana: The state of freedom from Karma, the extinction of desire, passion, illusion and the empirical self. The attainment of rest, truth and unchanging being: Salvation—contrasted with samsara.

Octagon: A person who is extremely conservative. 'Super square.'

Pot: Marijuana. A 'pothead' is a person who regularly smokes marijuana.

Psychedelic: Mind-manifesting

Rock: New rock-and-roll music, including rock-folk, etc.

Rub: A person who is conservative; 'old-fashioned' or square.

Sansara: Variation of samsara. Hinduism and Buddhism; the indefinitely repeated cycle of birth, misery and death caused by Karma.

Satori: A sudden enlightenment and a state of consciousness attained by intuitive illumination representing the spiritual goal of Zen Buddhism.

Scene: Situation; usually carries a good connotation unless preceded with the word 'bad,' as in 'bad scene.' Also, a scene goes down (happens); one can 'split the scene' (leave) or 'make the scene' (arrive).

Sebsi: Small pipe for smoking hashish.

Source: Contact, dealer or connection for purchasing drugs.

Spaced out: High on LSD; having an LSD experience.

Stash: Either the hiding place of a whole supply of psychedelic drugs, or one's extra supply hidden away.

Stoned: Denoting other than normal consciousness,

	usually induced by marijuana (as distinct from alcohol).
Straight:	In a state unaffected by any drug which could induce a psychedelic experience. Also, anyone who does not use or who has never used psychedelic drugs.
Toke:	One lungful of marijuana or hashish. A measured amount of marijuana or hashish, usually one pinchful, which is placed in the pipe for lighting .
Travel agent:	In the context of psychedelic use, the person who provides the trip.
Trip:	A psychedelic experience. Usually denotes usage of LSD, peyote or morning glory seeds, but not marijuana or hashish.
Turn on:	To alter awareness, with or without chemicals. Also, local usage includes 'turning on' to an idea, i.e., becoming aware of something new; taking on a new attitude; learning about psychedelic drug use whether or not the person has participated in such activity.
Ups:	Stimulants, or moods from taking stimulants.
Vodka acid:	Vodka that contains LSD, considered by many to be the most readily available preservative for the chemical.
Zero:	Non-effective dose of a psychedelic drug, including having no effect from marijuana. Also, generally a bad or unhappy mood, e.g., 'to feel zero.'

REFERENCES

BECKER, H. S. History, culture and subjective experience: An exploration of the social bases of drug-induced experiences. *The marijuana papers.* New York: Bobbs-Merrill, 1966.

HINCKLE, W. A social history of the hippies. *Ramparts,* 1967, February.

LINDESMITH, A. R. and STRAUSS, A. L. *Social psychology.* New York: The Dryden Press, 1949.

MERTON, R. K. *Social theory and social situations.* New York: The Free Press, 1957.

ROSE, A. M. *Sociology:* The study of human relations. Minneapolis: University of Minnesota Press, 1956.

SHIBUTANI, T. *Society and personality: An interactionist approach to social psychology.* Englewood Cliffs, New Jersey: Prentice-Hall, 1961.

SCHILLER, L., ALPERT, R., and COHEN, S. *LSD.* New York: The American Library, 1966.

CHAPTER 12

Language and Taboo

Oh perish the use of the four-letter words
Whose meanings are never obscure;
The Angles and Saxons, those bawdy old birds,
Were vulgar, obscene, and impure.
But cherish the use of the weaseling phrase
That never says quite what you mean.
You had better be known for your hypocrite ways
Than vulgar, impure, and obscene.

Psychiatric Quarterly, Jan. 1947

Terms like obscenity, as recent court battles have amply demonstrated, tend to defy easy definition. Obviously what is considered unclean, sordid or immoral will vary greatly from one sector of society to another. On the other hand, few authorities seem willing to take refuge from perplexity or responsibility in facile formulas such as "Obscenity, like beauty, is in the eye of the beholder." At any rate, social scientists have long since relinquished interest in essentially arid debates over the semantics of obscenity in favor of concern with a more fundamental and inclusive issue—the phenomenon of taboo.

This term has enjoyed the broadest application: to gestures, actions, objects and spoken or written language. Leach (in Lenneberg 1966) simply defines taboo as expression which is inhibited. While recognizing that the concept of taboo has manifold and complex ramifications, we shall confine our discussion to those aspects of taboo which extend primarily to linguistic considerations. One area of special concern is the use of tabooed words in psychological investigation—and we shall try to cover this topic in some detail.

Verbal taboos can be divided into several major categories: (1) words and actions related to sex and excretion; (2) blasphemy and profanity; and (3) animal abuse. (A case of sorts could be made for including a fourth category of homonyms or near-homonyms of taboo words, e.g., "circumscribe," "elicit," "mensuration," and "emasticate,").

SEX AND TABOO

In our culture today, taboo words are dependent upon prudery to maintain their special characteristics. Prudery is fear and hatred of pleasure, especially sexual pleasure—"a more or less organized interference with other people's rights," as Fryer (1964) views it.

Prudery's first line of action is the restriction of language. This restraint has been active all through history. The earliest suggestion of the suppression of taboo words can be found in the Bible. Moses and the law of the Hebrews influenced taboo words even up to the present time with one of the Ten Commandments, "Thou shalt not take the name of the Lord thy God in vain." Much farther along in history we find various evidence in records of famous persons who were influenced by taboo words. The great Roman orator, Cicero, for example, advised his friends not to say, "little pavements," by adding a diminutive to *pavimenta*. For the word so formed this way, *pavimentula*, would suggest *mentula* which meant "penis."

Noah Webster in 1833, offended by the coarse words in the Bible, set out to revise them. With World War I came a partial and short lived return to plain speaking, without the mid-Victorian taboos. By the 1930's, however, the influence of taboo words was tremendous. A Hollywood list of banned words in movies which came out in the 1930's testifies to this. The list included: "eunuch," "courtesan," "harlot," "slut," "tart," "trollop," "wench," "whore," "son-of-a-bitch," "sex," and "sexual." The words "virtuous" and "bum" were to be avoided and the expression "traveling salesman" might not be used in reference to a farmer's daughter (1964, Fryer). Philip Wylie has stated sarcastically that the end of civilization could come by the clouds forming a series of forbidden words, and that our culture would die when the stars start forming a huge "F" (Sagarin, 1962).

Euphemisms and dysphemisms are so closely tied to a study of taboo words that they cannot be excluded from discussion. Dysphemisms are the clear, meaningful, accurately descriptive and easy to learn and use words which represent the terms of body organs and functions and sex. Dysphemisms are the actually unadulterated taboo words. These forbidden words function to insult, emphasize importance and most especially to vent frustration.

Euphemisms, on the other hand, are society's way to avoid using blunt and shocking dysphemisms. Sagarin (1962) says that euphemisms are necessary to society because the thought of sex and the other taboo areas "is not shocking, only the sound; so if one can express the same thought, while not quite saying it, the objections are overcome" (p. 132). Carnoy's six reasons for euphemisms (given in *La Science Du Mot*) are reduced by Partridge (1934) to three: fear, kindness and delicacy.

A person who believes a word to be obscene mirrors his state of mind. To reduce this state of mind, the word itself must be changed through euphemisms which relieve tension. The problem with euphemisms is that in time each euphemism gets dragged into an endless cycle. When a new euphemism is initiated, it functions to relieve the unpleasant effect of the taboo dysphemism, but gradually these words become contaminated by association with the taboo words, and thus themselves become taboo. This process continues when a new euphemism is added to soften the old and now taboo euphemism, and the second one meets the same fate and so on.

It is quite obvious from this cycle that taboo words have tougher and longer lives than euphemisms. Euphemisms cause the growth in number of taboo words, for obscenity does not become uncontaminated, but euphemisms do become absorbed into the class of forbidden words.

The evolution of obscene words is often hard to trace with accuracy. There seem to be several routes a word may take to reach the dubious status of a taboo word. Quite often its birthplace is the language of slang. Slang has been called the poetry of everyday language, an observation which tends to be confirmed by the metaphorical nature of many slang creations. This seems especially true of slang words that deal with taboo areas. The function, location, appearance or other obvious characteristics of a taboo part of the body or bodily function, for example, furnish the major determinants for the slang term. These slang terms are applied arbitrarily by individuals and pass through the population by word of mouth, thus often becoming altered slightly. Groups such as the armed forces, however, can also initiate slang terms. The new language spreads fast and is tough enough to survive.

Another possible influence on the development of taboo words is onomatopoetic origin. For example, the word "piss" may have first been used because it sounded like the action (Sagarin, 1962). In addition, a small percentage of our dirty words come from other languages such as "shit" from the French word "chier." Still others are contaminated by a new or different association. The innocent child's word "bunny" recently has been slipping into the realm of taboo because of its association with Hugh Hefner's Playboy Clubs. Euphemisms in their cycle, however, seem to be the main instruments that perpetuate change into development of taboo words once a word is established as obscene.

After taboo words are created, these words generate their own phrases. By adding one or two common words, a taboo phrase is formed. "Up" added to the past tense of "fuck," for example, gives "fucked-up," which means fouled up. These phrases are not literally intended and are often quite illogical; for instance, "Go fuck yourself" is a hostile order, but Albert Ellis (1962) pointed out the absurdity of ordering someone to go and obtain the greatest pleasure known to man. He suggests that it would be more appropriate to say, "Go unfuck yourself."

The language of taboo words and phrases sometimes has unusual syntactical structures as compared with the English language. For example, in England, "bloody" is often used in the middle of a word (im-bloody-possible) or between two words (outside, out-bloody-side!). "God damn" and "fuckin" likewise are used in this same way. "Schizo-phrasia," a term employed by Sagarin, means this intrusion of one or two words into a phrase like "Shut the hell up." This illustrates that the "fluidity of slang is restricted by the internalization of the negative attitude toward all things sexual" (Sagarin, 1962, p. 151).

ANTHROPOLOGICAL PERSPECTIVES

Taboo words can be traced back to primitive societies in all parts of the world. Categories corresponding somewhat to our English-language obscenities were formed in pre-literate cultures not at all like contemporary Western society. Whether people uttered these words at certain times and suppressed them at other times because they considered the words obscene, is difficult to determine at present. It might be the case that this quality was given to them by early European travellers with their own moral judgments.

World-wide anthropological studies since 1900 support the idea that obscenity is not new. Sagarin (1962) offers a summary of the evidence: Duncan MacKenzie discovered that obscene language was used at death-wailing ceremonies in several primitive, ritual groups; Philip Han-neken found that obscenity was used at weddings in earlier Roman times; Henri A. Junod reported that obscenity plays the greatest part in the sacred rain-making ceremony of a South African tribe; Knud Leem observed that the Lapps ritualistically use obscenity while hunting; in India the priests of the Vedic religion repeat obscenities to the women at all sacrifices; and in a few pre-literate societies, the husband and wife are forbidden to say or even think their in-laws' names. Although not obscene, these words are tabooed to them. Bloomfield (1933) reports that in some Asian groups the names of the dead are tabooed.

A Russian anthropologist, Zelenin (in Sagarin, 1962), describes the use of taboo words in Eurasia. There the basis of taboo words is the belief that the utterance of them frightens away prey, which seems to be just the antithesis of the concept held by the Lapps. The anthropologist, Pritchard, feels that obscene language used by tribes or groups was probably accepted in ceremonies, but tabooed in all other contexts (in Sagarin, 1962).

European societies seem to share a common taboo word system with the United States. Although the words themselves differ, similar types of words are considered obscene. We can even see that some of the words which are presently taboo in Western civilization were also taboo in the past. For example, the word for ass in old English was *aers;* in old Persian it was *ers;* in old high German it was *ars;* and in old Norse it was *ars* (Fryer, 1964).

Our society, by the nature of the words considered to be taboo, reflects in its language a hostile attitude toward sex and the body. According to the Sapir-Whorf hypothesis, language not only mirrors culture, but is instrumental in shaping culture. Although the issues presented by the linguistic relativity hypothesis are far from settled, we can readily identify an integral tie between the attitudes in our society toward taboo words and what those words represent. For example, there is a need to express the idea of copulation in a short, concise term. All languages have such a term, but few are so threatened by it as to invoke taboos as strong as those found in the United States.

Though obscene words are subject to intense taboos, in our society, there are some circles in which such words are exalted. In male groups such as the armed forces and adolescent peer groups, the number of times dirty words are worked into the conversation is one of the criteria by which peers judge a member on such qualities as ribaldry, masculinity and sophistication.

Taboo words as well as prudish attitudes towards them can have detrimental effects on society. The very real harm of prudery can be demonstrated by the resistance of American and English officials to print or speak the words "syphilis" and "venereal disease." Efforts to reduce the great number of people afflicted by this disease were tremendously hampered by this prudery of communication (Fryer, 1964).

Because of embarrassment or great propriety, parents often fail to provide instruction for their children in matters of sex and excretion. Therefore, the children at an early age learn from their peers that the shunned areas in question have names that are forbidden in everyday usage. These words acquire an emotional charge for children. The forbidden characteristics of the words can come to be associated with the objects themselves.

Often obscene words that children pick up outside of the family have an extremely negative connotation such as "scum" for "semen." Children educated with terms surrounded by such negative emotionality have a hard time acquiring wholesome uninhibited attitudes toward sex. In this case language molds attitudes, yet at the same time the words are taboo because society has previously forbidden them. Since language acquisition corresponds in its beginnings with the Age of Innocence, children are not apt to discover the meanings of taboo words in experience, but rather the meanings that are imposed upon them. From that point on, ideas about taboo areas are already negatively established by the language. This can be seen as a cycle: Society molds the language, which molds society in turn, and the beginning and end of the process are extremely ambiguous.

TABOO WORDS IN PSYCHOLOGICAL INVESTIGATIONS

In 1935, Steadman sought to examine the language consciousness of college students. One aspect of his procedure was to request his subjects to compile a list of taboo words. Although the study may be slightly outdated and can be criticized for lack of construct validity, various observations were made which may have stimulated interest in this area. Steadman concludes that the avoidance of coarseness, obscenity and unpleasant connotations is one of the most powerful factors in language consciousness of college students, in spite of a tendency toward direct and forthright speech generally attributed to modern youth.

Included in the investigation was a theory by Bloomfield (1933), which has quite thought-provoking implications for the study of taboo words. In answer to the question, "Why does a taboo word come first to mind although a substitute word is spoken?" Bloomfield suggested that obscenity has an emotional force which makes the recall of taboo words easier. The forbidden word, though not spoken, is recalled and so persists in language longer than synonyms not possessing such an emotional aspect. "The flavor of 'forbidden fruit' reinforces the word" (Bloomfield, 1933, p. 97).

Three years later Hunter and Gaines (1938) studied verbal taboos in a college community. Using a check list of taboo words, two different independent variables were employed—educational attainment and sex. They found that by far the greatest resistance to obscene words was felt by the freshmen and greatest freedom by the seniors. Besides age and experience, one would say that the new student in a novel and uncertain environment tries to be accepted; to be on the safe side, he steers away from potentially controversial material. Women were found to show greater restraint than men in all ages.

McGinnies (1949) conducted a study in which he examined the relation between recognition of taboo words and the emotion aroused in the subject when responding. His measure of emotionality—galvanic skin response (GSR)—was recorded while a list of eleven neutral words and seven taboo words referring to sex and excretion were presented to the subjects. According to McGinnies' interpretation, perceptual defense was the factor responsible for delayed recognition of taboo words. Perceptual defense operates to keep the individual from visually responding to any stimuli that would arouse strong unpleasant emotional experience in the subject. The results of the experiment indicated that subjects had greater GSR's for the sexually taboo words than neutral words, and that recognition thresholds for the taboo words were higher. McGinnies explained his findings by stating that:

> . . . early in life, most individuals learn that words like 'whore' and 'bitch' are socially taboo. Since the use of such words by the child will generally result in chastisement by the parent, a conditioned emotional reaction to these verbal symbols is soon established. This pattern of conditioned emotional response may be considered one of fear or anxiety aroused by symbols having sexual, excretory, or otherwise unpleasant or 'immoral' connotations. Despite the fact that these words may be employed frequently at a later age, especially when communicating with members of one's own sex, the early emotional reaction persists, as revealed by the GSR, even when overt signs of anxiety or embarrassment are not observable (McGinnies, p. 249).

Having explained how perceptual defense worked with respect to recognition and threshold of taboo words, McGinnies broke his sample down according to sex and found that males had a higher recall ability on both taboo and neutral words than females.

Howes and Solomon (1950) reviewed and attacked McGinnies' study on several grounds. They maintained that the subjects he used (college students) were very impressionable and inhibited in their responses. Because they wished to avoid embarrassing themselves and/or the experimenter in the room, they would not immediately respond to a taboo word; rather they waited until they were positive of the word and took no guesses as they did with neutral words. This anxiety was also responsible for the larger GSR for taboo words than neutral words. The second line of attack was against McGinnies' concept of perceptual defense. Howes and Solomon asserted that the neutral words used occurred more frequently in the subject's vocabulary than did the taboo words and thus accounted for the lower threshold for the neutral words.

Dorfman, Grossberg and Krolkry (1965) conducted a study that dealt with recognition of taboo and neutral words as a function of exposure time and also included a study of frequent and infrequent word recognition as a function of exposure. In the part of the study dealing with frequent and infrequent words, it was found that the frequent words had a lower threshold. This would seemingly support Howes and Solomon. The second half of the study used neutral and taboo words and showed that at short durations the neutral words were recognized at lower exposure more often than taboo words. With increased exposure time, accuracy for taboo words increased also. The experimenters explained this by stating that a response bias was operating. Zajonc and Nierwenhuyse (1964) have suggested that response bias for taboo words diminishes with increased exposure time. This, then, would seemingly support McGinnies' idea of perceptual defense.

The third finding of the McGinnies study, that dealing with the sex variable, has also been the subject of much research. Using the same procedure of neutral and taboo word presentation Miller and Solkoff (1965) performed a study using male and female subjects. In this study the subjects were presented an equal number of taboo and neutral words which were matched for their frequency in the language. The subjects were required on some instances to write their responses and on other occasions to verbalize responses. When the words were written there appeared not only no sex difference in accuracy, but also no significant difference between neutral and taboo word accuracy. When oral responses were required, males had more errors for taboo than neutral words and males had significantly higher thresholds. Females showed no significant difference with the two methods. These findings were inconsistent with the McGinnies study and suggest that threshold recognition depends not only on sex, but familiarity, duration and method of responding.

Grosser and Walsh (1966) examined the effects of sex upon the recall of sexually taboo and neutral words. In the experiment, taboo words were used for the experimental condition and neutral words for the controls. Twenty words, randomly ordered with ten taboo and ten neutral words, were exposed for one second intervals to the subjects. It was determined that both male and female subjects were of equal recall ability, but that males recalled more sexually taboo words than did the females. It was felt that females would feel more threatened by sexually taboo words than males and also that more neutral words would be recalled than taboo words. However, the findings indicated that males recalled more taboo than neutral words and that females recalled more neutral words. While these results might point to a suppression variable, in that females suppress sexual words more than males, it must also be considered that the experimenter in this case was a male which may have served to inhibit the females' responses.

Regardless of the various loopholes left open in research on sexually taboo words, it appears reasonable to assume that there exists a sex factor as well as other variables and that these verbal taboos were transmitted to the various sexes. It consists of a learning process, whether it be the mid-Victorian taboos which prohibited a mention of a female's legs or the present taboos which prohibit the use of various sex words (e.g., penis, fuck) in common conversation. There are rules for expression in this category which culture has made and society attempts to enforce.

BLASPHEMY AND PROFANITY

The second category of taboo topics deals with blasphemy and profanity. This category reflects the misuse of sacred ideas and objects and borders on being, and in many cases is, sacrilegious. From earliest history, man has had his gods and the prescribed ways of speaking to and about them.

In earliest cultures, this was the most serious taboo category. Men were put to death for blasphemy.

A study by Dixit (1965) showed that there exists a significant difference in the rate of learning and retention of taboo and religious words based on association time. The greater the association time, the less efficiently the word was remembered. Words dealing with religion, then, would be retained more readily than other taboo words by virtue of a greater association with religion. It is not uncommon for a person to swear upon occasion, that being the first thing to come into his mind before a sexually taboo word. Phrases like "damn it," "Jesus Christ," etc., come to mind before phrases like "fuck it," "shit." Dixit also determined that there existed an indifferent attitude on the part of his subjects toward religion which would explain why presently this category of verbal taboo is not necessarily strongly enforced. It would appear that blasphemy as such, does not exist in the same framework as in earlier cultures. The sanctions are by no means as strict. Profanity, however, abounds in present day usage. The profanity of today is also tied up with the blasphemy of yesterday. "Damn it," for example, once had a religious connotation, but it is more readily placed in the profanity category than in that of blasphemy. Profanity is used as a collective term and, in general, describes "off-color" verbal abuse. This not only includes words that would have fallen into the blasphemy category, but also those contained in the sexually taboo words. It is really not a specific term and as such encompasses the three categories of taboo to some extent.

TABOOS INVOLVING ANIMAL ABUSE

The third, and perhaps most interesting, taboo topic concerns animal abuse. Phrases such as "son of a bitch," "jack-ass," "swine," etc., evoke much emotion when directed towards a person; whereas such phrases as "son of a mongoose" or "polar bear" have no meaning at all. A possible explanation would possibly be found in religion. Some animals are sacred as the Brahma bull, and others are referred to as unclean, as pork is in the Jewish religion. To use these terms in these cultures would border on the sacrilegious and are thus taboo. However, the problem remains that such verbal abuses as "pig" are not culturally bound.

Edmund Leach has formulated what might be called a general theory of animal abuse. "Taboo serves to separate the SELF from the world, and then the world itself is divided into zones of social distance corresponding here to the words farm, field and remote" (1966, p. 53). Leach sets forth a paradigm in which he depicts a social continuum stretching from the self to the stranger. He explains that the taboo concept operates in relation to the self and society. There exist certain rules for the associations between self and sibling, self and cousin, self and neighbor, and self and stranger. As an example, the incest taboo operates between self and sibling; but between self and cousin, the incest taboo is not as strong and there is an attitude of permissiveness between premarital intercourse and incest taboo. Cousins would then fall into a category half way between that which is forbidden and that which is permissible. In the same fashion, Leach organizes the relationship between self and animals. The continuum ranges from pets to wild beasts. Whereas the relationship between self and others is based on sexual intercourse, the relation between self and animals is controlled by categories of edible and inedible taboos. Self and pets, for example, are considered to be taboo if eaten. Pets are classified as inedible. On the other end of the continuum are the wild animals which are also inedible and belong in the zoo. This corresponds to intercourse with unknown strangers which are as remote from the self as are wild beasts. Placed between these ends of the continuum, animals are categorized as edible, but only under certain conditions. Farm animals are considered edible if castrated; certain other animals are considered edible only if killed during the hunting season; wild animals are considered inedible. (This corresponds to the discrimination of farm, field and remote animals.) The point that Leach makes with the above examples is that society has built into man certain taboos in relation to self which have been passed through the culture with no apparent reason in many cases. In America, for example, man would not think of eating his pet dog, except in the gravest circumstances, perhaps; but in other cultures, dogs are bred for the sole purpose of food consumption.

It would seem from the above, that the concept of animal taboo is contained in two major areas: that of an edible-inedible classification and that of a ritual classification. These have been passed through the culture, frequently with both categories applying to the particular animal abuse. As an example, examine the word, "jack-ass." This animal is produced by a cross of a donkey and a horse. Both of these animals would be placed in an inedible category as they are non-castrated farm animals. Ritually, the donkey is the beast of burden and Christ is placed upon it in several instances in the New Testament (e.g., on Palm Sunday). However, the cross-breeding of the two animals produces an animal which is neither a donkey nor a horse—it has no "status" if you will, in either species. It is a misfit; a degradation of species. Conceivably, the term "jack-ass" would be applied to a person with no status in a particular society; one who was a misfit and was considered a degradation to the human race.

"Swine" (or pig), however, is not so easy to analyze. Swine used to be fed from table scraps, as were other pets, such as dogs. To kill an animal with such close association with humans was considered, in English rural areas, almost a sacrilege! Now, however, swine are more often associated with the pig sty, grunting around in their own slop and mud, and physically, very dirty animals. To insinuate that one is a swine puts him in the same category as the sty, and all the physical characteristics of a dirty, smelly pig. But this is an edible animal now, and in some cultures it is forbidden even though other cultures classify it as a castrated farm animal and thus edible. Even in discussing this example, one encounters difficulties. Only castrated pigs are to be eaten and when eaten are referred to as "pork," not, for example, as a "pig chop." Ritually, some cultures (Jewish, Arabian) will not eat pork as their religion has stated that these animals are unclean and are not to be eaten. Perhaps the religious taboo on pork could account for some cultures labeling a man a "swine;" but how can it be explained in those cultures which do not place a taboo on eating pork, and yet the term "swine" means approximately the same thing?

In discussing Leach's continuum, one can view it as the distance from the self in a social system. Basically, both systems start with the self. Correlating the two continua, it is possible to illustrate the following: (1) the first category contains the relationship of self to sibling and self to pet. Intercourse with a sibling is prohibited by the incest taboo; pets are inedible because of their close association with man. (2) The relationship between self and cousins and self and edible animals is likewise controlled. Cousins, while eligible for intercourse, are not eligible for marriage. Farm animals are eligible for food, but only if castrated. (3) The third category controls the relationship between self and neighbor and self and sexually intact animals. Marriage is permitted with neighbor and thus obviously includes permitted intercourse. Also in the relationship are self's friends and enemies who are theoretically eligible for the same benefits. Sexually intact animals are categorized as friendly and hostile and are classified as edible. There do exist some restrictions as to when some of these animals are edible and these are governed by the hunting seasons. (4) The fourth category includes relationships with strangers and remote wild animals. Sex relations do not occur with strangers nor are remote wild animals considered edible as they belong in the zoo for observation. There are some instances when remote wild animals are hunted, but it is generally not for food purposes; rather the sport of hunting is the motive.

Leach's continua, then, are built upon self's distance from humans and animals and his behavior is regulated by this distance in terms of sex relations and edibility. In examining Leach's theory, it seems plausible to accept his idea that animal abuse is the equation of a human being with another species of animal; it is a degradation, if you will. It would seem that the nearer the species lies on the continuum to self, the more offensive is the abuse. The further along the continuum one travels, the less offensive the abuse becomes (e.g., son of a bitch, pussy, swine, horse, cow, buck, lion, etc.). The animal abuse is most certainly dependent upon the cultural framework for its classification of animals as edible or inedible. It is something which has to be transmitted in the same way as sexually taboo words or any other taboo topics.

Taboos are not restricted to subjects harshly sanctioned by society. Puns, for example, constitute a category of linguistic taboo and are usually looked upon as a talent. A pun violates linguistic rules:

> . . . by confusing two apparently different meanings of some phonemic pattern. The pun seems funny or shocking because it challenges a taboo which ordinarily forbids us to recognize that the sound pattern is ambiguous. In many cases, such verbal taboos have social as well as linguistic aspects (Leach, 1966, p. 25).

Verbal taboos do not necessarily have a causal relationship with behavioral taboos. The

> . . . association between deed and word is not so simple as might appear . . . It is not the case that certain kinds of behavior are taboo and that, therefore, the language relating to such behavior becomes taboo. Sometimes words may be taboo in themselves for linguistic (phonemic) reasons, and the causal link, if any, is then reversed: as behavioral taboo comes to reflect a prior verbal taboo (Leach, pp. 24–25).

Taboos, then, can be classified as behavioral or linguistic, with varying sanctions in both categories. There may or may not exist a relationship between the two, but both are controlled by culture and society which, through learning, transfers the rules for accepted behavior and proper linguistic use. Through the process of learning, the individual associates various emotions, situations, reactions to the taboo topics and forms a subconscious framework in which they may be used. It is for these reasons, says Leach, that "taboo is simultaneously both behavioral and linguistic, both social and psychological" (p. 26).

COMMUNICATION AND PROTEST: GRAFFITI

Graffiti are rude inscriptions, drawings or the like, found on fences, billboards, sidewalks or washroom walls. They can be distinguished from inscriptions, which are made with more care and are intended to be permanent. Executed by an unpaid citizenry, graffiti are usually scratched with sharp instruments or written in ink, paint, chalk or pencil. They are savored esthetically for their neo-primeval bitterness, commenting on a turmoil long past and now forgotten, even by their creators. These anonymous one-liners have usually ranked below limericks on the literary scale, but recently the messages have gained a new respectability.

A report at a professional convention of psychiatrists not too long ago concluded that people execute graffiti for a variety of reasons: to prove themselves, to hurl insults ("Hugh Hefner is a virgin"), for purposes of titillation ("Marian, $25"), to communicate an opinion ("Reality is a crutch"), or to render a sociological commentary ("James Baldwin eats watermelon").

The urge to make one's mark in the world is common to all social classes; among members of the American middle class, it is often expressed in "commercial graffiti," such as bumper stickers and buttons.

Inscriptions of Greenwich Village have inspired several recent movie and Broadway titles such as "Stop the World, I Want to Get Off" and "Who's Afraid of Virginia Woolf?" Newspapers are also no exception. After Yale released its map showing that Vikings rather than Columbus discovered America, the New York Times chose "Leif Erickson is a Fink" as its quotation of the day, a graffito from an Italian district in Boston.

The legendary "Kilroy" is being challenged by "Overby," usually only "Overby Lives." At times he appears as the unknown hand that works for the Selective Service, as in "Down With the Draft—Overby Strikes Every 7 Hours."

Since psychedelics are now one of the biggest teen-age hang-ups, "Take LSD and See" is a common inscription. Also the discovery that the world is not a Disneyland resulted in "Mary Poppins is a Junkie," "Donald Duck is a Jew," and "He's Not Dead—He's In the Hills—But He'll Be Back If We Need Him." Public personalities are subject to a heavy share of the wall commentary as in "J. Edgar Hoover Sleeps with a Night Light."

The standard graffito is a one-line opinion, with two-liners infrequent, and three-liners a true rarity. However, recently more and more grafficionados seem to enjoy commenting on the works of others. In a San Francisco bar, "My mother made me a homosexual;" beneath was written, "If I buy her the wool, will she make me one too?" And on a washroom wall in New York, "I Love Grils," to which was added, "It's Girls, Stupid, G-I-R-L-S," and finally the real wit, "But What About Us Grils?"

Another form of graffiti utilizing essentially the same figures, but expressing completely distinctive interpretations is based on the traditional valentine-shaped heart. One, both grammatically and psychologically correct, professes that even between lovers there exists a partition.

The other, lipsticked on a slate panel in a schizophrenic ward, was found near a slogan, "Support Mental Health."

From these examples, it is clear that there are two types of graffiti. The first type is writings scratched or scribbled on walls. This is of importance to the philologist studying ancient alphabets, dialects and languages, and to the social historian and archeologist studying everyday life and dating buildings and events. The second type is drawings which probably originated in Egypt, but were popular in Italy in the 15th and 16th centuries where whole buildings were decorated. In Egypt, names and short prayers were common. In Italy, graffiti were more varied, including humorous and amatory remarks, obscenities and many religious comments.

Pompeii, a small city on the Bay of Naples which is now best remembered as one of three cities covered by the eruption of Mount Vesuvius in 79 A.D., was a typical Italian mecca of graffiti. Two books (Tanzar, 1939; Lindsay, 1960) have undertaken to utilize the "writing on the wall" in order to reconstruct the daily lives of the citizens of Pompeii. Through the more than 15,000 inscriptions that have been uncovered, houses can be allocated to their owners, personal relationships understood, and a detailed account of all aspects of the life pieced together. One graffito reads, "Everybody writes on the walls but me," and it appears almost believable.

A tour of the city reveals many similarities between Pompeii and any modern American city. "Hermes recommends Calventius for Mayor" reminds one of our own "Vote for ——." Democratic government was of interest to the citizens of Pompeii and many notices proclaimed the fact. Lodgings and hotels also support political announcements along with their owners' names, as "Once You Come to Gabinius' Hotel, You'll Stay Here." Within the hotel, the bedrooms are full of scribbles. "Vibius Restitutus slept here all on his own and longed for his Urbana," from one who loved his own wife, an unusual situation in ancient Italy.

After securing quarters, a bath was in order. These walls contain greetings, as "Aegyptus wishes the best to his Gallus," and insults, as "Jarinus, you live here," implying that he is a lazy fellow who bathes several times a day. The bathkeeper of the Forum baths was a target for insults about his habits, as "Daddy Colupius Kisses the Ladies Where He Shouldn't." For a barber, expert with curling-tongs and liking the girls, was written, "Xanthe, the anointer's your dear, and practiced too at merry games: he smoothly tickles you." Money matters were also of importance in Pompeii, but not everyone was satisfied with its handling as two graffiti testify: "May he who serves the Gaecilii come to a bad end!" and "Here's my advice. Share out the Common Chest. For in our Coffers piles of money rest."

Eating places frequently contributed accounting and purchases to the wall, and one entry read, "He who wrote this did it because he wanted to." Customers scribbled also, as "I am yours for 2 coppers," and "Goddess, I won't want to sell the supper." And one obviously homesick traveler wrote, "Desirous we came; but more we desire, O Rome, to go. Please let us see the gods of home."

The theatre with its plays and concerts was a favorite pastime in Pompeii, and actors often got a big following. However, not all were favorites, "Oppius you interludeplayer you're a thief, a sneakthief." Theatre notices were also popular, as "Thirty pairs of gladiators and their substitutes on November 24th–26th; Fare you well Paris." Within the Forum gladiatorial troops performed, not always bravely, "Officiosus fled November 6th," but usually so, "Severus, freedman, 55 fights, has just won again," and "Anctus of the Julian Troop has won 50 times." But even the gladiators had their sense of humor, "Edict of M. Atius Primus: If anyone wants a little fishsnack, let him go after L. Asicius for it." Not everyone enjoyed the combat, "The philosopher Annalus Seneca is the only Roman writer to condemn the bloody games" was found in a barracks, proving that the fighters thought about the things they did.

"Teacher Sema with his boys recommends Julius Simplex as Commissioner" marked a school under the portico in the Forum. Schools were important to the populace, and thus one teacher wrote as encouragement to parents, "May He who gives me the fee for teaching get what he seeks from those aloft." As a reminder, one graffito reads, "If Cicero is a pain in your neck, you'll be whacked." When not in school, young students belonged to Youth Clubs. Exercises of all sorts, and parades on foot and horse took most of the time, "he rides like Romulus Son of Mars in the Heavens."

Most houses in Pompeii were modest affairs. A few rich folk had latrines on upper-floors, but most commoners used the public latrines, except for those who thought any quiet place would do. Hence many threats were inscribed on the walls, but usually to no avail. As one guest wrote in a lodging house, "My host, I've wet my bed. My sins I bare. But why? you ask. No pot was anywhere." And inside a hall, "Belch when you're happily drunk and dare to assert the bottom's rude delights. Blurt still, and blurt." The entrance to a house was rich with election notices, and special epigrams from the host, "Drop horrid brawls. With courtesy converse, please now. Go home, or else obey my verse."

In several cases, graffiti are not simply one-line verses, but instead couplets and even stanzas, which gives evidence to the literary achievements of the poetic citizens of Pompeii. Often seen are the lines, "O Wall, so many men come here to scrawl, I wonder that your burdened sides don't fall." Many of the graffiti were repeated by others who then claimed them, but occasionally someone produced an original line. The philosophy of these grafficionados seemed to have been, "It's right enough to imitate but don't give way to envy."

The market was a place of business, but a place of pleasure once the sales were over. Graffiti extend from the business-like "What may I do for you?" to a maxim to offset all disasters "The greatest evil becomes a trifle if you scorn it," to a threat "Woe to you, Colony!" and then back to the lighter side "Suavis the Barmaid has a thirst, I ask you and a very strong thirst it is." At once somebody's rude again "Chius, I hope your piles are chafed once more that they may burn worse than they've burnt before." The practical lover adds "I like a girl with a proper mat, not depilated and shorn. Then you can snug well in from the cold, as an overcoat she's worn." And someone with a morning-after feeling: "Once a man drinks, thereafter everything's in confusion." Then a contorted couplet: "She who smiles on my first letter's truly mine, she who names a price is anyone's, not mine." Lovers had spent a lot of time there judging by the verses, and at last there is one who seems to have worn down his girl's resistances, "What's harder than stone and gentler than water flowing? Yet hard stone is hollowed by flowing water."

The taverns of Pompeii were difficult to distinguish from the inns and restaurants, but generally the taverns were a place where snacks were drowned in wine or mead. Everyone loved a boozer as long as he was good-natured and hadn't reached the frowsy stage. "Good Luck to Comrade Proculus, long may he yet drink, though his ashes and bones are covered deep," refers to a drunken man who was killed when a wall fell on him during an earthquake. Pub-keepers were usually honest because their reputations were at stake. Very seldom would a drinker write "May you be cheated yourself and then repine. Landlord, you sell us water, while drinking wine."

Occasionally a man would write his own election opinions, but generally he left it up to signwriters with their neat lettering. Sometimes people would deface the notices so the signwriter would try to deter them. "If you are jealous and damage this, may you suffer for it." The election notices generally took two forms. Either the writer declared his support for a candidate, or he called on someone to take action on his behalf.

Pompeii had its share of lovers "Lovers like bees enjoy a life of honey"; but as usual, someone added a caustic diagnosis, "Lovers—sick creatures needing a cure." This latter citizen was the type who objected to the small scratches made by lovers giving public notice to some secret moment. Intending to catch out the person who read the words aloud was written, "It's the Lover who writes, the Sod who reads it, it's clear. The Listener twitches and itches, and he who goes by is a queer. And me, I'm the Bear's-dinner, I'm the Twerp who stands reading here." The boys did most of the writing, but occasionally a girl tried her hand, "Venerusa, I hope you may love him well." Now and then a warning appeared, "Look out for Wives!"

If one had no lover, a girl was easy enough to find. Any bar or inn could provide one, or there were single rooms along the streets. Paintings on the walls suggested various things one might do if he were energetic or young or drunk enough. Writings on the walls were mostly from satisfied clients. "Here I've had hordes of girls," "Felix twice did the deed on this spot," and "Phoebus the performer had a first-rate time here." The brothels were called lupanars, or wolf-dens because the word for whores was wolves. One young man understood why when he wrote, "Here I'd the luck a lovely girl to win. Folk call her beautiful. She's filth within." Not all were quite as boastful of their feats. "Here I recall I had a girl of late. The intimate details I shall not relate."

It is not remarkable that the walls of Pompeii were decorated with graffiti, but it is extraordinary that these notes should have been preserved, and that they should throw so much light on the minds and manners of these people of so long ago. They give the impression of a high degree of literacy even among the lower classes. Numerous quotations from Vergil and Ovid are found, showing a wide acquaintance with the best of Roman literature.

The reconstruction of Pompeii from the wall commentary represents a rather extended example of the first type of graffiti, that of writings. This is not to slight the second type, that of pictorial graffiti. The interior walls of Mayan temples in Tikal, Guatemala, Central America, are so direct in their graphic notations that they remind one of modern comic strips. Their representations of human types and activities are definitely not mural decorations. Many are only a few inches high, marked on the soft white covering the limestone plaster, with no directly related evidence of paints.

The closest parallels to the forms are found in Maya codices, the few remaining original books where a pictographic form of writing records calendar information. The graffiti represent humans, animals, buildings and decorative and symbolic designs which range from the sophisticated to the crude with no ordered plan.

There appear to be two forms. The first are the small scaled pieces of characteristic Maya types displaying masterful graphic skill found within the center of activity, the temple. The second type is large crude forms, sometimes spread over the smaller examples, which are found on the periphery of the ceremonial area. These include execution scenes with priests, warriors, profile versions of temples and dozens of left-facing profile heads (only a few face right).

The lack of organization and continuity of design rules out any esthetic intent on the part of the artist. They appear to be more in the nature of individual and informal comments or records about time, places, circumstances, customs or superstitions presented in graphic forms. It may well be a written language for which we have no key as yet.

REFERENCES

BLOOMFIELD, L. *Language*. New York: Holt, Rhinehart and Winston, 1933.

DEWEY, R. and HUMBER, W. J. *An introduction to social psychology*. New York: The MacMillan Co., 1966.

DIXIT, R. C. Learning and retention of religious and taboo words. *Archivio di Psicologia, Neurologia e Psichiatria*, 1956, 26, 188–193.

DORFMAN, D. D., GROSSBERG, J. M., and KROLKRY, L. Recognition of taboo stimuli as a function of exposure time. *Journal of Personality and Social Psychology*, 1965, 2, 552–562.

ELLIS, A. *The American sexual tragedy*. New York: Lyle Stuart, 1962.

FARBEROW, N. L. *Taboo topics*. New York: Atherton Press, 1963.

FRAZER, J. *The golden bough.* New York: Criterion Books, 1959.

FRYER, P. *Mrs. Grundy, studies in English prudery.* London: London House and Maxwell, 1964.

GROSSER, G. S. and LACZEK, W. Prior parochial vs. secular education and utterance tendencies to taboo words. *Journal of Psychology,* 1963, 60, 263–277.

GROSSER, G. S. and WALSH, T. Sex differences in differential recall of taboo and neutral words. *Journal of Psychology,* 1966, 63, 219–227.

HOWES, D. H. and SOLOMON, R. L. A note on McGinnies's "Emotionality and perceptual defense." *Psychological Review,* 1950, 57, 229–234.

HUNTER, E. R. and GAINES, B. E. Verbal taboo in a college community. *American Speech,* 1938, 13, 97–107.

LEACH, E. Anthropological aspects of language: animal categories and verbal abuse. In E. H. Lenneberg (Ed.), *New directions in the study of language.* Cambridge, Massachusetts: MIT Press, 1966.

LEE, I. S. *Language habits in human affairs.* New York: Harper and Row, Publishers, 1949.

LINDSAY, J. *The writing on the wall: An account of Pompeii in its last days.* London: F. Muller, 1960.

Local graffiti. *New Yorker,* 1956, 32, 44–45.

LOMAS, H. and WELTMAN, G. Washroom wit: An analytic study. *Newsweek,* 1966, 68, 110.

McGINNIES, E. M. Emotionality and perceptual defense. *Psychological Review,* 1949, 56, 244–251.

MILLER, M. E. and SOLKOFF, N. Effects of mode or response and sex of E upon recognition thresholds of taboo words. *Perceptual and Motor Skills,* 1965, 20, 573–578.

PARTRIDGE, E. *Slang yesterday and today.* New York: The Macmillan Co., 1934.

SAGARIN, E. *The anatomy of dirty words.* New York: The Macmillan Co., 1962.

STEADMAN, J. M. A study of verbal taboos. *American Speech,* 1935, 10, 93–103.

TANZER, H. H. *The common people of Pompeii: A study of graffiti.* Baltimore: The Johns Hopkins Press, 1939.

WALKER, L. C. Message from the Maya: Tikal, Guatemala. *Americas,* 1963, 17, 15–19.

WHITTAKER, E. M., GILCHRIST, J. C., and FISCHER, J. W. Perceptual defense or response suppression? *Journal of Abnormal and Social Psychology,* 1952, 47, 732–733.

ZAJONC, R. B. and NIEUWENHUYSE, B. Relationship between word frequency and recognition: Perceptual process or response bias? *Journal of Experimental Psychology,* 1964, 67, 276–285.

CHAPTER 13

Psycholinguistics and Language Style

Disorders in the communicative medium may be met in part by an attempt to overcome them, in part by an attempt to go around them. One will either try to say his say despite his handicaps, or he will say the sort of things that can best be said within the terms of the handicaps.

Kenneth Burke: *Permanence and Change**

I N A POWERFULLY EVOCATIVE METAPHOR, T. S. Eliot once captured an elusive but fundamental truth of inspired scholarship. Writing about Paul Valéry's *Meditations,* the poet observed that "the tower of ivory has been fitted up as a laboratory." His expressive figure was intended as a tribute to the work and accomplishments of a remarkable man of letters; but it might have been fashioned instead to describe the progress and direction of literary criticism in the twentieth century, especially in the field of stylistics.

Superficially, it seems easy enough to distinguish one style of writing from another and to characterize stylistic differences in terms that are generally intelligible. Beyond these considerations, there are questions that involve the comparison of writing styles according to specific content or historical period, and the evaluation of the relative effectiveness of various stylistic techniques and conventions. Such aspects of style

---

* Hermes Publications, Los Altos, California, 1954.

189

have formed the traditional province of literary criticism. To accomplish their task, critics have evolved their own specialized methods of investigation and technical vocabulary.

Within the past several decades, however, there has been a continually increasing receptivity among literary critics and analysts toward the use of concepts and methods which have originated outside the field of literary criticism. Stanley Edgar Hyman (1955) was among the first to give explicit recognition to this trend when he defined modern criticism as *"the organized use of non-literary techniques and bodies of knowledge to obtain insights into literature"* (p. 3). The "techniques and bodies of knowledge" which Hyman mentions refer primarily to linguistics and psychology, although note is also taken of the contributions received from sociology, anthropology, economics, historiography and other disciplines.

This, of course, is not to say that literary critics have failed in the past to apply such knowledge to the interpretation of literature. As far back as Aristotle, attempts have been made to study poetry and drama in the light of whatever information was available concerning the human mind and the nature of society. The key word in Hyman's statement is *organized*. Traditional criticism, according to Hyman, "used most of these techniques and descriptions, but in a spasmodic and haphazard fashion" (p. 3). Modern criticism, on the other hand, makes systematic use of such information. Says Hyman:

> From psychoanalysis critics have borrowed the basic assumptions of the operations of the subconscious mind, demonstrating its deeper 'wishes' through associations and 'clusters' of images; the basic mechanisms of dream distortion, such as condensation, displacement, and splitting, which are also the basic mechanisms of poetic formation; the Jungian conception of archetypes, and much else. They have taken the concept of 'configurations' from the Gestaltists; basic experimental data about animal and child behavior from the laboratory psychologists; information about the pathological expressions of the human mind from the clinical psychologists; discoveries about the behavior of man in groups and social patterns from the social psychologists; and a great deal more, from Jaensch's 'eidetic images' and purely subjective material to the most objective physical and chemical data reported by neurological and endocrinological psychologies. From competing sociologies, criticism has borrowed theories and data regarding the nature of society, social change, and social con-

flicts, and their relation to literature and other cultural phenomena; and from anthropological schools, theories and data regarding primitive societies and social behavior . . . (pp. 5–6).

Concomitant with these developments in criticism, the new approach toward the analysis of language and language designated *psycholinguistics* was evolving within the social and behavioral sciences. In viewing this evolutionary process, one is tempted to invert Hyman's characterization of modern criticism and suggest that psychologists and psychiatrists with interests in language phenomena have shown increasing receptivity to the contributions of literary criticism, both as an aid to formulating significant problems in research and as a potential source for achieving a deeper understanding of the psychological processes which underlie human communication.[1] It may be worth noting that an article on psycholinguistics by the distinguished psychologist George A. Miller (1964) appeared in a recent issue of *Encounter*—another indication, perhaps, of the narrowing gulf between literary and scientific interests in the sphere of language.

The psycholinguist takes for his object of study the larger part of the domain of language behavior in its written, spoken and graphic aspects. Unlike the literary critic who accepts the responsibility for making esthetic evaluations, the principal aim of the psycholinguist is understanding. He may therefore find the deviant or bizarre verbalizations of a schizophrenic patient as suitable an object for inquiry as the lyric poetry of the nineteenth century. But in the area of style and expression, the divergent paths of the literary critic and the psycholinguist came recently to a meaningful intersection.

Seminars are nothing new in the social sciences. Nor are they unknown, for that matter, in literary circles. In an article in *Bookman* in 1929, T. S. Eliot called for "the collaboration of critics of various special training, and perhaps the pooling and sorting of their contributions by men who will be neither specialists nor amateurs." Such seminars hold an important place in the advance of scholarship. After all, as Hyman (1955) reminds us:

Thomas Young, an English physician, optical physicist, Egyptologist, physiologist, etc., who died in 1829, is supposed to have been the last man who knew everything scientific

---

[1] *See* the articles by Forrest (1965) and Lorenz (1965) listed in the bibliography at the end of this chapter.

there was to know. No one since has come forward to dispute
the honor (p. 395).

But if seminar approaches are not particularly new, something of real
novelty was attempted in the 1958 Conference on Style in Language at
Indiana University. On this occasion, psychologists, linguists and cultural
anthropologists were joined by literary critics and philosophers, all of
whom pooled their special resources of knowledge in an effort to seek
answers to one specific problem: the nature and characteristics of style in
literature. In a foreword to the anthology of papers and articles contributed to this seminar, Sebeok (1960) states:

> Out of such discussions, it was hoped, might come a clearer
> perception of what literature is and what the constituent
> elements of style are. If literature is an aspect of behavior, is
> there any way in which these groups can reach a meeting of
> the minds on the nature of this behavior and its place in
> human culture? How can the understandings of one group be
> used to shed light on those of other groups and on the whole
> problem of style in literature?

With the visual acuity conferred by hindsight, it seems almost inevita-
ble that the convergence of mutual interests among psychologists, literary critics and linguists would come eventually to a sharp focus on the
question of style. In much the same way that psycholinguistics aims at
bridging the gap between linguistics and psychology, modern stylistics is
a borderline discipline that lies astride the boundary between linguistics
and literary criticism. More importantly, many of the problems which
claim the interests of the psycholinguist are restatements, in slightly
altered form, of problems that have long absorbed the attention of
students of style.

THE PROBLEMS OF STYLE

Language has been called a graveyard for dead metaphors. If this
description has any validity, the word *style* itself must be counted among
the illustrations. Originally it meant "a writing implement"; but, adds the
Oxford Dictionary (with unintentional irony), it could also be used "as a
weapon of offence, for stabbing, etc." This latter meaning may have
influenced Flaubert to "imagine a style which would enter like a stiletto
into the idea expressed."

In the past—and, particularly, the recent past—much has been written about the "subtle and elusive puzzle" of style. If one is seeking answers to specific questions he encounters as a result of his own literary endeavors, he cannot help but be frustrated by most of what he reads. He may find something intriguing about Buffon's widely quoted (and misquoted) utterance: "Le style c'est l'homme même," but discover little opportunity for a practical application of this dictum. He might experience some sense of uplift in Whitehead's assertion that style is "the ultimate morality of the mind," without being able to turn this observation to advantage in the preparation of an article, short story or technical report.

If he searches farther afield, he will discover that a prominent anthropologist like Kroeber (1957) views style as "a strand in a culture or civilization: a coherent, self-consistent way of expressing certain behavior or performing certain kinds of acts"—a formulation which seems to place literary style in the same category of behavioral consistency as mass calisthenics or synchronized swimming.

He may be more mystified than enlightened to learn that an expert in communications theory like Bloch (1953) sees the style of a discourse as "the message carried by the frequency distributions and transitional probabilities of its linguistic features, especially as they differ from those of the same features in the language as a whole" (p. 40), and be willing to argue that style is not always a deviation from some norm but may, indeed, represent the *achievement* of a norm.

Or he may find himself compelled to register strong objections to attempts on the part of some writers to divorce style from content or meaning, and insist that style is often equated with vocabulary or lexical choice in ordinary usage. (Such efforts to ignore the semantic dimension of language in favor of the easier regularities of syntax recall Schuchardt's criticism of Ferdinand de Saussure who, he claimed, had tried to divide the theory of coordinates into a theory of the ordinate and a theory of the abscissa.)

With the emergence of stylistics as an autonomous disciple, however, a new perspective on style was introduced. From the outset, writers in modern stylistics have emphasized the necessity for distinguishing between the *style of a language* and the *style of a writer*. In referring to the development of stylistics in the twentieth century, Ullmann (1964) observes that:

> One school of thought was interested in the stylistic resources of particular languages, in the expressive devices which they place at the disposal of the speaker and writer. The other school was more concerned with the use to which

these resources are put in the hands of creative authors (p. 100).

To this distinction it is necessary to add a third element: the complex processes involved in the conscious and unconscious *choice* which provide a basis for the intimate connection between the writer and the expressive features of the language code. What we are dealing with, in brief, are questions of encoding; and it would appear that in this crucially important area of inquiry, the interests of the psycholinguist and the stylist are synonymous.

To describe the stylistic resources of language requires the establishment, classification and evaluation of expressive elements implicit in the particular language code. Says Ullmann (1964):

> For the student of style, 'expressiveness' covers a wide range of linguistic features which have one thing in common: they do not directly affect the meaning of the utterance, the actual information which it conveys. Everything that transcends the purely referential and communicative side of language belongs to the province of expressiveness: emotive overtones, emphasis, rhythm, symmetry, euphony, and also the so-called *'evocative'* elements which place our style in a particular register (literary, colloquial, slangy, etc.) or associate it with a particular milieu (historical, foreign, provincial, professional, etc.) (p. 101).

Research on these features of language has generated an enormous, vital and fascinating literature,[2] and it is regrettable that the limited scope of the present discussion precludes even a cursory review of this material. Those who have special interests in this area of stylistics can find many worthwhile suggestions for further reading in the works of writers like Devoto (1963), Lucas (1962), and Ullmann (1964).

Regarding the stylistic study of individual authors and the complex problems of choice, approaches have been numerous and varied. It would be facile to summarize certain trends that are apparent within this impressive mass of literature and try to identify a *linguistic approach,* a *stylostatistical approach,* and a *psychological approach.* But classifications of this sort, which emphasize particular features of the analyst's orientation at the expense of ignoring others, are apt to prove a hindrance rather than a help to understanding. Instead of burdening the

---

[2] In the area of Romance languages alone, more than two thousand titles have appeared since 1962.

reader with such a latticework of categories, it seems more appropriate to present several psycholinguistic contributions to stylistic research—including several papers introduced at the Indiana University seminar on style—and let the contents of the articles speak for themselves.

VARIETIES OF PSYCHOLINGUISTIC RESEARCH

In the introduction to his paper entitled "Vectors of Prose Style," John B. Carroll (1960) identifies variation as a basic component of style:

> It takes little argument or evidence to secure agreement that there are different manners of writing, and that these differ among themselves not only by virtue of the content or the subject matter treated but also by virtue of a host of 'stylistic' elements which are present in varying degrees in samples of prose. But what, exactly, are these stylistic elements? Ever since man discovered the pleasure of commenting upon his own and others' oral and written compositions, he has been seeking a useful set of pigeonholes for classifying style. The tendency has been for the classifications to proliferate without design or system. *Literary criticism today does not have any well and sharply defined set of elements by which a sample of prose may readily be characterized* (p. 283). (Emphasis added.)

To remedy this need, Carroll proposes an objective investigation of literary style by means of *factor analysis*—a "statistical procedure for identifying and measuring the fundamental dimensions ('vectors') that account for the variation to be observed in any set of phenomena." Encouraged by the fact that this procedure has proven useful to the psychologist in systematic studies of individual differences, Carroll seeks to examine "the relations among a large number of indices of style" in an attempt to "identify the most salient ways of describing stylistic variation in prose."

The materials used in Carroll's study consisted of 150 passages of about 300 words or less chosen from a wide variety of sources: newspaper articles and editorials, novels, sermons, biographies, even some samples of high school compositions. The principal object was to cover the broadest possible range of prose styles and subjects.

These prose samples were then assessed according to both subjective and objective procedures. The objective measures included various "counts, indices and ratios" which were based on the "enumeration of

certain classes of words, clauses, sentences and other linguistic entities."
Subjective measures consisted of a series of 29 semantic differential
rating scales. These 29 scales were all applied to each of the 150
passages; and the SD ratings were made by 8 expert judges. According to
Carroll:

> In all, 68 scores were obtained for each of the 150 passages:
> the 29 averaged ratings of the 8 judges, and 39 objective
> measures . . . The resulting 68 × 150 scores formed the basis
> for the ensuing statistical analysis. The correlation of each
> measure with each other measure was determined—the re-
> sults being exhibited in a very large table with 68 rows and 68
> columns. This *correlation matrix* was then subjected to a
> factor analysis in order to determine how many fundamental
> dimensions would be needed, at a minimum, to account for all
> the inter-relations among the 68 measures (p. 288).

Upon the completion of this rather laborious analysis, Carroll was able to
identify six independent dimensions or "vectors" of style: General Stylistic Evaluation, Personal Affect, Ornamentation, Abstractness, Seriousness
and Characterization versus Narration. About these so-called vectors of
style, the author has a rueful confession to make:

> . . . that even he, after completing the study, remains skep-
> tical whether the dimensions identified here adequately repre-
> sent the aspects of style that truly make the difference be-
> tween great literature and the not so great, or even the aspects
> that serve to differentiate some of the recognized styles of
> writing (p. 284).

While one is disposed to agree with the author's evaluation of his own
project, he is apt to find other aspects of Carroll's study even more
distressing. His assertion that, "Literary criticism today does not have
any well and sharply defined set of elements by which a sample of prose
may readily be characterized," seems to reveal a surprising ignorance of
the achievements of more than a century's work in stylistics. Nor is it
reassuring to find the results of previous stylostatistical analyses dis-
missed in a few sentences. There is no mention, for example, of Herdan's
(1965) inclusive and detailed summary of research on the statistical
properties of language.

Nevertheless, Carroll's investigation has much to commend it as a
significant first step in the introduction of a potentially useful instrument

—factor analysis—for further research in stylistics. In addition, as Carroll (1960) points out:

> . . . the study points to some of the more obvious characteristics of prose which have to be observed, mentioned, and duly noted before the literary critic can really go to work. It injects a semblance of order into the study of 'readability' and suggests certain bases for guiding the teaching of English composition in schools. Further, it provides leads toward the psycholinguistic study of the 'encoding' processes by which the individual translates nonverbal prelinguistic states of behavior into linguistically encoded output (p. 284).

The latter statement might be considered a somewhat technical rephrasing of what we have already identified as the key problem of choice—the possibility of selecting among alternatives or "stylistic variants" on an unconscious or conscious basis—and, as such, bears directly upon the next paper to be considered, a study by Charles E. Osgood (1960) entitled "Some Effects of Motivation on Style of Encoding."

For the purposes of his investigation, Osgood defined style as *"an individual's deviations from norms for the situations in which he is encoding, these deviations being in the statistical properties of those structural features for which there exists some degree of choice in his code"* (p. 293). Using a carefully defined set of hypotheses derived from general behavior theory concerning the possible effects of motivation or drive upon language behavior, Osgood conducted a comparative study of genuine suicide notes and pseudocide notes in an attempt to determine which, if any, features of language code are responsive to qualitative and quantitative differences in motivational state. To control what the author calls "situational style factors," a sample of ordinary letters (from relatives, friends) was secured.

As one might have expected, the results of this investigation indicated that non-suicidal people "can intuit and encode the style of suicidal people to a considerable extent." The writers of these notes, it should be mentioned, were not professional authors in any sense. Unfortunately, no answer could be supplied for what would seem to be an obvious and crucial question: Were the writers of the pseudocide notes able to imitate the style of the suicidal writers by "generating the heightened emotional state and then encoding accordingly," or by the simple process of adopting an encoding style familiar to them from movies, plays, reading, etc.?

Of much greater interest, however, was the finding that certain features of the suicidal style were *not* easily intuited by the pseudocide writers. Says Osgood (1960):

> This applies particularly to the *noun-verb/adjective-adverb ratio* and to Skinner's *mands;* it applies somewhat to the *proportion of ambivalent evaluative assertions* and to the disorganization measures, *structural disturbances* and *length of independent segments.* The nonsuicidal person, asked to produce the note he might write just before taking his own life, *fails* to catch the true suicide's emphasis on simple, non-discriminative action statements, his demanding, command-ing, pleading character, his exaggerated emotional ambiva-lence toward himself and significant others, and his somewhat disorganized or distracted approach to encoding, leading to more errors and shortened, explosive segments. Whether a skilled writer—or perhaps a person who had himself experi-enced the suicidal state without actually taking his own life —would be able to intuit the suicidal state more completely, and thereby encode the style more faithfully, we do not know (pp. 305–06).

The point that should be stressed with respect to Osgood's study, how-ever, has relatively little to do with his success or failure in demon-strating the ability of his pseudocidal assistants to accurately encode according to genuine suicidal intent. The value of his contribution to psy-cholinguistics research on style rests, in the present writer's opinion, on his determined efforts to employ a series of explicit, theoretically derived, and experimentally testable hypotheses within the framework of a rigor-ous and controlled investigation. Whatever subtleties may be lacking in his approach, Osgood has presented us with the kind of psycholinguistic study which developments in the field of stylistics seem to demand.

Traditional methods of scholarship place an equally high premium upon the values of explicit statement, rigorous control and the processes of verification, as the work of Harry and Agathe Thornton (1962) serves to demonstrate. Their study is not only a pace-setting achievement in psycholinguistics for future investigators to emulate; it is also a model of thorough and insightful scholarship. One hesitates to do the Thorntons an injustice by risking a fragmentary and piecemeal review of their study —it should, by all means, be read in its entirety. But perhaps enough can be conveyed in a brief sketch to give some appreciation of their basic conceptions and procedures.

Their study employs a linguistic principle derived from the analysis of literary materials which the authors have identified as the "appositional mode of expression." Using classical Greek and Latin texts, they show how this appositional mode functions in a variety of authors, from Homer to Lucretius. Their concern is with the question of "how thought proceeds or moves" within the context of the literary presentation. As the authors note:

> Our method is to follow each sentence or paragraph or work as it unfolds in time. Thinking, like speaking and listening, requires the incessant redirection of attention, what we call 'movements of attention.' A sentence, for example, expresses the way in which the speaker's attention moves, and provides the clue to the way in which the listener's attention has to move in order to understand him . . . *The outcome of such a method is to show that a number of formal characteristics described in specialised investigations are in fact the result or form attained by one and the same mental process* (p. xi). (Emphasis added.)

In the first two chapters of their book, the Thorntons conduct a detailed analysis of the paratactic style of exposition, distinguishing "linear" from "appositional" modes of thought:

> The linear form of expression, proceeding step by step in an unswerving, swift and pauseless movement, using the simplest only of connecting words, is easily appreciated by us, although we, being used to an analytic and highly constructed language, could hardly write in that manner. A good example of this form of style is the narrative of the return journey of Odysseus and his friends (p. 1).

The appositional mode of expression, on the other hand, is much less familiar to us:

> . . . now and again the flow of events halts and something that has been mentioned is viewed more closely and characterized . . . In each case, we have the bald narrative of events followed by a descriptive adjective or participle, in 'apposition' to (and, of course, agreement with) a person or thing named in that narrative . . . When in this way the initial statement ('statement' in the widest sense) is fully differen-

tiated out into all its details, the thought returns to the beginning, and proceeds from there (pp. 1–2).

Having documented the linguistic principle of apposition with a wealth of insightfully selected literary data, the Thorntons next proceed to discuss the relationship between appositional expression and temporal experience. Here the analysis brings them to a consideration of psychological factors involved in temporal perception and discrimination:

> All utterance involves an experience of time in speaker and listener. What distinguishes appositional utterance is that it is an experience of a minimum of a future that is certainly to be expected and in part predetermined. As for the past, it is not strictly separated from the present as a past that has been and is no more, but it is always close behind the present intensifying and illuminating it . . . Two points emerge from our analysis of the appositional style. Time implied in it is not yet clearly or necessarily differentiated into past, present, and future. What differentiation there is, is rudimentary and partial. Expectation, as we have said, spans a minimum of the future, and the past is felt and experienced so vividly that it seems little removed from the present (pp. 119–20).

The concluding step in their investigation is "to consider whether this time-notion bears any relationship to the early Greek and Roman time-notion as known from other evidence." The reader will undoubtedly find this final chapter the most stimulating and absorbing part of their study, not only from the standpoint of the conclusions they reach on the concrete and qualitative nature of temporal percepts in Greek and Roman experience, but also as a demonstration of sound methodology in scholarship.

SOME TENTATIVE CONCLUSIONS

Now that we have considered a few samples of psycholinguistics research on style and expression, we might entertain a question of two concerning the meaning and significance of the developments represented by these papers. Is it premature to speak of trends in this field, or can we identify certain broad consistencies of viewpoint and approach? Does the psycholinguist have a definite and positive contribution to make in stylistics? If so, what is the nature of this contribution, and what are the most promising directions for further research?

In his review of stylistics, Ullmann (1964) makes the following observation:

> The general impression which emerges from this rapid survey of current trends in stylistics is that of an active and vigorous young science which is still somewhat inchoate and unorganized. There are many experiments, many ideas in ferment; at the same time there exists as yet no accepted terminology nor is there any general agreement on aims and methods. Under the circumstances it would be difficult to draw up anything in the nature of an interim balance-sheet (p. 130).

There is enough in common between stylistics and psycholinguistics to support an indorsement of Ullmann's remarks and relegate the whole problem to long suffering posterity.

Nevertheless, it is possible to take encouragement from T. S. Eliot's persuasive metaphor: "the tower of ivory has been fitted up as a laboratory." This figure expresses both a challenge and a commentary; and perhaps it even supplies part of an answer.

Hyman (1955) closes his critique of critics with a series of entertaining speculations on the Verry Parfait Literary Critic:

> If we could, hypothetically, construct an ideal modern literary critic out of plastics and light metals, his method would be a synthesis of every practical technique or procedure used by his flesh-and-blood colleagues. From all the rival approaches he would borrow as much as could be used in a synthesis without distorting the whole, he would balance one bias or excess or overspecialization against another so that both canceled out, and he was left with only neutral elements adaptable to his purpose (p. 386).

It is an article of faith with psycholinguists that the future of their interdisciplinary field ultimately rests upon younger scientists who, as Osgood and Sebeok (1954) have put it, "maintain in a single nervous system the habits of both sciences."

But Hyman warns that this:

> . . . ideal integration of all modern critical methods into one supermethod could not be on the analogy of stew, with everything thrown at random into the pot, but would have to be on

the analogy of construction, with the structure built up according to an orderly plan on some foundation, or around some skeleton framework (p. 388).

While it seems impossible, at this point, to supply a blueprint for that framework or foundation, it is transparently clear that psycholinguistics can furnish only a share of the preliminary sketches. One must record agreement with Hyman's assertion that:

> Few . . . individual methods or disciplines are even formulated so as to embrace other approaches, and where they are sciences or near-sciences, like psychology and anthropology, or clearly demarcated fields, like scholarship or biography, they obviously could not invade other territories without automatically losing their special character.

Despite the interdisciplinary character of his field—or perhaps, in a curious way, because of it—the psycholinguist must function as a specialist in any joint undertakings.

If these limitations are understood and accepted, it appears possible to give some cautious and highly personal answers to the questions raised earlier about the nature and direction of contributions from psycholinguistics to a deeper understanding of stylistic phenomena. In offering these observations, it is necessary to emphasize their idiosyncratic character.

To generalize from a dangerously small sample, we may note the following features of consistency in psycholinguistics research on style and expression:

1. Vigorous attempts to develop new methods of investigation which incorporate the specialized knowledge of several disciplines, and efforts to adapt older, more standard techniques to meet the requirements of the phenomena under examination.

2. An interest in rephrasing in a more precise form the questions with which traditional approaches in stylistics have dealt, i.e., in a form that lends itself to verification or refutation.

3. The readiness to use, wherever possible, empirical data supplied by systematic investigations, including laboratory or "brass instrument" studies.

4. An increasing recognition of the need and responsibility

for coordinating activities with those in other areas of academic or professional interest.

It has been said that no one ever erected a monument to a committee. However, at a time when powerful forces are being exerted within psychology to choose its models from reductionism, these signs of receptivity toward extracurricular contact can be seen as a source of strengthening the artistic and humane values without which any science is bound to develop sterility. Miller (1965) seems to be suggesting something along the same lines:

> If we accept a realistic statement of the problem [of language acquisition] I believe we will also be forced to accept a more cognitive approach to it: to talk about hypothesis testing instead of discrimination learning, about the evaluation of hypotheses instead of the reinforcement of responses, about rules instead of habits, about productivity instead of generalization, about innate and universal human capacities instead of special methods of teaching vocal responses, about symbols instead of conditioned stimuli, about sentences instead of words or vocal noises, about linguistic structure instead of chains of responses—in short, about language instead of learning theory.
>
> The task of devising a cognitive production model for language users is difficult enough without wearing blinders that prevent us from seeing what the task really is. If the hypothetical constructs that are needed seem too complex and arbitrary, too improbable and mentalistic, then you had better forego the study of language. For language is just that—complex, arbitrary, improbable, mentalistic—and no amount of wishful theorizing will make it anything else.
>
> In a word, what I am trying to say, what all my preliminary admonitions boil down to, is simply this: Language is exceedingly complicated. Forgive me for taking so long to say such a simple and obvious thing (p. 20).

REFERENCES

BLOCH, B. Linguistic structure and linguistic analysis. In A. A. Hill (Ed.), *Report of the fourth annual round table meeting on linguistics and language teaching.* Washington, D.C., 1953.

BROWN, R. *Words and things.* New York: The Free Press, 1958.

CARROLL, J. B. Vectors of prose style. In T. A. Sebeok (Ed.), *Style in language*. Cambridge, Massachusetts: MIT Press, 1960.

DEVOTO, G. *Linguistics and literary criticism*. New York: S. F. Vanni, 1963.

FORREST, D. V. Poiesis and the language of schizophrenia. *Psychiatry*, 1965, 28, 1–18.

HERDAN, G. *Language as choice and chance*. Groningen, Holland: P. Noordhoff, 1965.

HYMAN, S. E. *The armed vision*. NewYork: The Viking Press, 1955.

KROEBER, A. L. *Style and civilizations*. Ithaca, New York: Cornell University Press, 1957.

LORENZ, M. Criticism as approach to schizophrenic language. *Archives of General Psychiatry*, 1965, 9, 235–245.

LUCAS, F. L. *Style*. New York: Collier Books, 1962.

MILLER, G. A. The psycholinguists: On the new scientists of language. *Encounter*, 1964, 23, 29–37.

MILLER, G. A. Some preliminaries to psycholinguistics. *American Psychologist*, 1965, 20, 15–20.

MURRY, J. M. *The problem of style*. London: Oxford University Press, 1956.

OSGOOD, C. E. and SEBEOK, T. A. (Eds.), *Psycholinguistics: A survey of theory and research problems*. Supplement to the International Journal of American Linguistics, 1954, 20.

OSGOOD, C. E. Some effects of encoding upon style of encoding. In T. A. Sebeok (Ed.), *Style in language*. Cambridge, Massachusetts: MIT Press, 1960.

SAPORTA, S. (Ed.), *Psycholinguistics*. New York: Holt, Rinehart and Winston, 1961.

SPITZER, L. *Linguistics and literary history*. Princeton, New Jersey: Princeton University Press, 1948.

THORNTON, H. and THORNTON, A. *Time and style: A psycho-linguistic essay in classical literature*. London: Methuen, 1962.

ULLMANN, S. *Language and style*. New York: Barnes and Noble, 1964.

CHAPTER 14

Nonverbal Communication: Kinesics and Gestural Phenomena

Fie, fie upon her!
There's language in her eyes, her cheek, her lip,
Nay, her foot speaks; her wanton spirits look out
At every joint and motive of her body.

Shakespeare: *Troilus and Cressida*, Act IV, Sc. 5.

The LANGUAGE of words and numbers is the medium through which the accumulated knowledge and experience of our culture is transmitted from one generation to the next. The importance we attach to this transmission process is underlined by the fact that formal instruction in the schools is almost exclusively cut to patterns supplied by verbal language. Our educational practice is to spend some ten to twenty years indoctrinating students in specific ways of speaking, reading, writing and calculating, but without a corresponding regard for training along non-verbal, analogic lines. Thus we acquire a narrow orientation to solve complex and technical problems, but fail to develop a real capacity for understanding many of the actions, gestures and emotional expressions of other human beings. One anthropologist (LaBarre, 1947) bluntly charges that "Americans are characteristically illiterate in the area of gesture language" (p. 64). Another anthropologist (Hall, 1959) points out how our inability to read the "silent language" of other cultures has ntributed materially to the hostility and suspiciousness with which many of our actions abroad are greeted. Our bewilderment and chagrin at the growth of the "Ugly American" image have signaled the crucial need for fuller comprehension of the complex processes of nonverbal communication.

Gestures have a variety of uses. They can be employed to represent nonverbal substitutes for words, emphasize meanings or to express feelings. Gestures, in themselves, cannot usually gratify any immediate bodily need, nor can they be isolated from the verbal components of speech. Isolation of the gesture may result in a misjudgment of the communicative act.

The development of nonverbal communication is intrinsically related to developmental processes and changes in the motor system of the child. Nonverbal means of communication predominate during the first year of life. Despite the fact that the symbolic processes in the child's mind may be more advanced than his capacity for communication by means of words or actions, the child literally "speaks" with his entire body.

The relationship between gesture and the origin of speech is a source of dispute among language theorists and cultural anthropologists. Some writers have hypothesized that articulate speech is directly related to gestural activity. Their argument is that animal sounds are a product of movement of the oral musculature. Paget (in Eisenson, et al., 1963) elaborated oral-gesture theory as follows:

> The earliest human language most likely consisted of gesture signs. Through bodily movements . . . primitive man was probably able to express a variety of ideas and feelings, and to evoke responses from others. With the development of gesture, there was concomitant though unconscious development of laryngeal sounds (p. 15).

LaBarre, however, disagrees with this formulation. He states (in Sebeok, 1964) that the theory skips from the purely muscular gesture to the specifically vocal muscular reaction, leaving a chasm between the two. He maintains that one would have to postulate some kind of meaningful vocalization as an intermediate step.

A further breakdown of the origin of gestures (as opposed to those associated with speech predominating) was proposed by Holloway (1951). He suggests that some gestures are clearly acquired through learning and may contribute to the achievement of the same or similar ends as those of words. They may be presented to the individual through verbal definitions and explanations, and they may be offered either by themselves or in connection with some verbal utterance, as synonymous in meaning with some particular form of verbal expression. A second category of gestures includes those which could have been learned originally but may be acquired even by a person who is devoid of language, e.g., smiling, laughing or frowning.

Gestures are language. They may be determined by the way the human body is constructed, even those gestures that border on reflex and are necessarily elaborated in an interpersonal and social context. The individual, however, may develop his own personal idiosyncratic way or form that may be only discernible to those with whom he is in intimate contact. Their understanding is also dependent upon the familiarity one has with the broad spectrum of communication modes within a given culture. Like his words, the speaker's gestures derive from the speech community of which he is a member and should reflect something of this source. The observable components of speech are produced and controlled by the individual; consequently, they become his gestures.

The systematic study of gestures has made use of spatiotemporal and linguistic approaches. Efron (in Ruesch and Kees, 1964) has recommended that the formal analysis of gesture should include a spatiotemporal description, which includes such classifications as the parts of the body involved, the type and form of motion, the speed of movement and the transfer of gesture from one part of the body to another. Also of primary interest and concern is the linguistic aspect of gestures, particularly those which may be used as substitutes for words, e.g., when a person waves goodbye, points a direction or places his hand behind his ear as if to say "louder please." Within such situations, the accurate understanding of these movements must be based on previous agreement between persons. Gestures, however, may also be used as accompaniments to words, e.g., a person may give a passerby directions and indicate the location by illustrative movements of his hand.

Also, as Ruesch and Kees (1964) observe:

> Gestures may express both appreciation and sensuousness, as when two hands are curbed in the air to suggest an attractive female shape. Conversely, gestures may be used also as devices of punctuation conveying such abstract concepts as rhythm, timing, acceleration, or emphasis (p. 77).

Many types of occupations, such as surveying, radio production or construction have specific gestural languages of their own, since the verbal communication of the human voice may be hindered through noise, or distance. Certain social situations involve the discretion of verbal sounds and use of gestures becomes more mandatory as in hunting expeditions or wartime maneuvers among the military.

NONVERBAL CODIFICATION

Ruesch (in Smith, 1966) postulates three major categories of nonverbal codification: *sign, action* and *object language.* Sign language:

> . . . includes those forms of codification in which words, numbers and punctuation signs have been supplanted by gestures; these vary from the 'monosyllabic' gesture of the hitchhiker, to such complete systems as the language of the deaf (p. 209).

Action language comprises all movements that are not used exclusively as signals, e.g., walking and drinking. Object language includes all "intentional and nonintentional display of material things," such as machines, art objects and the human body. These three nonverbal means of communication differ with respect to the specific sensory modalities required for transmission. Silent sign language is perceived exclusively by the eye, whereas action language may be perceived by both the eye and the ear, and also mediated by the senses of touch, temperature and pain. Object language further includes the olfactory and gustatory senses.

These three types of nonverbal language also differ in effectiveness depending upon the distance between the participants in the communication. Sign and action languages depend on immediacy, requiring the persons to be within visual range of one another. Object language, however, closely resembles written language to the extent that a transmitter and perceiver need not be visible to one another in order for communication to be successfully completed.

Closely related to action language are sign language and gesture. Over the centuries every social group has developed systems of communication in which particular words, signs and gestures have been assigned communicative significance. There are, as stated before, gestures that assume the auxiliary role of providing emphasis, timing and direction. Because such denotation systems are not bound to phonetics, they enable persons who speak different languages to communicate with each other in ways analogous to the pictographic symbolizations that cut across verbal language barriers.

Certain social situations call for certain gestures. Where rapid motion is involved, gestures are mandatory because limitations of time would prevent a verbally coded message from being understood. Thus the language of traffic is based almost entirely upon nonverbal signals, such as the hand signal used by drivers to indicate direction. In addition, gestures may be employed whenever verbally coded messages prove inadequate on other grounds. A good deal of humor depends for its effects on the notion that gestures are more universal and so can convey ideas and moods when words fail.

Gestures are also used when particular kinds of verbal expression would be considered obscene or in bad taste. The dual nature of verbal and nonverbal communication makes it possible for the human being to create impressions based upon differences between what he expresses in words and what he communicates through actions and gestures. Hence, a person who integrates both the nonverbal components of language, those of action and gestures, and the verbal message has advantage over the person who selectively responds to only one, since he loses much information in the social situation. By doing this, he may misinterpret the message due to possible incongruity between the two components. A person who tends to solve incongruent relationships by disregarding part of the message is less capable of successful communication in society. Ruesch (in Smith, 1966) has noted that what we call "mental illness" is closely associated with disturbances in sign behavior, language and communication. Aberrations in nonverbal sign behavior tend to accompany more severe and longer psychopathological conditions than those which occur in verbal sign behavior. As Needles (1959) found in relation to mental functions, when an individual passes a certain emotional peak, speech breaks down and nonverbal communication (most commonly through hand gesticulation) becomes important as a means of communication.

Gesture languages are found in many parts of the world, and sometimes exist as a separate system where, for some reason, oral language is not readily possible or desirable, such as the system of gestures used by the deaf, certain monastic orders and some North American Indian tribes. These systems so resemble one another as to almost constitute a universal language.

Gestures like shaking hands in greeting and waving all seem very natural to us as Americans, yet they do not seem so to people in other countries. The gesture is only a significant means of communication when two persons attach the same meaning to the gesture; the person who initiates the gesture and the one receiving or perceiving it. The following mixtures of cross-cultural gestures representing "greeting" quoted from Hiller (in Lindesmith, 1951) serves to illustrate the shared and conventional character of human gestures:

Among the Wanyika, people meet by grasping hands and pressing their thumbs together; dwellers in the region of the Niger join their right hands and separate them with a pull so that a snapping noise is made by thumb and fingers. The handshake of the Arab seems to be a scuffle in which each tries to raise to his lips the hand of the other. The Ainus draw their hands from the shoulders and down the arms to the fingertips of the person greeted, or they rub their hands together . . . Polynesians stroke their own faces with the other person's hands . . . The Fuegians in saluting friends hug 'like the grip of a bear.' Some peoples greet by placing one arm around the neck of the person saluted and chucking him under the chin, or encircling his neck with their arms . . . Among the Polynesians, Malays, Burmese, Lapps, and others —a usual salute is that of smelling each other's cheeks p. 45).

These above gestures constitute not only sign language but also and mainly action language. Any observant traveler notes large and small variations in the gestures and other motor habits of different regions.

Certainly the expression of emotions and the circumstances arousing particular emotions vary culturally. A vivid example is presented by LaBarre (1947):

The sticking out of the tongue among Europeans (often at the same time 'making a face') is an insulting, almost obscene act of provocative challenge and mocking contempt for the adversary, so undignified as to be used only by children. In Bengali statues of the dread black mother goddess, Kali, the tongue is protruded to signify great raging and anger and shock; but the Chinese of the Sung dynasty protruded the tongue playfully to pretend to mock terror, as to make 'fun of,' the ridiculous and unfeared anger of another person. Modern Chinese in South China at least, protrude the tongue for a moment and then retract it to express embarrassment at a *faux pas*.

Kissing, as is well known, is in the Orient an act of private love-play and arouses only disgust when indulged in publicly.

In the language of the gesture all over the world there are varying mixtures of the physiologically based response and the purely cultural response, and it is frequently difficult to analyze out and segregate the two.

KINESICS

The twist of the foot, the interlacing of the fingers, the slump of the shoulder, the slant of the hip, the curl of the lip, the furrow of the brow, the direction of the gaze and the tilt of the head—all of these physical actions communicate nonverbally (Ekman, 1965). More specifically, they are "kinesic" forms of nonverbal communication dealing with postural-gestural cues as a source of communicative information. Kinesics, a term introduced by Birdwhistell, is generally the "systematic study of how one communicates through body movements and gestures" (Birdwhistell, 1955, p. 10). More precisely, it emphasizes the patterned and learned nature of aspects of body motion and their "independent" communicative value (Birdwhistell, 1963). This last point only serves to underline that body motion functions in a larger capacity than as a subsidiary to verbal communication. Rather than merely enhancing verbal communication, body motion is of equal importance to the understanding of the communication process. The basic assumptions underlying the study of kinesics have been outlined by Birdwhistell (in Sebeok, 1964):

1. Like other events in nature, no body movement or expression is without meaning in the context in which it appears.

2. Like other aspects of human behavior, body posture, movement and facial expression are patterned and, thus, subject to systematic analysis.

3. While recognizing the possible limitations imposed by particular biological substrata, until otherwise demonstrated, the systematic body motion of the members of a community is considered a function of the social system to which the group belongs.

4. Visible body activity like audible acoustic activity systematically influences the behavior of other members of any particular group.

5. Until otherwise demonstrated such behavior will be considered to have an investigable communicational function.

6. The meanings derived therefrom are functions both of the behavior and of the operations by which it is investigated.

7. The particular biological system and the special life experiences of any individual will contribute idiosyncratic elements to his kinesic system, but the individual or symptomatic quality of these elements can only be assessed following the analysis of the larger system of which his is a part (p. 158).

According to Birdwhistell, the status of "gestures" for kinesic analysis has been widely misinterpreted:

> Technically gestures are the stereotyped aspects of kime-morphs (a complex of abstracted motion particles from more than one body area) often a clear substitute for linguistic behavior (i.e., point, nod, head-shake, or hand-wave). (Sebeok, 1964, p. 159).

There were two senses advocated by Birdwhistell in which the meaning of the gesture should be analyzed. These are:

> . . . the situational context within a given cultural or sub-cultural setting, and the context provided by the paralinguistic kinesic and no doubt other as yet unanalyzed subsystemic materials which may or may not be present (in Sebeok, et al., 1964, p. 160).

While there is still a relative dearth of empirical studies in kinesics, a number of investigations have been reported in the literature which deal with body movements and gestures as a source of information in communication. Their subject is thus common to that of kinesics. However, in passing, it is important to note that this is the only connection that should be drawn between these studies and kinesics. For only in the general aspect of subject matter are they comparable with kinesics. A fuller study of kinesics reveals its more specific theoretical and methodological approach to the study of patterned bodily motion. This particular approach is adopted only by a minority of the investigators whose work we shall review in the remaining section of this chapter.

Beyond their mutual acceptance of bodily movements as the object of investigation, the studies tend to group themselves in terms of their differing conclusions about "what" is communicated by bodily gestures. Dittman (1962), Dittman, Parloff, and Boomer (1965), Ekman (1964; 1965b), Sainsbury (1955) and Thompson and Meltzer (1964) are concerned with the bodily cues revealing information about the interpersonal relationship between communicants. Postural cues as sources of information about role behavior interest Rosenberg and Langer (1965). Finally, Rosenfield (1966) looks at bodily movement which functions as an instrumental affiliative act.

Perhaps an even clearer organization might result from a categorization of these studies according to fundamental differences in methodology—the "traditional" versus the "contextual analysis" approach (Scheflen, 1965). The customary approach in psychological research involves a pre-study decision about what elements of behavior will be selected as variables. This is precisely what is done by the authors cited above—with the exception of Scheflen. They decide what behaviors they will look at (for example, facial or body expression) and set up a procedure whereby they can measure and count these behaviors and in this way derive the meaning of behavior. Using such techniques as free associations and judgment tasks, in which judges determine by intuition the meaning of behaviors in an interaction, the studies derive meaning from the qualities of the event itself (Scheflen, 1965). Meaning of a particular nonverbal body behavior comes from the judges' determination of it. Thus, in situations subject to varying degrees of control, judges are asked to rate the body cues on a particular dimension. Also the behavior of the judges being studied or the body cues being investigated may be correlated with other activities to discover the meaning behind the kinesic behavior. Behaviors are measured and counted, charts and statistics are presented, and the meaning of the interaction is abstracted from the statistical data on the judgment task.

In contrast to this rigorously statistical, judgmental, task-oriented approach to bodily movement, Birdwhistell and Scheflen study kinesic activity using the procedure of "contextual analysis." Contextual analysis is rooted in general systems theory, according to which the organization of living systems is conceptualized as a hierarchy of successively larger units. The visually sensible elements of kinesic behavior are examined "for structural configurations as they appear in the stream of behavior" (Scheflen, 1965, p. 246). The completely free stream of behavior is viewed. Posed behavior or experimentally controlled parts of interaction are not studied as they are in the traditionally oriented approach. The meaning of the behavior emerges from its function in the larger systems not in the event itself. The experimenter does not ask what does this gesture mean, but rather how does it fit into the interaction of the larger system (Scheflen, 1964). He does not measure and count behavioral events per se, but rather looks at the larger picture. Instead of charts and statistics, the results are simply descriptions and abstractions. The two groups of studies, then, reveal a fundamental difference in how they view behavior. The traditionalist watches behavioral events in restricted interactional processes and the contextual analyst interprets the behavior only in its full structural context. And this theoretical discrepancy leads to a second split in methodology. The traditionalist counts and quantifies behaviors in statistical presentations, whereas the contextual analyst gives behavioral descriptions (Scheflen, 1965).

TRADITIONALLY ORIENTED STUDIES OF NONVERBAL COMMUNICATION

In the interests of discovering possible interrelationships between emotion and verbal expressive activity, Sainsbury (1955) measured spontaneous gestural movements made by patients during psychiatric interviews in which topics judged to be disturbing or nondisturbing were discussed. His subjects included 16 depression and anxiety patients.

Recognizing that "spontaneous movements are closely dependent on emotional states," Sainsbury hypothesized that "gestural activity of patients will increase if they are affectively disturbed during the interview" (1955, p. 459). An electromyograph measured the action potential of the patient's gestural movements and an integrator synchronized them with tape recordings of the accompanying speech during the thirty minute interview. By concealing some of the recorder equipment in an adjoining room, he hoped to reduce self-conscious inhibition of gestural activity (p. 461). The interview was structurally planned to begin and end with a discussion of topics thought to be nondisturbing for the patient. During the intermediate stress periods, preselected problems of the patient were set forth for discussion.

A comparison of the number of body movements during periods rated as disturbing and undisturbing revealed that movement was greater in the disturbing period and that the differences were significant in 14 out of 16 interviews. The author also compared the proportion of body moves made to each topic and again found the gestural movement increased significantly during discussion of the disturbing topic in nearly every instance. In locating passages of affective states and measuring accompanying body movement, Sainsbury found movements consistently more numerous within periods marked by resentment and indignation, with passages evocative of anxiety also running up high movement scores. Finally, four patients were re-interviewed and it was found that topics accompanied by most gestures in the first interview were likewise accompanied by most gestures in the second interview. Although perhaps not terribly specific, these findings express something about the what (i.e., emotions) of kinesic communication and the how (i.e., amount of movement) of this type of communication. As a conclusive statement about gestural movement, Sainsbury suggests that one may infer "that the use of gesture increases with affective disturbance. Whether this is more the case with some affects than others did not clearly emerge from the results" (p. 468). Suggestions of this sort are only hinted at by findings such as the consistent accompaniment of a large number of gestures to emotional states like resentment.

The relationship between body movements and moods in patients' interviews was studied by Dittman (1962). In developing his nonverbal variables for use in "this interaction research in psychotherapy," Dittman studied frequency of body movement as it related to stated mood or feeling. His procedure marked a technical advance over that of Sainsbury in the employment of motion picture recording techniques. He also differed from Sainsbury in his choice of postural-gestural cues for study. Whereas Sainsbury concentrated on movements of the hands, Dittman studied three body areas (i.e., hands, head and leg movements) within five stated moods of the patient. "Frequency of movements differentiated these moods reliably, and an interaction effect appeared between mood and body area" (p. 480). Dittman described this interaction by showing that patterns of body movement differ across body areas for different moods. The depressed mood, for instance, revealed few movements of head and hands but many leg movements. These findings reveal that postural-gestural cues are informatively related to mood in that certain bodily cues are instrumental in showing feeling state.

Thompson and Meltzer (1964) studied communication of emotional intent by facial expression; whereas other authors studied spontaneous, interactional flow of bodily movements in the expression of emotion, the interest of these investigators lay in ascertaining the extent to which "expressors" can convey to judges (students), via facial expressions alone, their emotional content. Deliberate ability to express emotion is emphasized. The experimenters focus on the variable of expressor behavior rather than the behavior of judges. Differences in the ability of expressors to recognize and portray affect and possible personality correlates to such ability were of primary concern to the authors.

Choosing from a list of ten emotions: happiness, love, surprise, fear, determination, disgust, contempt, suffering, anger and bewilderment, judges decided what emotions untrained expressors were portraying. There were two enactments of each emotion over four judges, and thus eight separate scores for each emotion comprised its "enactment score." The results show that in over three-fifths of the trials, expressors were successful in communicating the emotion with this figure varying between 38 percent successful for contempt to 76 percent successful for happiness. It was found that contempt was less adequately communicated than love, happiness, fear, determination, surprise, bewilderment or anger. Thirdly, although the correlation was modest, expressor success in enactment of one emotion predicted success in further portrayals. However, any expected personality correlate of these individual differences as to success and failure in enactment ability failed to appear.

A final result involved the confusion between certain expressed emotions. Facial cues for certain affects were evidently more easily confused with another emotion. For instance, judges' ratings showed that contempt was easily confused with anger, disgust with anger and digust with contempt. Although the focus in this experiment is expressor behavior and not judge behavior, it certainly reveals the informative ability of kinesic activity, particularly with respect to emotional communication.

In a study of body position, facial expression and verbal behavior during interviews Ekman (1965a) dealt with the communicative value of these kinesic activities by measuring an observer's ability to detect a relationship between nonverbal and verbal interview behavior. He examined spontaneous interactive nonverbal behavior of the interviewee in the standard stress interview situation with its alternate ten minute stress and "catharsis" periods.

Ekman objects to the use of posed behavior (e.g., Thompson and Meltzer). Rather he feels:

> . . . any demonstration of communication or information [through posed nonverbal behavior situation] is not surprising, and [he is] doubtful of its relevance to the question of whether less artificiality induced nonverbal cues communicate accurate information (p. 391).

He also feels that the few studies which sampled spontaneous behavior "provoked subjects with bizarre stimuli," giving them an unbalanced picture of nonverbal behavior to judge (p. 391). Usually, the nature of the interpersonal relationship imposes constraints on the manner and extent of the nonverbal expression. Thus it is important to view elements of spontaneous interactive behavior and even more advantageous if bodily motions in action could be observed as opposed to still photographs of bodily movements. Ekman's study also differed from previous experiments to the extent that he dealt with variations in nonverbal behavior as a "communicative stimulus" and studied the observer's response to this stimulus. Previous studies treated nonverbal body behavior as a response to some other factor, such as the interview structure or patient's mood. Thus, Sainsbury and Dittman report relationships between changes in nonverbal behavior and changes in content and structure of the interview. They do not study the related question "what is communicated to observer by a change in nonverbal behavior?" (p. 296). Secondly, interjudge agreement about what is communicated, which is the principal concern of other studies, is rejected by Ekman and replaced by an emphasis on the interjudge accuracy in understanding communication through kinesic activities. Thus, his methodology focuses on having judges match nonverbal behavioral photos and verbal speech excerpts from previously recorded and synchronized interviews. More specifically, judges were presented with one short written speech sample and a pair of photos, either one or both being from one of the two periods of stress or catharsis. They were asked to match one photo with the appropriate speech sample.

In a series of four experiments, all using a similar procedure, Ekman tested a number of hypotheses dealing with judgmental discrimination between these photos and speech samples. Generally he varied the nonverbal bodily cue given the judge over the experiments among three cues: head, body and whole.

In the first experiment, Ekman tested the hypothesis that "untrained observers can discriminate from pairs of photos one taken during a given speech sample" (p. 297). The results confirmed the hypothesis. The second experiment tested whether "untrained observers can choose from pairs of photos one which is taken during a given speech sample when responding to pictures as a whole" (p. 297). He found that judges could accurately match whole photos and speech; and in fact, later it was found that the level of accuracy was greater when matching the whole person with verbal behavior than when matching body cues and speech. The third study tested whether or not observers could match speech with body cues. This was also confirmed.

Because different groups of judges were used for experiments one to three, no information was obtained about the relative accuracy in matching speech and photos as a function of the specific nonverbal cue presented. This is the subject of the fourth experiment which hypothesizes "that judges can choose from a pair of photos the one which is taken from a given speech sample when responding to either head or body position cues" (p. 297). A greater level of accuracy was obtained with the head cues than with body cues.

The study generally concludes that spontaneous body positioning and facial expression have a special communicative value in relation to the verbal behavior and are not just "noise." They especially mediate information about "momentary changes between stress and catharsis during an interaction consistent with concomitant verbal behavior" (p. 726). The amount of information does seem to vary according to the type of kinesic activity presented, since Ekman finds that the accuracy in matching materials was related to the type of cue information provided—head, body or whole person.

Following this first series of studies, Ekman conducted another series of ten experiments dealing with the communicative value of body gestural behavior with regard to information about the quality of the interpersonal relationship. Questions were raised concerning whether nonverbal behavior can accurately communicate information about the quality of the relationship, and whether it is capable of reflecting change in the relationship. Behavior in a standard stress situation was observed, as in the first series of studies. The judgmental task differed somewhat; judges were not asked to match photos and speech. Rather, using photos, they were instructed to respond in terms of how the interviewer was reacting to the individual.

In the first experiment, judges determined the phase of the interview apparent in the picture from a photograph containing both the interviewer and the subject. It was shown that judges can distinguish accurately stress and final periods. Pictures in the second experiment contained only the subject and the elimination of the interviewer cues proved to decrease accuracy. Judges in the third study judged several random photos of interviewers and subjects together, but were deprived of information derived from a sequential ordering of non-verbal behavior. Accuracy of judgment was significant beyond the level of chance. Experiment four was similar to three except that the photos contained the subject alone. Differences in accuracy of judgment were found between the photos of interview A and interview B, with greater accuracy in interview A. Experiments five and six reported the finding that judges can accurately distinguish the interview period on the basis of nonverbal cues, but that the accuracy of the judge varied over the stimulus persons presented. Results suggest that accuracy is affected by: (1) whether interviewer and subject or subject alone is shown; (2) which particular stimulus is shown, either interview A or B; and (3) which method of judgmental task is used, either a single photo or many photos.

Experiments seven through nine deal with the possible contaminating effects of practice upon the judgmental task. First, it is shown that untrained judges can accurately determine whether randomly selected and ordered series of photographs were taken during stress or catharsis periods. Stability over time of judgments of nonverbal behavior was tested as judges rated a random series of photos, then after a four-day interval rated the same series in a different random order. It was concluded that potential practice effects on accuracy were contaminated by individual differences of observers in judging behaviors. And although a positive correlation was found between judging ability across stimulus persons, it cannot be concluded that an increase in accuracy over trials results from practice over trials. A final study in this group involved an accuracy measure of judgments with a substantially increased and sequentially ordered sample of nonverbal behavior. No greater accuracy was obtained with sequential cues. Ekman concludes with a discussion of three kinds of information transmitted by nonverbal, postural-gestural cues: (1) information about subject affects; (2) knowledge of the interviewer's behavior; and (3) information about the quality of the interpersonal relationship between the interviewer and subjects. In fact, "the nonverbal behavior systematically changes as a function of gross modification in the quality of the relationship between the two people."

A third major study by Ekman (1965,b) involved four experiments showing that head and body nonverbal cues provide different affective information. Again, as in his earlier studies, he sampled nonverbal behavior in five standardized stress interviews as it occurred during the ongoing, verbally communicative, interpersonal relationship. Since previous studies evidence the communicative potential of nonverbal behavior as a carrier of diverse messages, Ekman wished to begin to specify the "link between particular nonverbal cues and the inferences drawn by an observer" (p. 726). By showing two broad categories of nonverbal cues (i.e., the head and the body) taken from photographs of the same stimulus person to a common group of observers and by subsequently comparing observers' ability to draw the same set of inferences about the affect from each of the two sources, the experiment aimed at specifying something about the link between cue and inference. More precisely, the hypothesis tested was:

> Head cues carry information primarily about what particular affect is being experienced . . . but provide relatively little information about the intensity of the affect or the level of arousal; body cues reverse this pattern communicating information primarily about the level of arousal or degree of intensity of the affective experience, but provide relatively few cues about what particular affect is being experienced (p. 727).

Schlosberg's three dimensions of affect—pleasantness dimension, a dimension of attending to or rejecting stimulation, and an intensity dimension from sleep to tension—provided a framework for testing the hypothesis. (Actually in testing the hypothesis, only the pleasantness-unpleasantness dimension and sleep-tension dimension were employed. Because these two dimensions have been demonstrated empirically to be independent, the hypothesis would now expect more information relevant to the pleasantness-unpleasantness dimension to be available from head cues and more information about sleep-tension to be available from body cues.) In each experiment, three separate groups of judges each received cne cue version: head, body or whole person. Each judge was required to rate the emotion being experienced by the person in each photograph on each of Schlosberg's three dimensions.

Coefficients of concordance determined the extent of judge agreement in rating different cue versions on the two dimensions and offered support for the hypothesis. Correlations between judgments of the head and body on each dimension showed nonsignificant correlations, providing additional support for the hypothesis. Because moderate correlations between the head and whole on the sleep-tension ratings were found, it was necessary to qualify the hypothesis to admit that some information about sleep-tension is communicated by the head. Ekman also questioned whether known changes in interpersonal interaction could be inferred from head and body cues. A difference in pleasantness-unpleasantness ratings between stress and catharsis photographs was expected when head judgments were measured. Conversely, a difference in sleep-tension between the two types of photographic stimuli was expected when measuring body cues. Pleasantness scores did differ for the head and not for the body. However, the predicted results did not occur on the sleep-tension dimension. A possible explanation is that "the two interview experiences [were] characterized by the same level of arousal" (p. 732). Thus the finding does not necessarily contradict the hypothesis. In conclusion, Ekman explains that only one class of information (i.e., affect) has been considered in this study. Further studies of other information classes and further subdivision into more specific cues within each of these stimulus classes (i.e., body and head) are needed (p. 735).

Dittman, Parloff and Boomer (1965) undertook to determine whether observers "differentiate and respond to bodily cues as distinct from facial cues" (p. 239). Their method placed facial and bodily cues in conflict so that an observer response to facial cues might be influenced by an incongruent message from the body.

The study emphasized the recognition of bodily cues rather than the recognition of subtleties of any inferences which might be drawn. For this reason, the experimental discriminatory task remained quite simple. Two groups of judges—psychotherapists and professional dancers—assessed the feeling state of subjects shown in short motion pictures on a continuum from pleasantness to unpleasantness. It is interesting to note that, unlike previous studies which employed still photographs, the Dittman study made use of motion picture segments of bodily motion. Three different series of these films, each with twenty segments, were developed. Fifteen segments were rated crucial by the authors and five others were inserted as buffers to reduce the judges' memory of specific segments. In five crucial segments, subject expression was pleasant for both face and body (P-P); in five, unpleasant affect was expressed in both (U-U);

and in the final five the subject's face expressed pleasant affect while the body expressed unpleasant affect (P-U) (p. 240). Cues were presented to the judges in one of two ways—whole person and body. Three random orders of these twenty segments comprised the three series.

An analysis of variance revealed the following significant results:

1. a difference between groups of judges;
2. a difference between affective stimulus types P-P, P-U and U-U;
3. a difference between methods of presentation;
4. an interaction between stimulus types and methods of presentation; and
5. a triple interaction (p. 242).

The dancers judged the subject's affect as somewhat more unpleasant than did the psychotherapists. Differences over the three stimulus types are accounted for by the less pleasant overall rating on U-U segments as contrasted to P-P and P-U segments, and the finding means that all judges were influenced more by the face than the body in their judgments. When looking at the whole person, all judges attributed more pleasant feeling than when looking at the body alone over all the three stimulus conditions. Both P-P and P-U segments were rated more unpleasant when the body cue was presented than when the whole person was shown. Also, body presentation of P-U and U-U segments were judged almost identically with P-P items being judged more pleasant. These findings seem to indicate the judges' greater difficulty with bodily expression than with facial cues. The final triple interaction was related to two puzzling differences in judges' responses. First, psychotherapists saw the body presentation of P-P items as far more pleasant than did the dancers, outweighing the dancers' tendency to view all the items as less pleasant. Secondly, the judges differed in their perceptions of incongruity. When first given the whole presentation P-U, both groups of judges saw the items as pleasant. When next shown the body presentation P-U, the judges marked them unpleasant. Then when shown again the whole person, psychotherapists marked them equally as pleasant, while dancers were more influenced by bodily cues and rated the segments as significantly more unpleasant than they had the first time (p. 243). The authors conclude that the results demonstrate the availability of information about affect in both body areas studied. Facial cues were easier for judges to use; and although bodily expression yields information, the groups of judges differed considerably in their ability to respond to it.

Rosenberg and Langer (1965) investigated the communicative value of postural-gestural cues in expressing the meaning of an idea without using words. By use of the Stick Figure Test, the authors sought to study gestures as a source of information independent of the situational context and independent of the human element. This test consists of 43 line-drawn stick figures depicting people in varying postures. To examine the meanings conveyed by the various bodily positions of the figures, each stick figure was rated on six dimensions: a feeling dimension (positive-neutral-negative), a vertical dimension (up-down), a horizontal dimension (backward-forward), an achromatic dimension (black-gray-white), a chromatic dimension (red-green-yellow-blue), and a stability dimension (flighty-stable).

Results dealt with areas of interjudge agreement. Highest interjudge agreement occurred in the matching of stick figures with the vertical dimension, the achromatic dimension and the feeling dimension of meaning. Lowest agreement occurred within the chromatic and horizontal dimensions. In addition, tick figures previously characterized by Sarbin and Hardyck as showing "intense inner dynamics," were precisely those stick figures which yielded the greatest interjudge agreement in the study. Similarly, less interjudge agreement was found among stick figures previously described as having "less emotionally intense inner dynamics" (p. 596). This finding is relevant to the communicative ability of postural-gestural cues in the area of affective information. The authors conclude that more study is needed of the configurational characteristics of postural-gestural activity which mediate model verbal perceptions (p. 597).

A final study in this first group of investigations characterized by their quantitative and detailed approach, is Rosenfield's (1966) study concerning the instrumental affiliative functions of facial and gestural expression. This nonverbal bodily component of social behavior was viewed as behavior instrumental in satisfying and expressing affiliative motives.

Female undergraduate subjects were stimulated to win approval or avoid approval from another female student. Five postural-gestural cues were recorded in both approval-seeking and approval-avoiding conditions of interaction. Frequency of smiles, positive head nods (i.e., bi-directional movement on a vertical plane), negative head nods (i.e., bidirectional movement on a lateral plane), gesticulation (i.e., arm, hand or finger moving freely), self-manipulation (i.e., scratching, rubbing, etc.), and postural shifts were recorded. Smiles were expected to characterize approval seekers; gesticulations were expected to inform about involvement and attention; and postural shifts and self-manipulation were expected to indicate discomfort and avoidance. Results showed a positive correlation between the number of smiles and positive nods but a negative correlation between these two behaviors and a third—self-manipulation. A nonsignificant number of negative head nods and postural shifts were recorded and these behavior measures had to be eliminated from the data analysis.

Generally, the study revealed that overall gestural activity was greater for subjects in the approval-seeking condition, especially showing a greater number of smiles and gesticulations. A second experiment to determine the stability of gestural behavior measurement over time revealed that the gestures were fairly stable (i.e., low positive correlations) with the exception of self-manipulation. Also, behaviors were correlated with need for approval. Smiles were found to have a positive correlation with need for approval. The remaining gestures initially correlated negatively with this need; but with repeated interaction, they correlated positively with need for achievement. Fear of rejection was related to postural shifts.

These findings indicate the instrumental function of certain gestures and their capacity to induce similar responses from others. They are not only signs of approval but are also instrumental approval seeking devices. Rosenfield made some additional comments about the possibility that smiles are informative of the nature of the affective state, whereas gesticulations inform about the intensity of the affect. He felt this was supported by the greater activity in the approval-seeking condition, which he characterized as having a higher intensity of emotion. The study concludes with the assertion that the smile, although having additional functions, is a nonverbal concomitant of approval-seeking behavior and thus serves an instrumental affiliative function.

CONTEXTUAL ANALYSIS OF NONVERBAL COMMUNICATION

Contextual analysis represents a recent innovation in the study of nonverbal communication. However, it has by no means replaced the more traditional quantitatively oriented methodology. Instead, both approaches have been employed in recent years.

Birdwhistell (1963) characterizes kinesics—the systematic study of patterned bodily motion—as not seeking its essence in parts of the whole. Rather, communication is a system of interaction with structures independent of the lexical and nonverbal behavior of the individual participant. It is a "*continuous* process [composed of] isolatable discontinuous units both lexical and behavioral" (1962, p. 192). But it is precisely the multifunction of these lexical and behavioral units which allows the above continuity-discontinuity paradox to exist. First of all, the behavioral elements must not be considered subsidiary to the lexical units with the latter performing the cognitive function and the former mediating the affective function. Secondly, Birdwhistell recognizes, as do the authors of the previous studies, the importance of the individual behavior in communicating new information. However, Birdwhistell carries the argument beyond the "oversimplified" new information function to the integrative aspects of the function. Serving this function, the "communicative units operate throughout the sequence of activity" to "relate the communicants to each other and to the content of the interaction" (1955, p. 11). The integrative function keeps the system in operation, gives continuity and predictability to the social system, regulates the interactional process and cross-references messages leading to comprehensibility in the content (1962, p. 196).

Birdwhistell does not seek to examine the individual behavioral units apart from their contexts. Rather the full communicative function of the unit lies in its relationship to the whole or larger system. And it is for this reason that Birdwhistell does not look at singular kinesic behaviors apart from their interactional system. He does not ask of the individual behavioral units: what does this behavior mean? A list of meanings of an independent unit of behavior is not valued. Just as "dictionaries of words may stand in the way of language in action so dictionaries of gestures stand in the way of kinesics——the human body in communicative action" (1955, p. 13).

Birdwhistell's early studies revealed that kinesic activity was patterned within the hierarchical structure of the communication system and its parts. As acoustic phoneticians achieved more precise descriptions of language, changes in pitch over the units of the sentence were shown to be in a functional relationship with these syntactic elements. The units of the sentence were marked by terminal changes in pitch. A rise in pitch denotes a question, a fall in pitch denotes completion and constant pitch denotes that the speaker is continuing. Birdwhistell found that movements of the head, eyes and hands accompanied these pitch changes throughout the syntactic unit. For instance, the eyelids as markers lowered at the completion of a syntactic unit, widened at the question and remained half open at points of continuation. More specifically, raising the eyelids at the end of the statement showed that an answer was expected. The eyelid raising is a postural cue for eliciting an answer. Similarly, the upward and downward movements corresponding to those of pitch changes characterized hand and head movements. Thus in establishing "postural-kinesic markers of the American syntactic structure," Birdwhistell has "effectively searched and found meaning of systematic kinesic activity within the structure of the communication system" (Scheflen, 1964, p. 321).

Scheflen (1964) directly continued Birdwhistell's work with postural-kinesic markers. In studying eighteen psychotherapeutic sessions by the contextual analysis approach, Scheflen noticed a striking structural similarity among the therapy sessions regardless of the schools of psychotherapy and the individual therapist. Generally, he noted that kinesic activity is a reliable indicator of at least three aspects of the communication situation. According to the level of behavior, units of kinesic activity:

1. demarcate the beginnings and endings of structural units of the communication system,
2. denote how individual communicants are related to each other, and
3. mark steps in the program of the interaction (p. 316).

In dealing with how postural cues mark structural units of the communication, Scheflen further conceptualized successively larger units in the hierarchy of the lexical communication system. Just as the syntactic sentence is preceded by the phoneme and morpheme, it is succeeded by the structural units of point, the position and finally the presentation in the therapy session. Scheflen found that posture and postural shifts mark the duration and termination of these structural units (p. 320). Successively larger body postures and postural shifts mark the duration and termination of successively larger structural units in the interactive communication system. After the syntactic sentence the next level of communication is the point, described as the making of a point in a discussion. Head and eye shifts mark the termination of one point and the transition to another point. Such shifts in the head posture as turning the head left or right, tilting it, flexing or extending the neck, mark the end of a point in the lexical interchange. These behaviors were found to be quite stereotyped and repetitive throughout therapy. Often themes could be associated with a particular head position. For instance, one head position could be consistently associated with explanation and another with interruptions. The position, or a sequence of several points forming a point of view, constitutes the next structural level in the communication. These periods and changes in them were marked by gross postural shifting involving half the body. Especially noticeable was the body shift from leaning back to leaning forward when changing from the listener to the speaker in the therapy situation. The largest structural level studied by Scheflen is the presentation, synonymous with the totality of one's positions in a given interaction. Postural markers involve a complete change in location. Thus, Scheflen has shown that one function of the individual's bodily activity in communication is marking units at multiple levels of the structure of a communicative system.

Secondly, Scheflen considered postural indicators of the quality of the interpersonal relationship and how individuals relate to each other. Three simultaneously occurring dimensions of postural activity were related to giving information about the social relationship among the members. The inclusiveness or non-inclusiveness of posture defines the space for activities and delimits access to and within the group. Vis-à-vis versus parallel body orientation give evidence about the types of social activities. Thirdly, congruence and non-congruence of the stance and the positioning of the extremities indicate association, non-association or dissociation of the group members. An example of how the inclusiveness of a posture delimits the space of activities occurs when three individuals sit side by side on the sofa. The outside two cross their legs inward across the space between them thereby "boxing in" the center person. Vis-à-vis positioning occurs in situations of reciprocal exchange of information and feeling between two persons. Watching television, persons assume a parallel positioning in relation to each other. This positioning can indicate that only one person is needed to complete the task. Finally, congruence of the posture of body extremities can reveal such information as similarity or dissimilarity in roles and views of the group members.

Scheflen concludes his article on the significance of postures in communication with remarks about postural indicators of progressive steps in the therapy program. On the part of the therapist, there are relationships between his therapeutic maneuvers and his body positions, making his postural cues a good source of information about the stage of the therapy session. The therapist's maneuvers are equated with the structural level of points and marked by head-eye positions. The therapist's tactics are equated with the level of positions and are marked by gross bodily shifts in posture. In conclusion, Scheflen supported the significance of posture in communication by outlining it as an indicator of structural levels in the communication system, of ways in which the communicants relate, and of steps in the therapy program.

A second article by Scheflen (1965) deals with quasi-courtship behavior in psychotherapy. Again, in using the contextual analysis technique to study the communication system, Scheflen discovered behaviors similar to those found in American courtship appearing in psychotherapy. In fact, these courtinglike elements in kinesic behavior appeared not only in psychotherapy but in business meetings and conferences (1965, p. 247).

Scheflen outlined three common activities of early courtship in America: courtship readiness, positioning for courtship and actions of appeal or invitations. Readiness for courtship combines certain organismic changes with token behaviors such as the tie preen in men. Positioning for courtship involves vis-à-vis configuration in a two-party group or a parallel configuration in a three-party group with the two courters forming a closed circle by each crossing his legs inward over the space between them. Actions of appeal are such characteristic body motions as swinging the hips in women and gaze-holding or head-cocking in both sexes (p. 240). Qualifiers of courtship behavior include what Bateson calls "metacommunications" (i.e., communications about communications) or signals which indicate that, although two sets of behaviors seem to be courtship, they are not. The metacommunication allows a person who knows the rules to distinguish between the two sets of seemingly identical behaviors. Reference to the inappropriate context, such as the comment "other people are present" suggests, is one qualifier of courtship. "Incomplete postural-kinesic involvement," exemplified by two communicants sitting opposite each other and one person's eyes roaming about the room, qualifies the relationship. The omission of important courting behaviors such as verbalizing love while leaning away from your partner is a courtship qualifier. Finally, "lexical disclaimers" and "bizarreness of the performance of the courtship elements" serve to qualify the relationship.

In discussing the quasi-courtship complex as an entity, Scheflen notes that a few elemental courting behaviors put together form a complex courtship pattern. "These same elements, arranged in a different way and combined with qualifiers, make up integrations that resemble courtship but have a quite different significance in an interaction" (p. 250). This set of behaviors is quasi-courtship and is distinguished from actual courtship by its integration of courtship and qualifier behaviors, its appearance in inappropriate situations, and its thwarted progression never concluding in sexual consummation.

Having established the identity of quasi-courtship, Scheflen demonstrated its appearance in psychotherapy. In the psychoanalytic and more conventional psychotherapeutic interview, quasi-courting was covertly postural and kinesic. To bring the patient's conflict to the surface, some psychotherapists employ more overt quasi-courting in a verbal as well as nonverbal manner. The following example from a British family therapy session exemplifies quasi-courtship behavior typical to psychotherapy.

Whenever . . . the therapist is in a conversation with either the daughter or the grandmother, the mother moves into courtship readiness and begins coquettish expressions and movements. Both of the other women immediately place a leg across the space between the mother and the therapist, 'boxing in' the mother who then decourts (p. 252).

In addition to bringing forth patient's conflicts, the quasi-courting is a device to maintain the system. It helps maintain the communication by balancing the group between too much and too little integration of the members. Quasi-courting occurs in two contexts of disintegration: when one participant withdraws or is excluded and when there is gender confusion. By soliciting the return of the member and by heightening gender identification, this behavior sustains the group's integration. Also, where the situation calls for it, quasi-courting allows for smooth decourting. When gender confusion persists, when courtship status-ambiguity continues, when quasi-courting is too intense by one member, when the group's state of tension is beyond toleration of further quasi-courtship, and when group members interfere actively with the behavior, then decourting is necessary and facilitated by the presence of the quasi-courtship complex. Thus quasi-courting not only integrates the group, but it helps maintain a favorable "range of relatedness" among the members. Serving this dual function, quasi-courtship behavior, Scheflen notes, becomes important to psychotherapy not only as a covert technique but also as a potential deliberate technique.

CONCLUDING OBSERVATIONS

Consideration of the preceding studies according to their results leads us back to our earlier suggestion of categorizing them according to the different kinds of kinesic information they report: affective communication, interpersonal relations, role behavior, and nonverbal behavior as an instrumental affiliative act. Beyond this simple grouping, overall coordination of the results seems difficult, not because the studies contradict one another but because they vary so in what they tell specifically about the communicative value of kinesic activity. Some studies are more precise than others in delineating which body cues communicate what types of information. This difference is especially evident within the group of studies concerned with the function of postural-gestural cues in affective communication.

In addition, the findings can be differentiated in terms of their comprehensiveness or breadth of scope. Thus the findings of Rosenberg and Langer, that postural-gestural cues function as a mediator of verbalized modal perceptions and those of Rosenfield that bodily cues function as an instrumental affiliative act, are simple and direct. In contrast, Scheflen's system of bodily cue functions is broader and derived from a substantially larger social context. Instead of denoting one particular function of kinesic cues, he outlines several. Just one of his studies shows that they are indicators of the structural levels in the communication system, of the quality of the interpersonal relationship and of the steps in the therapy program.

Not only is it hard to group the studies according to their results without oversimplification, but the task of clearly dividing the studies according to their methodology is quite difficult. At first the "traditional" and the contextual analysis approaches seemed straightforward and appropriate. However, a closer examination of the literature reveals a more ambiguous picture with some members of the two groups overlapping in some methodological concerns. While it is true that one group is more quantitative in its approach and the other more descriptive, their respective orientations toward related issues are far less distinct, e.g., interjudge agreement versus interjudge accuracy. It was noted that interjudge agreement was the concern of the first group, while the second group addressed itself to interjudge accuracy. However, Ekman, a member of the "traditional" group with a definite statistical approach, specifically rejected this interest in interjudge agreement, replacing it with a concern for interjudge accuracy. His judgmental task involved matching photos with speech samples of previous interviews, ignoring the specific affect depicted. In this respect then, Ekman is more akin to the contextual analysts.

Secondly, some "traditional" studies are closely aligned with group two in their strong emphasis on the study of spontaneous interactive bodily motion. The contextual analysts are precisely concerned with studying bodily motion or action as opposed to a body movement or a static act. And further, they emphasize the examination of these patterned bodily motions in the context of communication. The "traditionalists" study posed behavior or spontaneous interactive behavior in a still photograph. Dittman and associates, although members of group one by virtue of their quantitative orientation, break away in using segments of motion picture films of body motion as photographic stimuli.

Finally, although the contextual analysis approach seems more interesting for its novelty and comprehensiveness, one cannot conclude that it is decisively more valuable to the extent of backseating the "traditional" approach. Rather both approaches are informative in the study of kinesic activities, and especially so when elements of both approaches are combined.

REFERENCES

AUSTIN, G. *Chironomia or a treatise on rhetorical delivery.* Edwardsville: Southern Illinois University Press, 1966.

BERELSON, B. and JANOWITZ, M. (Eds.), *Public opinion and communication.* New York: The Free Press, 1953.

BIRDWHISTELL, R. L. Background to kinesics. *ETC Review of General Semantics,* 1955, 13, 10–15.

BIRDWHISTELL, R. L. An approach to communication. *Family Process,* 1962, 1, 192–201.

BIRDWHISTELL, R. L. Kinesic level of the investigation of emotions. In P. Knapp (Ed.), *Expression of the emotions of man.* New York: International Universities Press, 1963.

BRYSON, L. (Ed.), *The communication of ideas.* New York: Harper and Brothers, 1948.

DITTMAN, A. T. Relationship between body movements and moods in interviews. *Journal of Consulting Psychology,* 1962, 26, 480.

DITTMAN, A. T., PARLOFF, M. B., and BOOMER, D. S. Facial and bodily expression: A study of receptivity of emotional cues. *Psychiatry,* 1965, 28, 239–244.

EISENSON, J., AUER, J. J., and IRWIN, J. V. *The psychology of communication.* New York: Appleton-Century-Crofts, 1963.

EKMAN, P. Body positions, facial expression and verbal behavior during interviews. *Journal of Abnormal and Social Psychology,* 1964, 68, 295–301.

EKMAN, P. Communication through nonverbal behavior: Source of information about the interpersonal relationship. In S. S. Tompkins and C. C. Izard (Eds.), *Affect, cognition, personality.* New York: Springer Publishing Co., Inc., 1965. (a)

EKMAN, P. Differential communication of affect by head and body cues. *Journal of Personality and Social Psychology,* 1965, 2, 726–735. (b)

HALL, E. T. *The silent language.* Garden City, New York: Doubleday & Co., Inc., 1959.

HOLLOWAY, J. *Language and intelligence.* London: MacMillan, 1951.

LABARRE, W. The cultural basis of emotions and gestures. *Journal of Personality,* 1947, 16, 49–68.

LINDESMITH, H. R. and STRAUSS, A. L. *Social psychology.* New York: The Dryden Press, 1951.

LINDZEY, G. (Ed.), *Handbook of social psychology.* Cambridge, Massachusetts: Addison-Wesley Publishing Company, Inc., 1954.

MEERLOO, J. A. *Conversation and communication.* New York: International Universities Press, 1958.

NEEDLES, W. Gesticulation and speech. *International Journal of Psycho-Analysis,* 1959, 40, 291–294.

ROSENBERG, B. G. and LANGER, J. A study of postural-gestural communication. *Journal of Personality and Social Psychology*, 1965, 2, 593–597.

ROSENFIELD, H. M. Instrumental affiliative functions of facial and gestural expressions. *Journal of Personality and Social Psychology*, 1966, 4, 65–72.

RUESCH, J. and KEES, W. *Nonverbal communication*. Berkeley: University of California Press, 1964.

SAINSBURY, P. Gestural movement during psychiatric interview. *Psychosomatic Medicine*, 1955, 17, 458–469.

SCHEFLEN, A. E. The significance of posture in communication systems. *Psychiatry*, 1964, 27, 316–331.

SCHEFLEN, A. E. Quasi-courtship behavior in psychotherapy. *Psychiatry*, 1965, 28, 245–257.

SEBEOK, T. A., HAYES, A. S., and BATESON, M. C. (Eds.), *Approaches to semiotics*. London: Mouton and Company, 1964.

SMITH, A. G. (Ed.), *Communication and culture*. New York: Holt, Rinehart and Winston, 1966.

THOMPSON, D. F. and MELTZER, L. Communication of emotional intent by facial expression. *Journal of Abnormal and Social Psychology*, 1964, 68, 129–135.

CHAPTER 15

Sign Language of the Deaf

In the dusk the two mutes walked slowly home together. At home Singer was always talking to Antonapoulos. His hands shaped the words in a swift series of designs. His face was eager and his gray-green eyes sparkled brightly. With his thin strong hands he told Antonapoulos all that had happened during the day.

Carson McCullers: *The Heart is a Lonely Hunter**

COMMUNICATION by a system of gestures is not an exclusively human activity, so that in a broad sense of the term, sign language is as old as the race itself, and its earliest history is equally obscure. However, it is reasonably certain that, even in pre-historic times, whenever a human culture had the material resources, the familial patterns and the attitudes toward life and "the normal" which allowed the child born deaf to survive, there would grow up between the child and those around it a communicative system derived in part from the visible part of the paralinguistic, but much more from the kinesic, communicative behavior of the culture (Trager, 1958). Based on the patterns of interactive behavior peculiar to that culture, the communication of the deaf-mute and his hearing companions would develop in different ways from the normal community of the culture. To take a hypothetical example, a shoulder shrug, which for most speakers accompanied a certain vocal utterance, might be a movement so slight as to be outside the awareness of most speakers, but to the deaf person, the shrug is unaccompanied by

* London: The Cresset Press, 1943.

anything perceptible except a predictable set of circumstances and responses; in short, it has a definite "meaning." That shrug should certainly
become more pronounced, even exaggerated, in the behavior of the deaf-
mute, and perhaps also in that of his hearing partners in communication
(Stokoe, 1960).

The sign language is as much a real language as any other. It is one of
the oldest living languages, as is proved in the hieroglyphics, or picture
writing, of Egypt, and the famous "dumb shows" or pantomimes of
Greek and Roman days or again in the gestures of the North American
Indians. The conventional sign language, as used in this country today,
was brought here by Dr. Thomas Hopkins Gallaudet, on his return from
France in 1816, and by his companion, Laurent Clerc, the gifted French
deaf-mute. It was modified to suit American conditions, and has expanded naturally in the course of time as any living language does (Peet,
1934).

The history of the sign language as we know it today in North America
begins in the second half of the eighteenth century when the Abbe de
l'Epée, starting with the manual gestures that he found being used by his
first deaf pupils, proceeded to systematize this "natural language of
signs," and to employ it as the principal medium of instruction in the
school that he founded in Paris. The sign language, in this state of
development, was brought to the United States, as previously stated, by
Gallaudet, who used it as the medium of instruction at the American
School for the Deaf in Hartford, Connecticut, opened in 1817. (Mendelson, 1964).

The visual communication systems of the American deaf population
include the manual alphabet and signs. The manual alphabet consists of
26 digital symbols by means of which any word in the English language
may be finger spelled. The manual alphabet represents a simple transfer
system. The signs, however, constitute a language proper, definable only
with its own system, so that when finger spelled items occur, they are set
in the structural context of the signed statement.

A cursory examination of the vocabulary of the language reveals some
signs like those for book, eat and see, the meaning of which might be
guessed by an uninformed observer, if the signing occurred at a tolerant
speed. The sign for book looks like a book being opened; it is, in a sense,
an "onomatopoetic" sign, or it might be said to be "cognate" with the
physical visualization of the object it names. Other signs like those for
honest, white, when, who, because, for and nothing, cannot be understood by one who does not know the language. The items in this set
when signed will be as obstruse and incomprehensible to the naive
observer as any unknown linguistic quantity.

The sign language also has a high potential for the creation of occasional signs, signs that come into being in a discursive situation and then pass out of existence once the situation or a particular statement made in the situation comes to an end. Those nonce-signs might appear at first glance to be neologisms, but neologizing activity in sign language discourse must be weighed differently from the same phenomenon in English. The aspectual nature of the language, the relative magnitude of the organs of communication (fingers, hands, arms, upper body) and the factor of simultaneity (there are no sequential syllables) make possible the immediate inversion of a nonce-sign, like two every week for four weeks, which was recently reported to the author. Nonce-signs are immediately understood by users of the sign language and are not looked upon as being neologistic (Mendelson, 1964).

Until recently very little work had been done in the structural analysis of visual communication systems (Birdwhistell, 1960). Birdwhistell studied the visual aspects of non-verbal, interpersonal communication among hearing people and devised a notation system for experimenting with and recording kinesic behavior. In a study of playground gestures used by deaf children in a Dutch oralist school, Tervoort (1961) found that manual communication was effective only when gestures were accompanied by mouthing of the spoken word on the part of the gesturer, and by lipreading on the part of the observer. When the lower face was covered, the gestures produced by the child did not convey meaning to a second deaf child observing.

The linguistic structure of the American sign language has been studied by Stokoe (1960) along the lines of the method used by Trager and Smith in arriving at their description of American English structure. In a spoken language the smallest unit of speech that distinguishes one word from another is the phoneme, examples of which are the /p/ and /s/ in "pit" and "sit." Just as any word or syllable is composed of phonemes, so each sign is composed of units which are called *cheremes*, the *cher* of chereme being derived from the Greek for "hand," *cheiros*. The typical sign is composed of three cheremes, one of position, one of configuration and one of motion. Unlike the phonemes in a syllable or word which occur sequentially, the cheremes of a sign enter into simultaneous combination. The cheremes are considered separately only for purposes of analysis and description. By means of 57 symbols, including three for syntactically significant facial gestures, provided by Stokoe, we are able to notate any sign.

Although the analysis of the grammar and syntax for the sign language is still in the initial stages, certain basic patterns may be observed. There is, for example, a tendency for the most important constituent in a whole signed statement to occur initially. From the standpoint of linguistics, this might be accounted for by the absence of audible parameters of vocalization that control the antecedent parts of a spoken sentence until the gist is delivered by the speaker. A simple illustration of the latter may be found in the intonation pattern of the forepart of any sentence beginning with a dependent clause. Viewed psychologically, the phenomenon of antiperiodicity in signed statements might be attributable to the shorter duration of visual perseveration as compared to the relatively long duration of auditory perseveration.

Virtually every sign, because it is in motion, has the potential of a verb. Thus, though "buy a suitcase" would be translated from English by two signs, for "buy" and for "suitcase," the phrase "carry a suitcase" could be translated from English by only one sign, that for "suitcase" with a pronounced variation in the chereme of motion. Also since the sign language is aspectual and produces its morphemes in space without visible largeness of scope, the commencement at one point in space and ending at another point, may provide for an altogether unusual equivalent of the verb tenses as we know them in vocal-auditory language. But this characteristic remains to be studied in greater detail. It has already been noticed by investigators, that the sign language "verb" can express pronominal subject and object merely by beginning and ending at points in the space before the signer's body where the pronominal referents have been preestablished (Stokoe, 1960).

Sign language is economical and rapid, so that it can be executed or read three times as quickly as articulate speech. It is potentially graceful and pleasing to the eye, and a wide range of expressive or facial movements can accompany and enrich the manual signs in a manner which is supremely eloquent.

This manual speech is largely "international" and surmounts the barriers erected by race, religion or language. In other words, there is a striking similarity, often an identity, between the gestures employed by deaf mutes of different nationalities.

Some of the signs may be regarded as "instinctive gestures" in that they are obvious and possess a symbolism which is universally accepted and employed. Some other signs are more obscure and are apparently empirical in nature. Thus it is not easy to understand why pinching the lobe of the left ear should denote "yellow."

The sign language of deaf mutes possesses its own primitive syntax. Definite and indefinite articles are usually omitted, adjectives and verbs are not easily distinguished. The tenses are not differentiated unless the meaning of the phrase absolutely demands this. The order of words is logical rather than in conformity with local grammatical construction.

A good deal of facial expression movement usually embellishes this sign talk.

It is also interesting to note that when two or more deaf-mutes are in animated conversation, they evince in addition to their rapid sign talk little grunting, whining, whimpering and twittering noises, which are of course inaudible to themselves. These primitive utterances occurring among a speechless gesture making community may be of the greatest significance in our conceptions of the origins of verbal speech in man. We see here not only the traces of an interjectional beginning of languages (pooh-pooh hypothesis) but even something still more primitive, namely, the operation of crude muscular movements rendered audible (yo-heave-ho) theory (Critchley, 1939).

A proper understanding of the way signs operate in individual behavior demands an explicit recognition of the importance of signs other than those produced by vocal cords and heard by the ear. Sign language is a form of non-verbal behavior because it is neither spoken nor heard. It is a visual sign (Morris, 1942).

In broad terms, non-verbal forms of codification fall into three distinct categories. One of these is the sign language which includes all those forms of codification in which words, numbers and punctuation signs have been supplanted by gestures; these vary from the "monosyllabic" gesture of the hitchhiker to such complete systems as the language of the deaf.

Verbal language is based upon entirely different principles than non-verbal languages. In its denotative capacity a single word can refer to a general or universal aspect of a thing or event only. In order to particularize and specify, words must be combined with other words in serial orders. Words enable us to express abstractions, to communicate interpolations and extrapolations, and they make possible the telescoping of far-flung aspects of events and diversified ideas into comprehensible terms. Unlike nonverbal codification, sign language for example, which are analogic and continuous, verbal codifications are essentially emergent, discontinuous and arbitrary (Ruesch, Kees, 1956).

It is a combination pictographic and ideographic language. Each sign represents something concrete or an idea or the progression of ideas. It is the most natural and most effective means of communication for the deaf.

There are a few principles to follow:

    1. When interpreting, it is better not to form words with the lips. However, when talking to only the deaf, one should talk as he signs.

    2. The appropriate facial expression should be used with

the sign. One should not look happy when signing the words sickness or sadness, etc.

3. The signs should be made clearly and smoothly, without jerking the hands or arms.

4. The wisdom in using signs is not how many signs one knows or how fast he can use them, but how cleverly he can use them. One should learn the synonyms for various words.

5. This is a living language and will be different in various parts of the country (Cissna, 1965).

We are witnessing today an unprecedented boom in sign language classes. The "Berlin Wall," which for so long has separated the deaf from their hearing contemporaries, is crumbling readily, as society discovers a formidable tool of communication so easy and so dramatic to use in the everyday intercourse of human affairs. The tool is old, but it gains in stature, dignity and effectiveness when people with their faculties intact are skillfully instructed in the three phases, language-colloquial, conventional and dignified platform usage.

Under the sponsorship of the United States Vocational Rehabilitation Administration, the District of Columbia Association of the Deaf has conducted classes in sign language instruction for the past two years. It has helped immensely to narrow the long standing gap between deaf and the hearing world.

For many years, publications of books on sign language have been few and far between. Sign language, like any other language, is dynamic. It is constantly undergoing changes. Obsolete signs are being dropped, new ones are embraced and put into wide circulation. Those once labeled as slang find ready modern acceptance. So the urgent need for an up-to-date manual on sign language in both illustrated and written form is underlined. Several dictionaries on dactylology have recently appeared on the market, but so far, few have been prepared for classroom instructional purposes.

The purpose is to provide an introduction to the system of manual communication used by almost all adult deaf people in the United States. Although the title of this book focuses attention on the hands, much more is involved than merely the movement of the hands.

In ordinary interactions, deaf people use formal signs, finger spelling, pantomime gestures, facial expressions, body movements and speech to convey meaning. All of these must be part of the student's introduction to manual communication and they obviously transcend the confining limits of sign language.

Estimates have placed the number of formal signs variously from fifteen hundred to two thousand. Though this may appear to the student as a formidable number of signs to master, it is actually very small considering the vast number of ideas to be expressed.

A very critical skill which the student must develop is the ability to evaluate a deaf person's educational and culture level. This enables him to sense whether he is getting through to the deaf person. The language handicap and cultural restriction which deafness imposes frustrate communication far more than the inability to sign clearly or finger spell fluently.

Many professional workers with deaf people have observed that as deaf people move up the ladder of educational achievement and broaden their social and cultural horizons, they tend to use fewer signs and more finger spelling. Conversely as they move down the ladder, and their experiences are far more restricted, then the signs increase, and finger spelling decreases. If the student observes the deaf person using more or fewer signs, he has one measure by which to gauge that person's level and he can adjust his communication accordingly.

A sign represents a concept. It may also, but not necessarily, represent an English word. When one makes the sign for "no," it represents the concept of prohibitiveness as well as the word "no." However, when one makes the sign for "tired," it represents the concept of tiredness, but it may be represented by such English words as weary, fatigued, all-in, exhausted, etc. The question of how deaf people think has not yet been adequately researched. However, many professional workers believe that deaf people make no attempt to "translate" signs into English words. Their minds comprehend that the concept tiredness, for example, is intended by the sign for "tired," and this is sufficient for their understanding.

An example of the misunderstanding that can take place occurs in the word "take." There are many concepts represented by this one English word. We take a letter to the post office (carry); we take medicine (swallow); we take courses in college (study, register, attend); we take sick (contract, catch); and so on. Each of these concepts had a different sign. Consider the illogicality of the sentence, "I will take the bitter pill of experience," when take is signed "carry." In other words, just because the English word take is used to express these various concepts, is no reason to use a simple sign to express all of them. Quite the opposite is true. It is important to know the precise English word intended, then finger spelling must be used. This is why the better educated deaf person with rich cultural experiences prefers to use more finger spelling than signs. He appreciates the importance of words and their fine shades of meaning. He has overcome his language handicap, whereas those deaf people on the lower rungs of the ladder have not. For them the general concept is sufficient. They do not care if the person was fatigued or exhausted, just the fact that he was tired is adequate. This is due to their language handicap, not to lack of intelligence or ambition.

Each letter of the alphabet can be represented by a configuration of the fingers. In the United States, we use only the fingers of one hand, while in some countries, the fingers of both hands are used. Finger spelling is nothing more than English spelled on the fingers. It has great merit for teaching English to deaf children. Signs do not necessarily represent words, but concepts. Since a verb sign such as "go" represents a concept, the only way one knows whether go, going, goes, gone or went is intended is through context or finger spelling. By using finger spelling, the emphasis is upon words and their arrangement, not just concepts.

Just as there are colorless and monotonous vocal speakers, there are colorless manual speakers. The ability to mix into signs and finger spelling other aspects which add color and life, and thus more meaning, is truly the distinguishing hallmark of a good manual communicator.

As deaf people communicate, their attention is focused on the face. They do not look at the hands. The face is the focal point. Therefore, it carries most of the burden of enriching the meaning of signs and finger spelling. It must become automatic for an individual signing "bad" to, at the same instant, have a deep furrowed frown on his face, or if the meaning dictates, a raised, questioning eyebrow. Our voices, as hearing people, rise and fall to add meaning to our words. The face functions for manual communication, as the inflections of the voice for words. Facial expressions are not just amusing and entertaining, they are vital.

There are other parts of the body that play important roles, especially the shoulders. Hundreds of ideas are suggested even among hearing people by the merest shrug of the shoulders.

Strange as it seems, the legs also play important roles. The bending of the knees, the hunching of the shoulders, the strained facial expression on the bowed head can turn the sign "sick" into "desperately ill." One's knees are valuable adjuncts in adding depth to a sign.

Even the lowly feet must be ever alert to add their emphasis. Standing one foot on tiptoe, knees bent, etc., can change the sign for "perfect" into "precisely" or "exact." Shifting the feet often makes clear the person's speaking in a dialogue.

The hands and arms of course play the leading role. They express the noun, as it were, and the other parts of the body supply the modifying aspects. The vigor with which a sign is made may express anger or docility, fear or joy. The speed with which the sign is made may convey the feeling of great haste or fear, or peace, or laziness.

Although different teachers at different times and places have made efforts to standardize the sign language, no widespread concerted standardization program has been undertaken. Because of this, some signs in one locality might not be used in another locality. There are, however, not so many of these signs as to make comprehension difficult.

Dr. William Stokoe, Chairman of the English Department of Gallaudet College, points out in his book, *Sign Language Structure*, that most signs have three parts: (1) the shape of the hands, (2) the place where the hands move to and from and (3) the movements (Fant, 1964).

REFERENCES

BALLIN, A. *Sign language: The deaf mute howls.* Los Angeles: Grafton Publishing Company, 1930.

BENSON, E. E. *The language of signs.* Washington, D.C.; 1961.

BIRDWHISTELL, R. L. *Kinesis and communication.* Boston: Beacon Press, 1960.

BLISH, I. S. Historical overview on language teaching. *Exceptional Child,* 1964, 30, 345–348.

CISSNA, R. L. *Introduction to the sign language.* Jefferson City, Missouri: Missouri Baptist Convention, 1961.

CISSNA, R. L. *Basic sign language.* Jefferson City, Missouri: Missouri Baptist Convention, 1963.

CRITCHLEY, M. *The language of gesture.* London: Edward Arnold and Company, 1939.

DARCY, W. J. *Symbology.* New York: Art Directors Club, 1960.

FANT, L. J. *Say it with hands.* Washington, D.C.: Gallaudet College, 1964.

FAUTH, B., FAUTH, L., and WESLEY, W. Sign language. *American Annals of the Deaf,* 1965, 100, 253–263.

MENDELSON, J. *Disorders of communication.* Washington, D.C.: Public ARNMD, 1964.

LONG, J. S. *The sign language.* Washington, D.C.: Gallaudet College, 1961.

MORRIS, C. W. *Signs, language and behavior.* Englewood Cliffs, N. J.: Prentice-Hall, 1946.

PEET, E. The philology of the sign language. *Buff and Blue,* 1934, 1–4.

RUESCH, J. and KEES, W. *Nonverbal communication.* Berkeley: University of California Press, 1956.

Sign Language Bibliography. Gallaudet College, 1967.

Some candid opinions of the sign language. *Occupations of the Deaf,* 1910.

STOKOE, W. C. Sign language structure: An outline of the visual communication systems of the American deaf. *Occasional Papers,* 1960, 8, 1–7.

TERVOORT, B. T. Esoteric symbolism in the communication behavior of young deaf children. *American Annals of the Deaf,* 1961, 106, 436–480.

TRAGER, G. Paralanguage. *Studies in Linguistics,* 1958, 13, 1–12.

CHAPTER 16

Drum Communication in Africa

. . . do but start
An echo with the clamour of thy drum,
And even at hand a drum is ready braced
That shall reverberate as loud as thine;
Sound but another, and another shall
As loud as thine rattle the welkin's ear
And mock the deep mouth'd thunder.

Shakespeare: *King John*, Act V., Sc. 2

THE TECHNICAL, artistic and social elaboration of signal drumming in Africa is characteristic of that continent, and the use of the drum as a technique of communication is intricately interwoven with many aspects of African social life and structure. Like much other content of native cultures, the drum system is bound soon to disappear under the increasing pressures of contact with Western civilization. Therefore, while the opportunity is still afforded, linguistic study of the drum language is important as a potential source of insights on the genesis and psychology of language development in primitive cultures.

Drum signaling is to some extent a technical language; it also represents a complex and subtle relationship between language and music. As a language, it is highly poetic in nature, bound up with the heroic connotations of warfare in various regions and with the style of the language symbols associated with offices of high prestige. An example of

241

the awe and mystery that surrounds the drums is given by Doob (1961) in reference to the Nhole of Uganda:

> In this society, the royal drums, the only drums allowed, receive daily offerings of milk from a herd of sacred cows. This diet is varied with beer or cattle which a man provides after the birth of a son or after some other joyful occurrence, such as promotion to office or a successful expedition. The drums also have their own special guardians and their own sacred spears. In addition in earlier times, when the skins were changed upon the succession of a new king, they were rubbed with papyrus ashes as well as with the blood of a young boy deliberately sacrificed for that purpose (p. 284).

Thus, when these drums are sounded, they are insured a respectful audience.

The drums can perform different functions in the various regions of Africa. In at least one tribe (Van Valen, 1955), the only messages sent are "danger, return to village" and "end of danger." In this case, the message has been reduced to a standard code and the language connection, which many of the tribes have as we will see later, is lost. Much more commonly, the drums are used for any type of message and they usually have other communication functions as well. Gossip, announcements of sporting and other events, sorrow, celebration, hunting calls, jokes and other entertainment, insults and probably most of the African functions of spoken languages are duplicated on the drums.

The big drums can also be an important instrument of propaganda in time of war. A tremendous psychological effect is created when the great drums say "War! War! War!" for two or three days without stopping.

They are also used in the various dances such as those described by Armstrong (1954) among the warlike secret societies of the Oglenye or Ichahoho.

> At a dance the chief drummer maintains a running commentary on the dance, controls the line dances with great precision, calls particular persons by name to dance solos, tells them what dance to do, corrects them as they do it, and sends them back into line with comment on the performance. He does this by making his drum talk even above four or five other drums (p. 360).

Drumming is a highly skilled profession and is regarded in a proprietary fashion by certain families. They are usually reluctant to talk about their methods, and one must watch for opportunities to practice on important drums. The drummers are usually paid for their services and often feel that their importance to the community is not properly appreciated. They are quite capable of holding up a big dance while they bargain.

Every male member of the community has, or at least is allowed to have, a drum name which is quite elaborate and may be entirely distinct from his spoken one. According to Van Valen (1955), the drum name has three components: (1) a phrase or epithet characteristic of the individual; (2) the first part of the father's name; and (3) the village of maternal origin. The name is given either at initiation ceremonies or when the boy is first old enough to understand the drum (5 or 6). In the latter case, the name is sometimes changed at his initiation. For a woman, her drum name is the expression for "girl" or "wife" combined with the drum name of the father or husband respectively. Most women understand all that is said on the drum, but it is out of their province to send a message, consequently they never touch the drums.

The chief of a tribe may have the prerogative of silencing all other drums in the area by sounding his special name. This is a valuable privilege because there may be several messages in one village being drummed at the same time, in addition to clearly audible ones from nearby villages. In some areas, only the chiefs and their close male relatives may be permitted to use the drums at all.

A complete message usually consists of five parts (Van Valen, 1955):

1. a signal for attention or a chief's refrain.
2. the name of the desired recipient (repeated 3 or 4 times)
3. the name of the sender (omitted if the chief's refrain is used)
4. the message itself (repeated 3 or more times)
5. the signal for the end, either a single sharp beat or a series of low notes.

This pattern of course varies in different areas. The entire message usually takes five to fifteen minutes to transmit, but it may take well over an hour if the drummer is feeling in the mood and plays the drums for effects.

The best time for sending is usually early in the morning or late in the evening because of the reduction in vertical thermal convection currents (Van Valen, 1955). The maximum audible range for one drum is usually five to seven miles but there have been reports of up to twenty miles (Carrington, 1955) under optimum conditions. It is legendary that messages are transmitted over hundreds of miles by relaying, but this happens very rarely since in most cases the relay drummers do not consider the message of sufficient importance to warrant transmitting and also language barriers exist between the different areas. Communication between tribes speaking different dialects or languages is, of course, feasible, and is practiced; but it requires that the drummers in the border areas be to some extent bilingual. They often learn to identify a number of signals in the neighboring language together with their approximate meanings, without knowing the text in the other language or its exact translations.

Since the drum language is for the most part an echo of the spoken language, the many local dialects and languages, which have their corresponding drum language, may extend only over a few square miles. But in a few areas, a single drum language is used by the people of several different small dialect regions.

The signal drums may be grouped into two major types: the more common all-wooden slit drums which are usually called gongs and those with a skin which often occur in pairs and are called twin drums by the natives. In the various regions of Africa there are different variations of these types, but each tribe customarily uses only one variety for signaling purposes.

The slit drum or gong (Good, 1942) is a hollowed log of wood usually of one of three types of hardwood tree: 1) barwood, 2) ebae and 3) olom. They are all equally good to use. Some small drums are two feet in length but most drums are about three and a half to four feet with a few exceptions. The Tiv (Armstrong, 1954) are proud owners of a tremendous gong which is some nine feet long and three to four feet in diameter.

The log is hollowed out roughly through a longitudinal slit while still lying in the forest. The slit is three or four inches across and runs nearly the whole length of the log. After its weight has thus been reduced, the log is slung on a pole, brought into the village and the finishing touches are then added. The sides are carefully hollowed to the required thinness and smoothed off by the use of a chisel-like tool inserted always through the same slit. The thinness of the walls is very important and while making final adjustments, workers will chisel off a little wood from one inner side and then tap the log to get the tone. In other words, the drum is tuned in much the same manner as the piano is tuned, by adjustment of the strings. The curved walls of the finished drum will be but a half inch or less in thickness and the ends are left about two or three inches thick. This makes a hollow cylinder with closed ends, highly resonant when dry, and the only opening being the slit along the top.

When the slit is first made, a small section of the wood is left connect-

ing its opposite edges, a little to the left of the middle. Later this small
section is separated into two blocks of different size, each adhering to its
side of the slit, and separated from the other by a crack one-fourth of an
inch wide as is shown in the illustration below.

These blocks seem to have a great effect on the tones that are produced, and they are placed slightly to the left center since this location
appears to help produce the clearest tones. One of the blocks, known as
the "man," is nearly twice as broad as the other, called the "female," and
it seems to have a more forceful and penetrating tone.

Technologically, these gongs are not really drums, but bells. Says
Herzog (1965):

> They are not considered as drums proper since they have no
> tensed membranes, but bells since the vibration decreases
> from the periphery, in this case the blocks, toward the dead
> center (p. 312).

To secure the best resonance and carrying power (Good, 1942), the
gong should be supported on ropes roughly woven from the outer fibers of
plantain or banana plants, or from the dried fronds of the same plants,
and upheld by a frame of sticks driven into the ground. A small thatched
roof may be built over it for protection from the sun and rain. The
drumsticks are usually kept in the cavity of the drum. At the close of a
drum call, it is characteristic to hear the thump of the sticks as they are
dropped in.

The skin or membrane drums are usually of two types. They can be
roughly cup shaped with a skin over the top or they can be open at one
end. With either type, the drummer produces different tones by beating
either the center of the head, or a place nearer the edge which gives a

higher tone since the skin is more taut there. The difference in the weight of the two beating sticks can also enter into the tone difference. He can produce other tones by hitting the wooden frame and by using his heel against the membrane to alter the tension.

With either type of drum, skin or slit, beating sticks covered on the end with a ball of latex from a forest creeper are preferred, although bare sticks are used as substitutes. On at least one variety of skin drum, bare hands are used.

In most of Africa, the wooden gongs are used for the purpose of signaling due to their better production of tones, but in some areas the tribes still prefer the skin-covered type.

Now that we have briefly considered the functions, types and making of drums, let us look at some characteristics of the actual drum language itself. The general principle which underlies the "talk" of the drum is understood to lie in the tonal quality of most of the spoken languages and in the fact that the drum reproduces the tones, stresses and number of syllables in the various utterances (Armstrong, 1954). In other words, every word and syllable has its own tone which is as integral a part of the word as its other phonetic constituents. This tone may change only according to set phonemic, morphophonemic or grammatical rules. What the drums transmit, therefore, is an abstraction from the total speech utterance and not usually a code or cipher. There is for this reason a tendency towards standardized messages which are fairly long since short, non-standard transmissions can be ambiguous unless the social context lends itself to easy interpretation. As Van Valen (1955) points out:

> There is by no means as strong a correlation between this element of tone or pitch and stress as in English. In fact, there may be none. Tonal relationships do to some extent influence the sentence as a whole, but the grammatical tone is often quite subordinate to the semantic tone or that tonal character of the words themselves (p. 252).

Each syllable has a definite relative pitch or tone which is basically either high or low, although there may be one or more middle levels related in some way to these. This tone is unmodified by the context, except in a few clearly defined grammatical situations. Thus tone is actually part of the word. Some words may differ only in tonal pattern. An example of this (Van Valen, 1955) letting (') be a high tone and (.) be a low tone, can be shown in one dialect since lisaka (...), lisaka (..'), and lisaka (.'') mean respectively puddle, promise, and poison. In this dialect, the words for finance and rubbish pit are also phonemically idential, liala (.'.) and liala (...).

Many of the Bantu spoken languages (Good, 1942) are tonal in character. There are five different tones in the basic Bantu language, but most words are either in the two lowest tones of the register which are not far apart or in the two highest ones, likewise close together. The middle tone is used with relatively few words, and so is practically negligible. Roughly speaking, nearly all words can be classified as either high or low. This basic two tone system is the basis of most African drum languages.

In the slit gong, the two sides of the drum, chiefly because of the difference in thickness and also because of the two blocks of wood left in the slit (man and woman), produce two distinct tones, one of which is considerably higher than the other. The high and low drum tones can be made to correspond to the high and low tones of the spoken language by striking on the appropriate side of the slit (Good, 1942). Occasionally the drummer with simultaneous beats on both the high and low tones can produce a middle tone with considerable stress if needed.

Since progression of tones must be by steps rather than continuous, a problem develops when tonal glides must be represented. Several alternative solutions have arisen for the problem, says Stern (1957):

> The Luba of the Belgian Congo try to avoid words containing glides, but when they must, they reduce them to one of the two register tones. The Yaunde, on the other hand, replicate a glide by means of two rapid successive strokes representing the termini of the glide (p. 497).

Another feature which may pose difficulty is quantity or length, frequently phonemic in the base languages involved. If vowel length is to be represented at all, it must somehow be conventionalized. According to Stern (1957):

> The Yaunde reproduce a long syllable as they do two successive short ones; by two strokes, the renditions are distinguished by tempo. On the other hand, the Tshi signals of the Ewe use the system that the interval between strokes reflects the length assigned to the first one. If it is followed at some length, the initial stroke is long; followed closely, it is short (p. 497).

There seems to be no standard tempo. Just as one person may talk more rapidly than another, so may he beat the drum with a quicker tone

(Clarke, 1934). Many times the rate of discourse of the message may be maintained by the drummer humming the message as he is sending it. Pauses are usually used at set places where syntactical or expressive pauses are apt to occur in speech. As Stern observes:

> While the drummer is sending the message, the rhythmic bodily movements of playing are likely to lead to stylistic elaborations of the essential message and this occurs particularly in the case when similar playing is employed for purely musical ends. The stylistic features are sometimes interspersed between segments of the message itself as when the Tumba drummers add extra beats between phrases in order to maintain the proper rhythm (p. 501).

The wording of the message on the drum is usually longer than the oral statement of the same language since it is almost never possible to transmit directly a thought or sentence from common speech. This is due to the fact that many of the words in each language have the same tonal pattern and they are distinguished from another, only when they are accompanied on the drums by other words which together can produce a relatively distinct pattern (Doob, 1961). In brief, not words, but the tonal pattern of characteristic short phrases are encoded. Thus the idea behind the sentence to be transmitted is really reduced to one of the sequences in the spoken language that is so common or stereotyped that the people are likely to recognize it.

An example of this is the message, "The missionary is coming up the river to our village tomorrow; bring water and firewood to his house." As translated into the language of the drum, this message would read:

> White man spirit from the forest of the leaf used for roofs comes up river, comes up river, when tomorrow has risen on high in the sky to the town and village of us. Come, come, come, bring water of (a specific type) vine, bring sticks of firewood to the house with shingles high up above of the white man spirit from the forest of the leaf used for roofs (Doob, 1961).

Other times a drummer may not even know the meaning of a word or two in an explanatory phrase either if it has passed out of use in the more flexible spoken language or if it was introduced from outside into the signal language years before and the rest of the phrase modified around it (Van Valen, 1955). Their everyday speech does not need these identifying comments, so they are not found in it. They are present only in the signal languages.

It must be borne in mind that the drum language has never been transcribed, so there is little emphasis on verbal accuracy. This fact plus the difficulty which is encountered in comprehending the tones of the words, all add up to make it very difficult for a novice to learn to understand drum language (Clarke, 1934).

Now that we have looked at some of the general characteristics of drum language, let us see how they lend themselves to an example of a system; in particular, the Jabo drum language of Eastern Liberia as investigated by Herzog. The Jabo spoken language is, as most African spoken languages, a tone language which is basically monosyllabic. Therefore, as we saw before, most of the words are distinguishable only by tone. Since the lengthening of a vowel often results from the existence of an identifiable syllable suffix, the notion of the "mora" has been introduced in the spoken language to complement that of the syllable. Thus the mora in Jabo is a basic unit in the language which has tone, duration and voicing as its minimum content (Herzog, 1965).

The mora also carries over as a basic unit in the drum language of the Jabo. As a rule, each beat on the wooden signal drum represents a single mora. Occasionally though, one may be omitted or both beats may be shortened if two full vowels follow each other. Also a technique called "scraping" is sometimes used to represent a mora. It consists of two quick beats given by the two sticks in alternation. It is mainly considered as an ornamental device since it occasionally occurs where linguistic reasons do not seem to account for it.

Scraping is also sometimes used to represent true diphthongs, although a single beat is more commonly used. They do not seem to be very consistent in which one they use since the same word in the same signal may occur in both forms at different places in the message. Herzog (1965) observes that the drummers would give the grammatically appropriate prose forms, in some instances, and in other cases would give the shorter forms which agree better with the signal.

The Jabo spoken language is basically a four-tone register system. In the drum language, only a three-tone system is used since the spoken tones 3 and 4 are usually made to coincide when they are produced on the drum. This is the case despite the fact that these two lower tones could be kept apart on the drum without too much technical difficulty. The contrast between speech tones 3 and 4 is to some extent preserved in that tone 3 can be beaten at two places on the wooden drum with one of them giving a lower pitch. Which of the two tone variants the drummers use seems to depend upon their convenience and on aesthetic factors involved. Tone 1 is also sometimes given with drum tone 2, but this is the case not nearly as often as with tones 3 and 4. Tones 2 and 3, on the other hand, are kept apart consistently. So we see that which tones a drummer uses seems to depend a lot on his convenience. Herzog concludes that the Jabo four-tone language grew out of an older three-tone system by splitting the lower register. He notes that must of the surrounding tribes (including the Grebo, from whom the Jabo derived their signaling system and much of their music) employ a three-tone language.

Occasionally some types of emotional effect in speech, symbolic "sound painting," or accoustical representations of non-vocal sounds are reproduced on the drum. One signal, for example, consists of rubbing a drum stick repeatedly back and forth along the wooden lips of the drum. This signal is used to represent the anger of the army (Herzog, 1965).

On the skin-covered drum only two tones, the 2 and 3, are used in the Jabo drum language. Within this limitation, the agreement between the speech tones and drum tones is not too great. Accordingly, the messages tend to be more of the coded type. Herzog proposes that the reasons for this are probably technical in nature. Since considerable force is required for beating the drum effectively, the drummer tends to use the right hand and left hand strokes alternately, leading to a mechanical alternation of tones 2 and 3.

In the area which the Jabo inhabit, there are comparatively few specialists who play the drum. This situation compares with other regions in Africa, for instance the Cameroons or the Congo regions, where many men know how to play the signal drum.

REFERENCES

ARMSTRONG, R. G. Talking drums in the Benue-Cross River region of Nigeria. *Phylon*, 1954, 15, 355–363.

CARRINGTON, J. F. *Talking drums of Africa*. London: Cary Kingsgate Press, 1949.

CLARKE, R. T. Drum language of the Tumba people. *American Journal of Sociology*, 1934, 40, 34–48.

CUDJOR, S. D. Techniques of Ewe drumming and the social importance of music in Africa. *Phylon*, 1953, 14, 280–291.

DOOB, L. W. *Communication in Africa*. New Haven: Yale University Press, 1961.

GOOD, A. L. Drum talk is the African's wireless. *Natural History*, 1942, 50, 69–74.

HERZOG, G. Drum signaling in a West African tribe. In D. Hymes (Ed.), *Language in culture and society.* New York: Harper and Row, Publishers, 1965.

STERN, T. Drum and whistle languages: An analysis of speech surrogates. *American Anthropologist,* 1957, 59, 487–506.

VAN VALEN, L. Talking drums and similar African tonal communication. *Southern Folklore Quarterly,* 1955, 19, 252–256.

WHITE, C. *Drums through the ages.* Los Angeles: Sterling Publishing Co., Inc., 1960.

Index

BOOK MANUFACTURE

Language Behavior and Communication: An Introduction was typeset, printed by offset and bound by Kingsport Press, Inc.. Internal and cover design was by John Goetz. The paper is Perkins & Squier's Glatfelter Old Forge. The type is Caledonia with Bulmer display.